Select Books By Andrew Podnieks

Kings of the North: Kawhi, Kyle, and the Toronto Raptors' Championship 2018-19 Season (Moydart Press, 2019)

Fast Ice: Superstars of the New NHL (ECW Press, 2017)

IIHF Guide & Record Book 2018 (Moydart Press, 2017, 8th edition)

Great Moments in Canadian Sports (Moydart Press, 2017)

Little Book of Stanley Cup Stories (Moydart Press, 2018)

Little Book of Hockey Stories (Moydart Press, 2017)

Canada's Team: Celebrating the Toronto Blue Jays' Incredible 2015 Season (Moydart Press, 2015)

The Toronto Maple Leafs' Ultimate Book of Facts, Stats, and Stories (Fenn/M & S, 2015)

The Decisive Moment: Photographs from the Dennis Miles Collection (Moydart Press, 2015)

NHL: 100 Years of Hockey Glory (Moydart Press, 2015—with Rob Del Mundo)

The Complete Hockey Dictionary—Updated & Revised (Moydart Press, 2015)

Where Countries Come to Play: Celebrating the World of Olympic Hockey and the Triple Gold Club (Fenn/M & S, 2013)

Team Canada 1972: The Official 40th Anniversary Celebration of the Summit Series (Fenn/M & S, 2012)

The Timeline History of Hockey (Worth Press, 2012)

Sid vs. Ovi: Natural Born Rivals (M & S, 2011 hardcover/trade paperback 2012)

NHL Records Forever: Hockey's Unbeatable Achievements (Fenn/M & S, 2011)

Hockey Superstitions: From Playoff Beards to Crossed Sticks and Lucky Socks (M & S, 2010)

Retired Numbers: A Celebration of NHL Excellence (Fenn, 2010)

Canadian Gold: 2010 Olympic Winter Games Ice Hockey Champions (Fenn, 2010)

Triple Gold Club: Inaugural Ceremonies 22 February 2010 (IIHF, 2010)

Canada's Olympic History 1920-2010 (Fenn, 2009)

Honoured Canadiens (Fenn, 2008 English and French editions)

IIHF Top 100 Hockey Stories of All-Time (Fenn, 2008—with Szymon Szemberg)

World of Hockey: Celebrating a Century of the IIHF 1908-2008 (Fenn, 2007)

A Canadian Saturday Night: Hockey and the Culture of a Country (Greystone, 2006)

Silverware (Fenn, 2005)

The Little Book of Hockey Sweaters (Key Porter, 2005)

Messier: Dominance on Ice (Key Porter, 2005)

Players: The Ultimate A-Z Guide of Everyone Who Has Played in the NHL (Doubleday, 2003)

The Goal: Bobby Orr and the Most Famous Goal in NHL Stanley Cup History (Triumph, 2003)

Honoured Members (Fenn, 2003)

A Day in the Life of the Maple Leafs (HarperCollins, 2002)

Canadian Gold 2002: Making Hockey History (Fenn, 2002)

The NHL All-Star Game: 50 Years of the Great Tradition (HarperCollins, 2000 hardcover/trade paperback 2001)

Hockey's Greatest Teams: Teams, Players, and Plays That Changed the Game (Penguin Studio, 2000)

The Great One: The Life and Times of Wayne Gretzky (Doubleday, 1999)

Red, White, and Gold: Canada at the World Junior Championships, 1974-1999 (ECW Press, 1998)

Shooting Stars: Photographs from the Portnoy Collection at the Hockey Hall of Fame (Doubleday, 1998)

Portraits of the Game: Classic Photographs from the Turofsky Collection at the Hockey Hall of Fame (Doubleday, 1997 hardcover/trade paperback 1998)

Canada's Olympic Hockey Teams: The Complete History 1920-1998 (Doubleday, 1997)

The Blue & White Book 1997: The Most Complete Toronto Maple Leafs Fact Book Ever Published (ECW Press, 1996)

Return to Glory: The Leafs from Imlach to Fletcher (ECW Press, 1995)

THE GREATEST
WEIRDEST
MOST AMAZING
NHL DEBUTS
OF ALL TIME

Andrew Podnieks

Published by ECW Press
665 Gerrard Street East
Toronto, ON M4M 1Y2
416-694-3348 / info@ecwpress.com

Cover design: Michel Vrana
Text design and typesetting: Kathryn Zante
Cover images: © Claus Andersen / Stringer / Getty Images Sport

Purchase the print edition
and receive the eBook free.
For details, go to ecwpress.com/eBook.

LIBRARY AND ARCHIVES CANADA CATALOGUING
IN PUBLICATION

The greatest, weirdest, most amazing NHL debuts
of all time / Andrew Podnieks.

Podnieks, Andrew, author.

Canadiana (print) 20190127090
Canadiana (ebook) 20190127104
ISBN 978 177041 515 7 (softcover)
ISBN 978 177305 435 3 (PDF)
ISBN 978 177305 434 6 (ePub)

LCSH: National Hockey League—Biography.
LCSH: Hockey players—Biography.

CC GV848.5.A1 P63 2019
DDC 796.962092/2—dc23

The publication of *The Greatest, Weirdest, Most Amazing NHL Debuts of All Time* has been generously supported by the Government
of Canada. *Ce livre est financé en partie par le gouvernement du Canada.* We also acknowledge the contribution of the Government of
Ontario through the Ontario Book Publishing Tax Credit, and through Ontario Creates for the marketing of this book.

PRINTED AND BOUND IN CANADA   PRINTING: NORECOB   1   2   3   4   5

Contents

Ottawa's Drake Batherson was one of only 11 players to score in his NHL debut during the 2018–19 season.

Introduction

It wasn't easy tracking the dates and statistics for every player's first NHL game, but it was certainly worth the effort. It's an area of research that has long fascinated me because for that one specific game, every player is the same.

Whether it's Gretzky or Crosby or a mid-level player or a small note in the history of the game, every player has a first game. But, of course, those first games come in so many shapes and sizes. Many Hall of Famers had quite unremarkable first games while many obscure players had sensational debuts.

The variety and scope of these games is such that I knew I could fill an entire book with interesting stories. My ambition was to break down "the debut" into every possible category. The more I looked, the more I found, and the more I found, the more interesting it got (to me, anyway).

The first part of the research was to understand how each player got into that initial game in the first place. For some, the answer is easy. If you're a first overall draft choice, your debut is likely only a few short months away. For others, it comes because of an injury to a roster player; it comes because of a player's excellent play in the minors or in junior; it comes in desperation, as an emergency replacement.

But no matter how you slice it, every player who gets into a game is a quality player who has had some combination of skill and luck to get there.

We can laugh at some of the names. We think of Lefty Wilson, longtime Detroit trainer, who is from an era when the game was so archaic the emergency replacement was to be found at the end of the bench—sometimes of the other team. We laugh at a high-school student coming out of the stands to take over for a badly injured, maskless goalie during the days of the Original Six.

And yet, it was only in early 2018 that the Blackhawks had to use Scott Foster, a local shinny goalie, for half a period. And we cheer his incredible success, playing shut out hockey for 14 minutes.

Some players not only get into a game but excel beyond their, or anyone else's, wildest dreams. The greatest debut of all time? Al Hill of Philadelphia. Three points in a period, a record five points in the game, and a Gordie Howe hat trick, all in his first game. And after? Nothing nearly as accomplished.

Other players got no more than a handful of shifts, and others still just one shift. Some did well and never played again in the NHL. Others played well, yet did little with their other opportunities.

Ask virtually any NHLer about his recollections of that first game, and the first thing that comes to mind is a connection to family. Every player who gets that call to play then in turn calls those he's closest to. That first game represents a lifetime of preparation, a lifetime of practice and sacrifice, of dedication and determination. For some, it is the very pinnacle of an ambition; for others, it's the start of a long career.

One of my favourite sections in the book is called "First Goal, Only Goal" because it looks at players who further enhanced their dream by scoring a goal in their debut—and then never scored again. A magical start, a career full of apparent promise—and then a black void. Not *schadenfreude*, just a shame.

In the century-long history of the NHL, there have been almost 7,900 players who have appeared in at least one game, and several categories of my research list only one player. The granddaddy of this group is surely Wayne Hillman.

Consider that of those 7,900 players, only 144 made their debuts in the playoffs. Of those 144, only 20 debuted in the Stanley Cup Finals. And then comes Hillman, who not only slots into these categories but one all his own—his debut, one single shift, came during the Cup-clinching game! One shift, a Cup win, and his name stamped on the game's most prized trophy.

Some players scored on their first shift with their first shot. Two scored in their first game with an empty netter. Several goalies earned assists in their debuts and only 23 earned shutouts. One goalie, Ron Loustel, allowed ten goals and, as one might unfortunately expect, never played in the NHL again.

One player, Kellan Lain, had a "debut" that lasted but two seconds, and another, David Koci, incurred a record 42 minutes in penalties in his debut (fighting, roughing, fighting, charging major, fighting, game misconduct). One goalie, Marc D'Amour, incurred 12 penalty minutes as the backup, thus earning statistics in a game he didn't actually play. That was his debut—no minutes, no shots, no goals, but a minor and misconduct.

And so this book sifts through 7,900 debuts to extract the purest, weirdest, most amazing first games ever played. All the records herein are supremely special because any player who wants to break them has one chance, one night, and perhaps only one shift to do so. But on that first night, any player can be as great as Howe or Orr or Lemieux. He just has to be quick about it!

Andrew Podnieks
Toronto, September 2019

Day One Debuts

The First Skaters, 1917–18

The National Hockey Association was founded in 1909 and was the pre-eminent professional league in Canada. Pro hockey of any sort had started only in 1904, but the NHA had the best teams and attracted most of the top players. In fact, NHA teams won the Stanley Cup every year of its existence except 1915 and 1917.

But a dispute with Toronto owner Eddie Livingstone incited the other owners to start a new league from which he would be excluded. Thus was born the National Hockey League, on November 26, 1917.

Most of the teams were ostensibly the same during this transition, so although every player who appeared in the NHL during the 1917–18 season was a "rookie"—i.e., a player in his first year in the NHL—most were not rookies in the spirit of the word as we know it (new to the professional game after playing junior hockey or some significantly lower level).

Of the 45 players to skate in the NHL during its inaugural season, only four players were playing pro for the first time—Jack Adams, Morley Bruce, Gerry Geran, and Raymie Skilton. Interestingly, none of these players recorded a point in their first games.

As well, most of the players who scored in their 1917–18 debuts were in their late twenties or older and had several years of pro experience upon which to rely. Probably the most impressive debut during this year was Reg Noble. He scored four times and was only 22 years old, but even still he had played a full season in the NHA the previous year. In fact, he was the only player to score who had started his pro career as late as 1916.

The upshot is quite simple. Given that the NHL was basically the same league as the NHA, but with a different name, it is more correct to consider a player's debut as his first NHA game (not NHL), if that was the league he started in prior to playing in the NHL.

Morley Bruce was one of the true rookies on opening night in 1917.

1917-18 NHL Skaters	Debut Age	League, First year pro	NHL Debut Stats			
			G	A*	P	Pim
Jack Adams	22	NHL, 1917	0	0	0	0
Billy Bell	26	NHA, 1913	1	0	1	0
Louis Berlinguette	30	NHA, 1909	0	0	0	3
George Boucher	21	NHA, 1915	0	0	0	0
Morley Bruce	23	NHL, 1917	0	0	0	0
Harry Cameron	27	NHA, 1912	2	0	2	0
Bert Corbeau	23	NHA, 1914	0	0	0	3
Jack Coughlin	25	NHA, 1916	0	0	0	0
Bill Coutu	25	NHA, 1916	0	0	0	0
Rusty Crawford	32	NHA, 1912	0	0	0	0
Jack Darragh	27	NHA, 1910	0	0	0	0
Corb Denneny	23	NHA, 1914	2	0	2	0
Cy Denneny	26	NHA, 1914	3	0	3	0
Gerry Geran	21	NHL, 1917	0	0	0	0
Eddie Gerard	27	NHA, 1913	1	0	1	3
Joe Hall	36	NHA, 1909	0	0	0	14
Harry Hyland	28	NHA, 1909	5	0	5	0
Newsy Lalonde	30	NHA, 1909	1	0	1	0
Jack Laviolette	38	NHA, 1909	0	0	0	0
Ed Lowrey	26	NHA, 1913	0	0	0	0
Joe Malone	27	NHA, 1910	5	0	5	0
Jack Marks	37	NHA, 1911	0	0	0	0
Jack McDonald	30	NHA, 1910	1	0	1	0
Harry Meeking	23	NHA, 1915	0	0	0	0
Horace Merrill	33	NHA, 1912	0	0	0	0
Harry Mummery	28	NHA, 1912	0	0	0	6
Frank Nighbor	24	NHA, 1912	1	0	1	3
Reg Noble	22	NHA, 1916	4	0	4	6
George O'Grady	26	NHA, 1913	0	0	0	0
Evariste Payer	29	NHA, 1910	0	0	0	0
Didier Pitre	34	NHA, 1909	1	0	1	3
Ken Randall	30	NHA, 1911	0	0	0	14
Dave Ritchie	26	NHA, 1914	2	0	2	0
Art Ross	31	NHA, 1909	1	0	1	9
Hamby Shore	31	NHA, 1909	0	0	0	0
Raymie Skilton	28	NHL, 1917	0	0	0	0
Alf Skinner	23	NHA, 1914	1	0	1	0
Phil Stevens	24	NHA, 1914	0	0	0	0
Ken Thompson	36	NHA, 1916	0	0	0	0

*the NHL did not award assists in 1917-18

blue=true NHL rookie

The First Goalies, 1917-18

Although the first NHL season can clearly be marked as 1917–18, it came during a time of change and evolution in the game. It was only in 1910 that games went from two 30-minute halves to three periods of 20 minutes; in 1911, the rover was eliminated, reducing on-ice manpower from seven to six players; in 1917, goalies were only now allowed to fall to the ice to make a save.

But in 1917–18, there was still only one centre red line, dividing the rink into two equal zones. Penalties were three minutes and had to be served in full, and the league consisted of only three teams (Montreal Canadiens, Toronto Arenas, Ottawa Senators) after the Montreal Wanderers' arena burned down and the team decided to withdraw from play after only four games.

In all, there were only 24 games played that season, and goalscoring averaged 9.83 a game, almost double what it is today. The Canadiens averaged 5.79 goals a game while the Senators surrendered an average of 5.64 goals a game, both exaggerated totals by today's standards.

Harry Hyland scored five goals on the first night of the NHL's first season.

NHL history, scored by Dave Ritchie of the Wanderers, and it proved to be the Wanderers' only win ever. The team lost the next three before its arena burned down.

Each other goalie who made his NHL debut had also had significant experience in the NHA. Georges Vezina was in the middle of perhaps the most special career in hockey history. Clint Benedict, another Hockey Hall of Famer, was just as magical in the goal. Sammy Hebert, Hap Holmes, and Art Brooks all played for Toronto in 1917 but had very limited careers.

The legendary Georges Vezina had a long pre-NHL career.

Only six goalies played in 1917–18, producing a wide range of crazy and historic results. The first game ever played featured Toronto in Montreal to play the Wanderers. It was memorable for many reasons: it featured the first goal in

The First NHL Game

Two games were on the NHL's schedule for Wednesday, December 19, 1917: one in Ottawa, with the Sens facing the visiting Montreal Canadiens, and the other at the Westmount Arena in Montreal, where the host Wanderers played the Toronto Arenas.

The Wanderers game started at 8:15 p.m. and as such represents the first game in league history. It was also one of the wildest. The first period alone featured eight goals. After Dave Ritchie opened the scoring, Jack McDonald made it 2–0 for Montreal, but Toronto tied the game 2–2 before the game was six minutes old. Harry Hyland made more history by scoring three goals, the NHL's first hat trick, in the first period and two more in the second to bring his total to five on the night.

Toronto fell behind 10–6 in the third but scored three in a row, two by Noble who counted four in the game, to make it close. In the end, the hometown Wanderers won, 10–9, before a sparse crowd of about 700.

Interestingly, all the penalties occurred in the first period. Ken Randall had three minors and a major; Art Ross had three minors; and Reg Noble had two minors.

What is amazing about this game is that although it was the first NHL game ever played, it is also to this day one of the highest scoring. Indeed, only four games of the more than 60,000 played from that date to the present have featured more goals than the 19 goals in this one.

Bert Lindsay was the winning goaltender despite giving up nine goals. Even today that represents the most goals surrendered by a winning goalie. Lindsay was the father of the even greater Ted Lindsay and, ironically, signed with Toronto the next year, the final season of his NHL career.

1917-18 NHL Goalies	Debut Age	League, First year pro	NHL Debut Stats		
			Mins	GA	Decision
Clint Benedict (OTS)	25	NHA, 1912	60:00	7	L
Art Brooks (TOR)	28	NHA, 1916	40:00	5	L
Sammy Hebert (TOR)	24	NHA, 1913	20:00	5	nd
Hap Holmes (TOR)	29	NHA, 1912	60:00	4	W
Bert Lindsay (WAN)	36	NHA, 1909	60:00	9	W
Georges Vezina (MTL)	30	NHA, 1910	60:00	4	W

Clint Benedict was one of six goalies to usher in the new NHL in 1917.

The One and Only

Four Special Players

One of the magical aspects of a player's NHL debut is imagining the post-game phone call between player and parents. Just as with the call leading up to the game—"Mom, I got called up!"—there is that special moment when a young man shares and celebrates such a momentous event with the two people who most closely can be credited with the player's first success.

But in all the century's-worth of NHL games, only four players can be known to have had the right to call their parents and declare, "I got the only goal of the game!"

That quartet of heroes includes Bill Cook, Stan Brown, Connie Brown, and Daniel Corso. Each of their debut games ended in a 1–0 score, and in each case the newbie scored the goal. More interestingly, while the first three were achieved in the game's early years, Corso scored his lone goal in 2000.

// Bill Cook, New York Rangers
November 16, 1926

Sometimes the bare facts obscure a greater reality, and in the case of Bill Cook that obfuscation is easily cleared up. However, it is but a very small number of players who can say that they played their first NHL game as team captain.

Bill Cook is one such player, but it's not as wild a stretch as it might first sound. The 1926–27 season was the inaugural one for the New York Rangers, and general manager Conn Smythe wanted to build a winner right away. He travelled to Winnipeg to meet Bill and Bun Cook, two brothers who had been playing pro with the Saskatoon Crescents of the Western Canada Hockey League. Smythe signed them on the spot and named Bill, 31 years old, team captain.

The Montreal Maroons, reigning Stanley Cup champions, travelled to Madison Square Garden for both teams' first game of 1926–27. It was a battle from the get-go, and referee Lou Marsh doled out a total of 18 penalties (11 to the Maroons), but it was the Cook brothers, with linemate Frank Boucher, who accounted for the only goal of the game late in the second period.

Bun saw Bill in front of the Maroons goal and got his brother the puck, and Bill made no mistake in beating Clint Benedict at 18:37, much to the delight of the 13,000 fans. Benedict fell awkwardly on the play, hitting his head on the goalpost and cutting his ear. He had to leave the game for a few minutes for medical attention, during which time play was stopped.

// Stan Brown, New York Rangers
January 6, 1927

Some 9,000 fans at Madison Square Garden witnessed history on this night, when newcomer Stan Brown scored late in the game to give the home side New York Rangers a 1–0 win over the Montreal Canadiens. Lorne Chabot (called Chabotsky by the *New York Times*) was brilliant in goal for the Blueshirts, stoning the whirlwind play of Howie Morenz and Aurele Joliat from start to finish.

Ironically, it was while Joliat was serving a penalty for roughing that Brown scored, his power-play marker coming with only 1:57 left in the game. It was an unassisted effort, and a sensational one at that. He rushed up ice with the puck, split the defence with great speed, and beat goalie George Hainsworth with a hard drive.

Brown was substituting for the great Ching Johnson when he scored.

// Connie Brown, Detroit Red Wings
January 26, 1939

The *Detroit Free Press* made a banner headline of Brown's heroics: "Rookie's One-Night Stand Brings Wings 1–0 Victory."

The actual events were somewhat less exemplary, but a goal is a goal.

Brown, a centre, was called up from the farm team in Pittsburgh because the Red Wings' lineup had been decimated by injuries. He ended up playing on a line with veterans Syd Howe and Charlie Conacher, and it was those two stars who created the play that led to Brown's goal at 18:48 of the second period.

The trio moved the puck up ice when Brown found himself going down the left boards. When he got near the end red line he simply fired the puck across ice. Goalie Mike Karakas tried to play the puck, but it hit his stick at an odd angle and caromed into the net for what would be the only goal of the game.

The other hero of the night was Detroit goalie Tiny Thompson. He was spectacular in the third period in keeping Chicago, the Stanley Cup champions, at bay and ensuring Brown was the hero on the scoresheet.

// Daniel Corso, St. Louis Blues
December 5, 2000

You get the opportunity, you have to do something with it. St. Louis ran into injury problems—Scott Young and Tyson Nash were unable to play—so coach Joel Quenneville called up Daniel Corso and Pascal Rheaume from the Worcester IceCats, the Blues's AHL affiliate. Rheaume had played in the NHL previously, but it was Corso's first game.

Rheaume had made his debut almost four years earlier and scored on his second career shift. He challenged Corso to match that. Corso came up short, but he scored the only goal of the game, which was even more special.

His goal came on the power play at 14:28 of the second period. Michal Handzus took the initial shot, but goalie Guy Hebert couldn't control the rebound and Corso whacked in the loose puck.

"He brings speed and skill," said Quenneville of Corso after the game. "It was a chance for him to play, and for us to get a look at him, too. He took advantage of his chance here tonight."

The Blues played their next game four days later. Young and Nash were back in the lineup—and Corso and Rheaume were back in the minors with Worcester. In all, Corso played 77 regular-season games in the NHL and scored 14 goals, but none bigger or more memorable than his first.

Daniel Corso (left) is the most recent first-gamer to score the only goal in a game.

Extra, Extra! Read All About It!

Of the 36 players to make their debuts on the night of the first games in NHL history, December 19, 1917, an incredible 16 were later inducted into the Hockey Hall of Fame—Clint Benedict, George Boucher, Harry Cameron, Rusty Crawford, Jack Darragh, Cy Denneny, Eddie Gerard, Joe Hall, Harry Hyland, Newsy Lalonde, Jack Laviolette, Joe Malone, Reg Noble, Didier Pitre, Art Ross, Georges Vezina.

But if you had to pick one name from that list as the game's first superstar, it would surely be Lalonde (the name Vezina is perhaps even more famous, but goalies don't hold the same attraction as skaters).

Lalonde was 29 years old by the time the NHL started operations. He had been a star wherever he played, notably in Cornwall and Renfrew, and later Vancouver, but he had been with the Canadiens most of the time since the club's inception in 1909. He even scored the franchise's first goal that year, in the NHA, and led the team to the Stanley Cup in 1916.

Indeed, the *Ottawa Citizen* started its game report with: "'Newsy' Lalonde and his champion Canadiens opened the hockey season at the Arena last night and made up for some of Quebec's recent disappointments by defeating the Ottawas by a score of 7 to 4."

The Habs started the 1917–18 season on the road, in Ottawa. Lalonde, the team captain, scored the team's second goal midway through the opening period to give the Habs a 2–0 lead. It was his first of what would turn out to be 23 goals in just 14 games that season, and it was the first of many that would make him the premier player of the NHL's early days.

The great Newsy Lalonde made a great first impression.

Did He, or Didn't He?

The Curious Case of Paul Jacobs

Of all the players to have skated in the NHL, there is none more enigmatic than Paul Jacobs because, quite simply, no one can say for certain whether he played in the league or not.

From day one, the NHL made game reports for every game. These reports consisted of three parts: rosters; goals and assists; penalties. Over time, however, the earliest sheets slowly disappeared from the NHL's offices. So in 2019, here's what we know about Jacobs.

First, he was definitely listed in the roster report for five games—January 7, 14, 21, and 31 and February 4, 1919.

However, these references don't make clear whether he played in the game or not. In later years the official scorer at every game would add a check mark beside the name (played) or an x (didn't play). For many game sheets in that year, there are no such marks to confirm participation.

Complicating matters, it was clear from newspaper reports of the day that he neither factored in on a goal nor incurred a penalty, leaving his participation further obfuscated.

There are only two clues that indicate Jacobs played at all. There are two references to Jacobs in the *Globe and Mail*, one on the day Toronto played its season opener for 1918–19, December 23 against the Canadiens, and a second the next day (but not in the game story). The first:

"Randall and Cameron will play defence, with Paul Jacobs, the Indian player, as substitute."

The next day, after the Canadiens rallied to beat the Arenas, 4–3, a second mention of his name was made:

"Paul Jacobs, the Leaside Indian defence player, who has been trying out with the Toronto Arenas, will not be available this season. He is leaving for Montreal tonight and will reside in that city in future."

The second possible game Jacobs played was on December 31, 1918, if only because the NHL referenced this date after it had published online the game-by-game stats of every player in league history. But there is no mention of him at any time in the days prior to or after this game.

In all likelihood, the NHL has kept Jacobs in its database, simply figuring if it were to make an error, better to include him than exclude him.

In the end, however, it seems unlikely Jacobs ever did play in the NHL. But the absence of proof that he did play cannot necessarily be taken fully as proof that he didn't play.

Lightning Unleashed

Howie Morenz

MONTREAL CANADIENS // DECEMBER 15, 1923

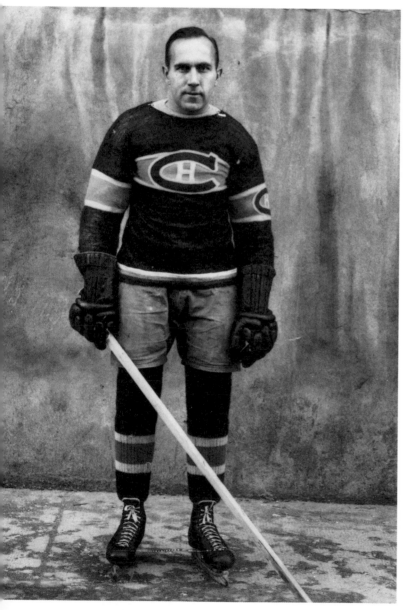

"The Stratford Streak" earned his nickname honestly. Howie Morenz was not only born in Stratford, Ontario, he also was a dominant player on the local junior and senior teams in the late 1910s and early 1920s.

By the time the 21-year-old made the starting lineup for the 1923–24 season with the NHL Canadiens, he had earned a reputation as a great skater and stickhandler, and his debut only further added to his burgeoning legacy.

Commented the *Montreal Gazette*: "Morenz fitted right into the Canadiens machine, and the manager thinks so well of his ability that he started him at centre in place of Odie Cleghorn."

Morenz played on a line with Aurele Joliat and Billy Boucher and was lightning fast from start to finish, although the team lost 2–1 to the hometown Toronto St. Pats.

The Streak was held off the scoresheet, but that was not to be a trend. He scored 13 goals in 24 games as a rookie in 1923-24 and became one of the greatest hockey players of the pre-WWII era.

Howie Morenz was perhaps the first superstar of the NHL.

Naughty, Naughty

Nels Stewart

MONTREAL MAROONS // NOVEMBER 28, 1925

The contrast was pronounced, but it was also representative of the era. The Maroons' Nels Stewart was such a great hockey player that he was inducted into the Hockey Hall of Fame in 1952, among the first players considered legends of the game. Not the smoothest of skaters, he was strong as an ox and had a hard shot and deft touch around the net.

Yet, in his first career NHL game, on November 28, 1925, he did what no player before or since has done—he incurred as many as five minor penalties in one game. These transgressions contributed to the final game summary, which showed that the visiting Montreal Maroons lost to the Ottawa Senators by a 3–2 score.

Stewart took three minors during a scoreless first period, and in the second the Maroons took an early 2–0 lead. But referee Lou Marsh called fouls both ways, and the Senators scored twice on five-on-three situations to tie the game, Stewart, one of the Montreal offenders on both occasions. Soon after, the Sens scored again to win the game.

Game reports suggest that Stewart and other rookies Babe Siebert and Hobie Kitchen, "took their bumps and handed them out in a manner that well demonstrated that they have come into professional ranks to stay," according to the *Montreal Gazette*.

Today, five minors in a first game would produce banishment to the minors, but in 1925, it was thought that Stewart showed fight. This was only the second season for the expansion Maroons, and thanks to the incredible play of Stewart, the team went on to win the Stanley Cup.

Stewart, in fact, led the league in scoring to win the Art Ross Trophy and was also named winner of the Hart Trophy. He led the league in goals, with 34, and his 121 penalty minutes were just behind Bert Courbeau (125) to lead the league in that department as well.

In the Cup Finals, against the Victoria Cougars, champions of the west, the Maroons won the best-of-five in four games. Stewart, playing variously defence and centre, scored seven of his team's ten goals, including the game winner in each victory. He was nicknamed "Ol' Poison" because of his deadly touch around the enemy goal, so despite incurring the most minor penalties in his NHL debut, he went on to craft one of the game's greatest careers.

Fast Facts

Of the 7,863 players to skate between 1917 and 2019, some 1,439 incurred at least a minor penalty in their debut. In all, 1,009 had just one minor while another 171 took two minors. Another 108 incurred a fighting major and 29 players had three minors. Some 48 players took a minor and major.

Best Goalie Debut Ever

Tiny Thompson

BOSTON BRUINS // NOVEMBER 15, 1928

Of the 775 goaltenders to play in the NHL, only 23 played the full game and recorded a shutout in their debut. But no goalie debut was greater than that of Tiny Thompson's.

It was billed as the largest crowd to attend a hockey game at Duquesne Garden in Pittsburgh, and on November 15, 1928, some 7,000 fans watched the local Pirates lose a 1–0 game to the visiting Bruins in the first night of play of the 1928–29 NHL season.

Thompson earned the shutout for the Bruins, of course, but he had to play 70 minutes to earn the historic win. Between 1927 and 1942, games that were tied after 60 minutes of regulation went to a mandatory 10-minute overtime (i.e., the full 10 minutes were played, and any number of goals could be scored in that fourth period).

So, it wasn't enough for Thompson to stave off the Pirates, in their third NHL season, he had to go a full half period extra to win the game. As it turned out, Dit Clapper scored at the 7:30 mark of the overtime, beating goalie Joe Miller with a high shot. That was all the Bruins needed.

Interestingly, four players were making their NHL debuts this night—Thompson, Cooney Weiland, Eric Pettinger, and Dede Klein. The latter two players didn't amount to much, but Thompson and Weiland were just starting what turned out to be Hall of Fame careers.

Thompson led the Bruins to the Stanley Cup in his rookie season. It turned out to be the only championship during his 12 years in the NHL. He retired in 1940 with 81 shutouts, tied for second most all time. Even to this day his career shutout number is tied for the sixth highest.

Tiny Thompson was small in stature but big in performance in the crease.

Debut Shutouts

The Complete History

Of the 775 goalies who have appeared in an NHL game, only 23 have recorded a shutout in their debut.

Goalie (Team, Age)	Date	Score	Opponent	Mins	Shots
Hal Winkler (NYR, 32)	November 16, 1926	1-0	Maroons	60:00	–
Tiny Thompson (BOS, 25)	November 15, 1928	1-0	Pirates	70:00	–
Alfie Moore (NYA, 32)	January 30, 1937	4-0	Canadiens	60:00	–
Dave Gatherum (DET, 21)	October 11, 1953	4-0	Maple Leafs	60:00	22
Bob Perreault (MTL, 24)	December 17, 1955	5-0	Black Hawks	60:00	18
Claude Pronovost (BOS, 20)	January 14, 1956	2-0	Canadiens	60:00	31
Marcel Paille (NYR, 24)	November 2, 1957	5-0	Bruins	60:00	23
Andre Gill (BOS, 26)	December 23, 1967	4-0	Rangers	60:00	41
Wayne Thomas (MTL, 25)	January 14, 1973	3-0	Canucks	60:00	20
Gary Simmons (CAL, 30)	October 11, 1974	3-0	Flames	60:00	24
Mario Lessard (LA, 24)	October 26, 1978	6-0	Sabres	60:00	18
Robbie Moore (PHI, 24)	March 6, 1979	5-0	Rockies	60:00	22
Mario Gosselin (QUE, 20)	February 26, 1984	4-0	Blues	60:00	26
Daren Puppa (BUF, 20)	November 1, 1985	2-0	Oilers	60:00	37
Mike Fountain (VAN, 24)	November 14, 1996	3-0	Devils	60:00	40
Jussi Markkanen (EDM, 26)	November 28, 2001	2-0	Mighty Ducks	60:00	27
Michael Leighton (CHI, 21)	January 8, 2003	0-0	Coyotes	65:00	31
Yann Danis (MTL, 24)	October 12, 2005	2-0	Thrashers	59:50	32
Mike Smith (DAL, 24)	October 21, 2006	4-0	Coyotes	60:00	22
Al Montoya (PHO, 24)	April 1, 2009	3-0	Avalanche	59:48	23
John Gibson (ANA, 20)	April 7, 2014	3-0	Canucks	59:51	18
Troy Grosenick (SJ, 25)	November 16, 2014	2-0	Hurricanes	59:56	45
Garret Sparks (TOR, 22)	November 30, 2015	3-0	Oilers	59:37	24

Toronto's Garret Sparks is the most recent goalie to earn a shutout in his NHL debut.

NOTES

// Winkler was 32 when he made his NHL debut only because he had played senior hockey in Winnipeg and pro hockey in the western leagues for many years previous. He was the first goalie to earn a shutout in his debut and he remains the oldest (32 years, 241 days).

// This was the only shutout of Alfie Moore's 21-game career. The same can be said for Andre Gill (five career games) and Mike Fountain (11 career games).

// Gatherum also shut out Chicago for 40:21 in his next start, and his 100:21 to start a career without allowing a goal was a record that lasted nearly six decades. Gatherum played only three games in the NHL.

// Pronovost was the youngest to earn his historic shutout. He was 20 years, 176 days old. He played only three career games, earning this one shutout.

// Lessard had the easiest shutout of the 23 on two counts. One, his Kings won 6–0, the highest score, and two, he needed to stop only 18 shots, the fewest among this list (tied with Gibson and Perreault).

// Robbie Moore played only six career games but had two shutouts.

// Leighton is the only goalie to earn a shutout in his NHL debut but not earn a win. Unfortunately, he had to share the glory with Phoenix Coyotes goalie Zac Bierk, who also earned the shutout after 65 minutes of goalless hockey. Leighton is also the only goalie other than Thompson to have to play more than 60 minutes to earn the shutout.

// Still active, Troy Grosenick has only two NHL games to his credit, this shutout win and a 4–1 loss to Buffalo two nights later. His shutout was the most difficult in that among this group of goalies he stopped the greatest number of shots—45.

// Jussi Markkanen is the only European goalie on this exclusive list.

Averaging a Goal a Game . . .

. . . For One Game, Anyway

Yes, there have been hundreds of players to score a goal in their first NHL game, but only four fall into a unique group: players who scored in their only NHL game!

Imagine the frustration. You get called up to play in your first game—it's a dream. You score a goal—not only a dream for the player but surely also for the coach. And then, no sooner have you lived your dream and done everything possible to succeed—you're summarily dismissed, never to return.

// Rolly Huard, Toronto Maple Leafs
December 13, 1930

The Leafs were hurting. Charlie Conacher, Joe Primeau, and Harold Cotton were all injured, and coach Art Duncan needed warm bodies for a game at Maple Leaf Gardens against the high-flying Boston Bruins.

GM Conn Smythe recalled Rolly Huard, a centre, and Hap Hamel, a winger, from the Buffalo Bisons of the International League and put the newcomers on a line with Roger Jenkins. The trio not only played well but clicked for the opening goal at 9:10 of the first period. But to read into Lou Marsh's colourful description of the goal, Huard got lucky:

"Then Duncan trotted out his sub forwards and Rolly Huard, the little Frenchman—he looks like his name—set the house afire by scoring on a sneaker from the blue line."

In other words, Huard managed to put a soft goal past Tiny Thompson, an assessment made blunter by Bert Perry in his game report for the *Globe and Mail*: "Huard's goal was the first of the game. He fired a knee-high drive from outside the blue line. 'Tiny' Thompson attempted to catch it but muffed, and the rubber ended up in the net."

Charles Querrie, the former Toronto Arenas coach turned *Toronto Star* journalist, offered this assessment: "Of the three recruits, the stout little fellow with the

moustache named Huard was the best. He scored the first goal of the game a minute after he was out and checked well."

Unfortunately the goal was of little significance. The under-manned Leafs lost, 7–3.

But because Huard came to the team as an emergency loan, and the Bisons needed him in the IHL, he went back to his old team after this one game and never played in the NHL again.

// Dean Morton, Detroit Red Wings
October 5, 1989

It was nearly 69 years after Huard's one-and-done game that the feat was replicated, but the circumstances were different in every way.

Dean Morton was drafted 148th overall by Detroit in 1986, and after one more year in junior and two in the AHL the team thought the 21-year-old was ready for the big time. They named him to their opening night roster for the 1989–90 season, and he seemed set to begin a respectable NHL career.

The Red Wings opened their season on the road, in Calgary, where the reigning Cup-champion Flames unveiled their banner in a lavish pre-game show. But the Wings had their own optimism after having signed Borje Salming and Bernie Federko in the off-season, two stars well-known for their careers with other teams (Toronto and St. Louis, respectively). And, team captain Steve Yzerman had committed long term to the team after signing a five-year, $6 million contract in the summer.

Coach Jacques Demers thought he had the makings of a solid outfit, but the hometown Flames had a 3–0 lead before the game was 12 minutes old. It was Morton, a defenceman, who got the visitors on the board when his point shot found its way through a maze of players and beat goalie Mike Vernon cleanly. Marc Habscheid and Yzerman drew the assists, but the goal mattered only a little. By the end of the night Calgary had won a slugfest by a 10–7 score.

The next day Demers despaired over his team's weak defence and vowed changes, one of which was to sit Morton in favour of 30-year-old veteran Chris Kotsopoulos. Kotsopoulos, however, played only the next two games and was demoted, ending his career. The Wings ended up using 12 defencemen that year and finished well out of the playoffs.

And Morton? He kicked around in the minors for several years before becoming an NHL referee.

// Brad Fast, Carolina Hurricanes
   April 4, 2004

Brad Fast was selected 84th overall by Carolina in the 1999 Entry Draft just before starting a four-year career at Michigan State University. After graduating, he played for the Hurricanes' farm team in Lowell, but on the final day of the NHL's 2003–04 season he was called up to play in "The Show."

The defenceman was in the lineup against Florida for an afternoon game and was making a solid impression. The 'Canes built a huge 4–0 lead after the first period, and Fast was taking a regular shift on the blue line alongside Sean Hill. But over the course of the next 27 minutes the Panthers scored six unanswered goals and were ahead 6–4 midway through the third.

Eric Staal made it 6–5 at 15:04, and two and a half minutes later Fast tied the game. He joined the rush with Rod Brind'Amour and Erik Cole, but the play was broken up. Rather than motor back to the point, Fast circled and went to the net. "Brind'Amour fed me the puck," Fast recalled years later. "I kicked it up to my stick, and I think it hit something in front and beat Luongo up high."

Five minutes of overtime solved nothing, and the game ended 6–6. The next year was lost entirely because of the lockout, and when NHL play returned in October 2005, the league had instituted a shootout. That means Fast scored the tying goal in the final tie game ever played in the league.

Nice bit of trivia aside, that lockout killed momentum for Fast. He was back with Lowell during the lost season and ended up going to Europe. His one end-of-season game proved to be his only game.

// Samuel Henley, Colorado Avalanche
   December 1, 2016

Hockey fans of the 21st century have the luxury of using a multitude of video sources that capture players' best (and worst) moments, so it's easy to watch Samuel Henley make history. He and the Colorado Avalanche were home to the Columbus Blue Jackets on December 1, 2016, and the visitors jumped out to a 2–0 lead after the first period.

Blake Comeau brought the home side to within one midway through the second, and then Henley tied the game at 14:25. Jackets goalie Sergei Bobrovsky played the puck behind his own goal, firing it around the boards, but Avs defenceman Tyson Barrie got a piece of it and kept it in. Henley was right there. He turned and fired a shot at the goal without looking, and it beat a surprised Bobrovsky cleanly.

Henley's story is nothing if not inspirational. The Val d'Or native loved hockey and wanted to play in the NHL, but those feelings were not reciprocated. He played five years in the Q, during which time no NHL team drafted him. But he had a really good playoffs in his final season with his hometown Foreurs, captaining the team to the Memorial Cup. The Avs signed him to a contract after that tournament, in May 2014, and Henley spent the next three years playing in the AHL.

Finally, in late November 2016, Henley got a break. Avs team captain Gabriel Landeskog was put on the injured reserve list, and the 23-year-old Henley and 25-year-old Gabriel Bourque were recalled from San Antonio, the team's AHL affiliate.

Henley called his family, and they had enough time to drive from Val d'Or to Denver for the game. Making the trip was his mom, Manon, girlfriend, Andree Ann, and brother, Cedrick. His father, Rock, was too ill to travel, but he watched on television as his son scored.

Wearing number 42, Henley got just 5:18 of ice time, but he made the most of it. Unfortunately, the Blue Jackets scored the only goal of the third period and won the game, 3–2, putting a bit of a damper on Henley's special night.

The next day, though, Henley was back in the AHL with the Rampage. At season's end, he announced he was taking a year off to figure out if he wanted to continue his career and to spend more time with his father, who was battling cancer.

Still in his mid-twenties, Henley might return to the game, might get another NHL shot, and might have his name removed from this exclusive list. But for now, he has one game—and one goal—to his NHL credit.

Colorado's Samuel Henley (No. 42) scored a goal in his first NHL game. The problem is that it's still his only NHL goal.

You're Playing!

Only 15 players have been fortunate enough to play their first game on their birthday, and five of the 13 skaters (two goalies) managed to score.

// Fred Hergert, New York Americans
January 29, 1935

Precious little is known of his debut except that it came in this game and the visiting Boston Bruins won, 4–0. It appears as though Hergert either did very little of note or didn't play much, but regardless he did see his first NHL action on his 23rd birthday.

// Jacques Richard, Atlanta Flames
October 7, 1972

There was double importance for Jacques Richard in his NHL debut. Not only did the game fall on his birthday, but it marked the start of two franchises. Richard dressed for the Atlanta Flames, and their opponents were the New York Islanders. Both teams were playing their first-ever games in the NHL, a league that went from six teams to 12 in 1967, 14 in 1970, and now 16 in 1972. The visiting Flames won, 3–2, and although Richard was held off the scoresheet, apart from a penalty, he did manage two shots on goal.

// Claude Vilgrain, Vancouver Canucks
March 1, 1988

The Calgary Olympics had ended the previous week, and the timing couldn't have been better for one of Canada's players, Claude Vilgrain. The Haitian-born Canadian had devoted two years of his life playing for the National Team in preparation for the Games, but Canada finished a disappointing fourth on home ice.

Nevertheless, the Vancouver Canucks were desperate. Their season was spiralling out of control and general manager Pat Quinn knew he had to do something to shake up the lineup. Quinn signed Vilgrain, a Detroit draft choice from 1982 but currently a free agent, to a contract, along with teammate Ken Berry. The GM also acquired Paul Lawless that same afternoon, March 1, 1988, and all three were in the lineup that night for a home game against the Flyers.

The moves made little difference as Vancouver was hammered, 7–3, before a sparse and unhappy crowd of 10,616, but Vilgrain made his NHL debut on his 25th birthday—and scored a goal. He beat Ron Hextall early in the first period, giving the Canucks a short-lived 2–1 lead, but that was pretty much the only good news on the night for the home side.

// Patrice Brisebois, Montreal Canadiens
January 27, 1991

It was a simple case of cause and effect, but on January 27, 1991, 20-year-old Patrice Brisebois was recalled from his junior team in Drummondville. The cause? Two of Montreal's top defencemen—Eric Desjardins and Mathieu Schneider—had been injured in the team's previous game. As a result, Brisebois and Luc Gauthier (from the AHL) were summoned on an emergency basis.

The Bruins were in town for a Sunday afternoon game that has become an annual Super Bowl day tradition in Montreal (Habs game early afternoon, football later in the afternoon). It was Brisebois's 20th birthday, but that event, and the assist he drew on the tying goal in the second period, were massively overshadowed by an injury to goalie Patrick Roy, who had to be carted off the ice on a stretcher. The Habs went on to lose the game, 3–1, and Roy was lost to the team for more than a month, but Brisebois made a little history of his own.

Montreal's Patrice Brisebois is an NHL debut birthday boy.

// J-M Pelletier, Philadelphia Flyers
March 4, 1999

Jean-Marc Pelletier is one of only two goalies to make his NHL debut on his birthday, and in his case it was a matter of helping the struggling Philadelphia Flyers. Losers of eight of their last 11 games, coach Roger Neilson and general manager Bobby Clarke decided to bench John Vanbiesbrouck and Ron Hextall and call up Pelletier from the AHL farm club on March 4, 1999.

Full of confidence and excitement—"Not a bad birthday present, eh?" he asked reporters rhetorically the day of his first start—Pelletier was brought down to earth by the pitiable play of his teammates. The visiting Ottawa Senators manhandled Philly to the tune of 5–0.

Alexei Yashin scored just one minute into the game, but Pelletier settled down and played well for the next 40 minutes. Yashin scored again early in the third, and the Sens added three goals later in the period, by which time the game was more or less over anyway.

Pelletier was demoted before the next game and didn't play in the NHL for another four years.

Jean-Marc Pelletier is one of only two goalies to make his NHL debut on his birthday.

// Stephen Weiss, Florida Panthers
April 3, 2002

Weiss scored a power-play goal midway through the third period to tie the game, 2–2, and the Panthers scored later to defeat Pittsburgh, 3–2. He had been called up from the Plymouth Whalers of the OHL after his junior season was over.

// Mike Rupp, New Jersey Devils
January 13, 2003

On his 23rd birthday, Rupp put the puck in the net three times. Only two counted, but that's also okay, as he helped the Devils beat the hapless Florida Panthers, 6–2. Rupp got his first goal in the opening period, but referees deemed it was scored with a high stick and waved it off. Early in the second, he scored a nice one that counted, snapping a high wrist shot that beat Roberto Luongo cleanly. Eight and a half minutes later, on a power play, he converted a nice pass from Patrik Elias. Rupp's play impressed coach Pat Burns, who could hardly send him down to the minors after a night like this. "He forces our hand with what we're going to do with him," Burns acknowledged.

// Jeff Heerema, Carolina Hurricanes
January 17, 2003

Heerema's goal in the third period was the 'Canes' only one of the night in this 2–1 loss to New Jersey. His goal, though, was lost to history because earlier in the evening Joe Nieuwendyk scored his 500th career goal for the Devils. It was Heerema's 23rd birthday, but more significantly Niuewendyk was the 32nd player to hit 500.

// Mike Green, Washington Capitals
October 12, 2005

A defenceman, Green was recalled from Hershey on the same day that forward and team captain Jeff Halpern announced he'd miss the Capitals' game on this night because of Yom Kippur. The one-two whammy of losing a top player and playing a 20-year-old, on his birthday, didn't help the team's cause, and they went down meekly to Carolina by a 7–2 score. Despite the seven goals allowed, Green played 14:14 and didn't look out of place. Impressively, he was even in plus-minus.

// Tom Gilbert, Edmonton Oilers
January 10, 2007

Daniel Tjarnqvist's pain was Tom Gilbert's gain. Tjarnqvist was nursing a sore groin, so on January 10, 2007, in advance of Edmonton's road game in San Jose a day later, Gilbert was recalled from Wilkes-Barre with the opportunity to play his first NHL game, on his birthday no less.

In fact, three rookie defencemen were inserted into the lineup—Gilbert, as well as Mathieu Roy (three career games) and Jan Hejda (14 games). The result was

Ray Sawada played his first NHL game on his 24th birthday.

a success as the Oilers held on for a 3–2 win. Gilbert had scored the NCAA Frozen Four championship-winning goal for the University of Wisconsin the previous spring and was developing at an impressive rate in the AHL. He played 13:23 on his birthday night and played in 12 games for the Oil that season.

// Ray Sawada, Dallas Stars
February 19, 2009

When Brad Richards of the Dallas Stars broke his wrist, Ray Sawada benefitted. The 52nd overall draft choice by the Stars back in 2004 had been playing in the AHL, with the Manitoba Moose, but he got the call to replace Richards for a home game against Edmonton on February 19, 2009, his 24th birthday.

Sawada didn't disappoint, firing a shot between Dwayne Roloson's legs late in the first period to give the Stars a 2–0 lead. It was his first NHL goal on his first shot in his first game. Sawada had only 6:58 of ice time that night and played four more games, without a point, before being sent back to the Moose. In all, he played but 11 NHL games and scored just the one goal.

// Jared Spurgeon, Minnesota Wild
November 29, 2010

Spurgeon and the Wild were in Calgary for his 21st birthday, and although he played 14:42 he couldn't generate much offence, nor could anyone else, and Minnesota lost, 3–0. It was the team's fourth defeat in five games and was spurred on by two quick Calgary goals early in the second period.

Spurgeon, a defenceman, had signed as a free agent with the Wild in September. Although he had been drafted by the New York Islanders in 2008, he never played with them. The defenceman was recalled for this game from the Houston Aeros of the AHL. The promotion, though, came at a cost. His good friend, Justin Faulk, was scratched to make way for him.

Unfortunately, Spurgeon's parents were in Austria watching another son, Tyler, play, but for the Edmonton-born Jared it didn't matter. Some 600 games later, he's still with the Wild.

// Brian Foster, Florida Panthers
February 4, 2012

Making his way from the ECHL to the AHL to the NHL in one season, Brian Foster saw his dream come true on his 25th birthday, but for the wrong reasons and with the wrong result. The intra-state battle featured the Florida Panthers and Tampa Bay Lightning, and on this night Tampa's diminutive sensation Martin St. Louis was unstoppable, scoring three goals in a 6–3 win.

The game turned in the second period when the Bolts took a 1–1 game and built a 5–2 lead by 15:08 of the period. Coach Kevin Dineen tried to stem the tide by making a goalie change, pulling starter Scott Clemmensen and inserting the birthday boy.

Foster played the rest of the period and faced only one shot, making the save. The Panthers scored late in that period to make it 5–3, so Dineen put Clemmensen back in. St. Louis, however, completed his hat trick in the third, and Foster's stats line read 4:52 of playing time and no goals allowed.

That night, however, has been his only NHL action, a seeming one-game wonder with that one game coming on his birthday.

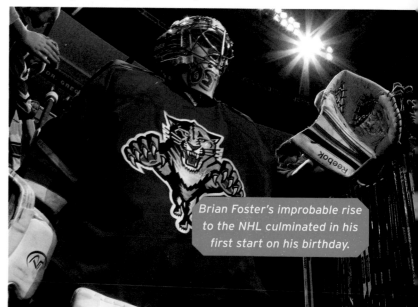

Brian Foster's improbable rise to the NHL culminated in his first start on his birthday.

Seth Jones (right) grew up in the world of the NBA but fell in love with hockey.

Player/ Goalie	Team	Age	Debut Date	G/ Mins	A/ GA	P	PIM/ Decision
Fred Hergert	NYA	23	January 29, 1935	0	0	0	0
Jacques Richard	ATF	20	October 7, 1972	0	0	0	2
Claude Vilgrain	VAN	25	March 1, 1988	1	0	1	0
Patrice Brisebois	MTL	20	January 27, 1991	0	1	1	0
Jean-Marc Pelletier	PHI	21	March 4, 1999	60:00	5		L
Stephen Weiss	FLO	19	April 3, 2002	1	0	1	0
Mike Rupp	NJ	23	January 13, 2003	2	0	2	0
Jeff Heerema	CAR	23	January 17, 2003	1	0	1	2
Mike Green	WAS	20	October 12, 2005	0	0	0	0
Tom Gilbert	EDM	24	January 10, 2007	0	0	0	0
Ray Sawada	DAL	24	February 19, 2009	1	0	1	0
Jared Spurgeon	MIW	21	November 29, 2010	0	0	0	0
Brian Foster	FLO	25	February 4, 2012	4:52	0		nd
Seth Jones	NAS	19	October 3, 2013	0	0	0	0
Yanni Gourde	TB	24	December 15, 2015	0	1	1	2

// Yanni Gourde, Tampa Bay Lightning
December 15, 2015

Gourde represents a classic feel-good story. The small Quebecker had a fine junior career with Victoriaville in the Q but was never drafted. He persevered, though, and eventually signed an AHL contract with the Syracuse Crunch. He played well and led the team in scoring in 2014–15. As a result, the Tampa Bay Lightning invited him to their training camp in September 2015, but he was returned to the minors before the start of the NHL season.

Still, Gourde continued to score, and in mid-December 2015 the Lightning experienced a rash of injuries. Called up, Gourde didn't dress for Tampa's game the night of December 14, but a day later, when the team travelled to Toronto, his name was in the lineup. Happily, it was also his 24th birthday.

His first shift didn't go as planned. He had to wait four and a half minutes to get onto the ice, and he promptly took an interference penalty on Tyler Bozak. The Leafs didn't score, though, and Gourde settled down. Early in the third, he assisted on Mike Blunden's tying goal, and the Lightning ended up with a 5–4 overtime win, making Gourde's night a happy one.

Gourde played one more game before returning to Syracuse. It took him four more years before he became a regular, but his sensational 2017–18 season led to the Lightning signing him to a six-year, $31 million contract. Not bad for someone no team wanted just a few years earlier.

// Seth Jones, Nashville Predators
October 3, 2013

Seth Jones was no call-up, no emergency injury replacement. The son of NBA star Popeye Jones, Seth was drafted 4th overall by Nashville in 2013, a star defenceman in the making. He impressed coach Barry Trotz at training camp and was in the lineup for the team's season opener, October 3, 2013, which also happened to be his 19th birthday.

Trotz also went outside the box in his use of Jones. Rather than putting him with a veteran player, Trotz paired Jones with another rookie, Swede Mattias Ekholm. Despite the 4–2 loss in St. Louis, the blueliners played well together. Jones had 18:35 of ice time and was on ice for both Nashville goals but none of the Blues' scores.

From his birthday debut to today, Jones has never played a game in the minors.

Goalie Playoff Debuts

Seven Special Goalies

Of the 7,863 NHLers in league history and the 144 who made their NHL debuts in the playoffs, only seven have been goalies.

// Jim Franks & Earl Robertson, Detroit Red Wings
March 27 & 30, 1937

One playoff series, two playoff debuts.

The Detroit Red Wings won the Stanley Cup in 1936, and a year later they were looking good again. Facing Montreal in the semi-finals, they had won the first two games, 4–0 and 5–1, and were hoping to lock up the best-of-five series at the Forum on March 27.

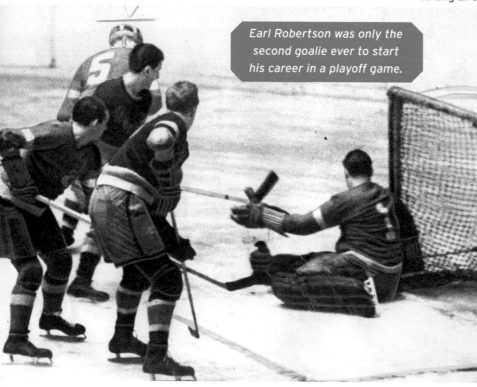

Earl Robertson was only the second goalie ever to start his career in a playoff game.

As happens so frequently, things didn't go as planned. The Habs opened the scoring early on a goal by Johnny Gagnon, but it was a play later in the first period that changed the game and series.

In a mad scramble around the Detroit net, goalie Normie Smith was badly injured. Teams went to their dressing room, agreeing to play the final seconds of the opening period after intermission, while Smith was helped off the ice, unable to move his left arm.

Doctors called it a temporary nerve paralysis. After several minutes, Smith could move his arm a bit and valiantly tried to play when the game got going again. But by the midway point of the second, he was in too much pain and knew he couldn't continue.

The Wings were granted 10 minutes so that their spare goalie, 22-year-old Jimmy Franks, could dress. He had been recalled from the farm team in Pittsburgh. Sensing an opportunity, the Canadiens threw everything they had at the inexperienced goaler, but Franks stood tall. After two periods, it was still a 1–0 game.

Early in the third, the visitors tied the game on a goal by Marty Barry, and by the midway mark, Franks had continued his brilliant play. It was not to be, though. Babe Siebert and then Gagnon again scored, and Detroit had no answer, losing the game, 3–1.

The next morning, the news was no better. Dr. C.L. Tomsu re-examined Smith's arm and reported categorically: "There isn't a chance in the world for him to play Tuesday night. He might be able to play Thursday, if necessary."

GM Jack Adams sprung into action, recalling Earl Robertson from the Pittsburgh Hornets. Despite never having played a minute in the NHL, Robertson was considered a star goalie. The problem was that the Hornets were in an AHL playoff series against Syracuse, so Adams had to send Franks down to replace Robertson.

Game 4, at the Forum, was a goalies' battle of sorts, one that was won by Montreal netminder Wilf Cude. The Red Wings outplayed their opponents, but Cude was sensational and Robertson just a little less so. The result was another 3–1 Montreal win. Robertson, in the dressing room after, was heard to mutter, "I'm better than that."

Smith made an amazing recovery and played in the deciding game of the series, won by the Red Wings, 2–1, in overtime. He then played every minute of the finals, leading the team to its second straight Cup with a 3-2 series win over the New York Rangers.

Smith was the hero of the playoffs, but his injury allowed Franks and Robertson to become the first goalies ever to make their NHL debuts in the playoffs.

// Paul Goodman, Chicago Black Hawks
April 7, 1938

See page 32

// Bob Champoux, Detroit Red Wings
March 29, 1964

"Rookie in Net, Wings Still Win!"

Such was the headline in the *Detroit Free Press* after a most unexpected NHL debut for goalie Bob Champoux, who remains to this day the only goalie to make his NHL debut in the playoffs and win the game.

Daniel Berthiaume was sensational in his playoff debut with Winnipeg.

Champoux responded to the pressure, that's for sure. The 21-year-old had just finished his first year of pro hockey, and it wasn't pretty. Goalie for last place Cincinnati of the Central Hockey League, he had a staggering goals-against average of 5.34. He was Detroit property, and he was in the stands as the Red Wings played Chicago in Game 2 of the 1964 Stanley Cup semi-finals, at the raucous Stadium.

Minding his own business, Champoux was watching Terry Sawchuk in the Detroit goal, but just a few minutes into the game, the legendary goalie had to leave because of a pinched nerve in his left shoulder.

Not only did Champoux have to race down to the dressing room to put on his equipment, he entered with Chicago on a power play and the fans going nuts. But the youngster held the fort, and in the second period his mates staked him to a 3–0 lead.

The Hawks stormed the goal thereafter, drawing to within one and threatening to tie it late in the second, but Champoux was fantastic. In the third, Detroit pulled away with two early goals, to make it 5–2, but the game wasn't done yet.

Two quick goals made it 5–4, and then the Hawks got a power play. Champoux, though, made a great glove save off a patented Bobby Hull blast and another in tight off Bill Hay. Final score, 5–4 for Detroit.

Sawchuk played the next game but was hurt later in the series, to be replaced by Roger Crozier. Incredibly, Champoux didn't play again in the NHL for nine years, until after expansion, with the lowly California Golden Seals. In between, he played in a variety of leagues—AHL, WHL, CHL, EHL, CPHL—but this one heroic moment when Sawchuk was injured gave him his greatest moment of NHL glory.

// Daniel Berthiaume, Winnipeg Jets
April 12, 1986

The Winnipeg Jets were on the ropes in their first round match of the 1986 playoffs against the mighty Calgary Flames (technically, the series was called the Smythe Division semi-finals). The Flames took the first two games of the best-of-five, 5–1 and 6–4, so Game 3, in Winnipeg, on April 12, was a must-win game for the Jets, playing at home.

In an effort to shake things up, coach John Ferguson said the day before the game that he was "seriously considering" starting untested Daniel Berthiaume in goal. This was both crazy and a real possibility given that he had used three goalies—Dan Bouchard, Brian Hayward, and Marc Behrend—in the first two games.

But Berthiaume had just finished his junior hockey season in Chicoutimi, and the 20-year-old had never played pro anywhere, at any level.

Sure enough, though, Ferguson honoured his threat—and Berthiaume was sensational. Yes, the Jets lost, 4–3, in overtime, but it was largely thanks to the goalie's play that the game was so close or even got to OT. He stopped two breakaways in overtime, one by Joel Otto, another by Hakan Loob, who also couldn't beat Berthiaume on two other breakaways during regulation time.

Two of the shots that beat him were deflections, and overall Berthiaume stopped 39 of 43 shots. The Flames were high in their praise of the newcomer and were glad he hadn't played earlier in the series.

// Mike Richter, New York Rangers
April 9, 1989

Thanks to the antics of general manager Phil Esposito, the New York Rangers were pretty much the laughingstock of the NHL in 1988–89. Nicknamed "Trader Phil" by fans and media, he bought and sold players like they were records at a garage sale. Over the course of the year, some 40 players got into at least one game for the Blueshirts.

Then, four days before the start of the playoffs, he fired coach Michel Bergeron and took over the bench-bossing duties himself. The team had lost 10 of its previous 13 games, and under Espo they lost the last two of the regular season.

The Rangers were set to face Pittsburgh in the first round of the playoffs, and that made for added controversy. The problem was that Phil had consulted his brother, Tony, about whether or not to fire Bergeron, but Tony was the general manager of the Penguins! Familial assistance aside, this was a major breach of trust.

The Rangers continued to lose in the playoffs, going down 3–1, 7–4, and 5–3 in the first three games and needing a win in Game 4 to stay alive in the series. Esposito continued to perplex supporters and critics alike by electing to start Mike Richter in that pivotal game. (Richter had been playing with the Denver Rangers in the IHL and had no NHL experience.)

And so, on April 9, 1989, Mike Richter played his first of many NHL games. He was the first Rangers player to make his debut in the playoffs, and he was starting ahead of incumbents John Vanbiesbrouck and Bob Froese.

Richter got off to a rough start, allowing three goals on seven shots in the first 11 minutes of play, but he settled down and got better as the game went on. The damage had been done, though. The Rangers rallied a bit but still lost, 4–3, bringing their record under coach Phil to 0-6 and sending the team home for the summer.

"I'm a little frustrated because I had a bad first period," Richter lamented later. "That was the margin of victory. I wish I could have stopped those early shots. But our team never gave up, and we almost overcame that first period."

Jake Allen's playoff debut didn't last long—just 67 seconds.

Esposito was not apologetic in the least with his decision-making. "The reasons for using Richter were twofold," he said, analytically. "First, he had a heck of a season. Everybody in the league knows Mike is a superb goaltender, an NHL goalie. And then we thought we'd try to shake things up. We felt that with Mike we wouldn't lose anything in goal. I can't blame Mike Richter [for the loss]."

// Jake Allen, St. Louis Blues
April 30, 2012

Like snowflakes, no two NHL debuts are the same, and Jake Allen goes in the books as having the shortest playoff debut ever—just 67 seconds. And to make it more special, he didn't even have to stop a single shot.

The Western Conference semi-finals included a St. Louis–Los Angeles best-of-seven, and the Kings won Game 1, 3–1, in St. Louis. They were also dominating Game 2 when, in the third period, the Blues were in a five-on-three situation.

Detroit's Bob Champoux is the only goalie ever to make his debut in the playoffs—and win the game.

Wanting a time out to keep his number-one power-play unit out, but having already used it, coach Ken Hitchcock used the old "change the goalie" strategy. He called Brian Elliott to the bench and told Jake Allen to go in goal.

Allen was so shocked that he didn't even have time to think about making his debut. He went to his crease, did a few stretches, and the Blues went back to their power play. At the next whistle, Hitchcock changed goalies again, and Allen was done. He played 1:07 of game time, didn't face a shot, recorded only zeroes on the game sheet, and left.

Goalie Playoff Debuts

Goalie	Team	Date	Mins	GA	Decision
Jim Franks	DET	March 27, 1937	29:32	2	L
Earl Robertson	DET	March 30, 1937	60:00	3	L
Paul Goodman	CHI	April 7, 1938	60:00	5	L
Bob Champoux	DET	March 29, 1964	54:38	4	W
Daniel Berthiaume	WJE	April 12, 1986	68:25	4	OTL
Mike Richter	NYR	April 9, 1989	58:17	4	L
Jake Allen	STL	April 30, 2012	1:07	0	nd

Making History

The 1938 Stanley Cup Finals was a crazy affair. It featured Toronto and Chicago, one team that clearly deserved to be there and another that somehow survived to get there. The deserving team was the Maple Leafs. They finished first in the Canadian Division with a 24-15-9 record and then swept Boston in three games to make it to the finals.

The Hawks had the opposite record to the Leafs, 14-25-9, but they won two best-of-three series, against the Canadiens and New York Americans. In the final game of the latter, goalie Mike Karakas broke his toe and was unable to play the first game of the finals.

Rules of the day allowed the Hawks to bring in a replacement, but only if the opposition agreed. The Hawks wanted Rangers' superstar Dave Kerr, but the Leafs refused, suggesting Alfie Moore instead. Moore had played with the Pittsburgh Hornets in the AHL but his season was over, so on the afternoon of Game 1, he was in a Toronto tavern quaffing some beverages.

Moore scrambled down to Maple Leaf Gardens, got dressed in a room of his own, and then went out and played a sensational game, leading the Hawks to a 3–1 victory.

Chicago brought in two recruits for Game 2. Pete Palangio, a 29-year-old who ran a tour bus to the home of the Dionne quintuplets in North Bay, was brought in to replace right winger Mush March, and Paul Goodman was brought in as a backup to Moore.

George Strickler, in the *Chicago Daily Tribune*, was unabashed in describing Goodman's role: "Goodman, however, will sit on the bench. No manner of argument could persuade the Black Hawks to switch from Moore."

Strickler's confidence was no match for Conn Smythe's resolve. The Leafs' owner, incensed by the opening-game loss, had Moore barred from the rest of the playoffs, and Chicago coach Bill Stewart had no choice but to turn to Goodman, who hadn't played in three weeks.

Nervous and lacking game condition, Goodman was no match for a determined Leafs team. The Hawks may have lost the game, 5–1, but Karakas returned for Games 3 and 4, both Chicago wins, and won the Cup.

Still, on April 7, 1938, Goodman made history. He became the first goalie, then or since, to make his NHL debut in the Stanley Cup Finals. And, despite the loss, he got his name on the Stanley Cup after playing just one game!

Rocket Launch

Maurice Richard

MONTREAL CANADIENS // OCTOBER 31, 1942

Think of the incredible excitement in 1979 when young Wayne Gretzky came into the league, or just a few years later when Mario Lemieux was drafted first overall. Think of "franchise savers" like Sidney Crosby, Connor McDavid, and Auston Matthews. They were superstars before they took their first shift.

Not so with 21-year-old Maurice Richard. When he made his debut on Halloween night in Montreal in 1942, the *Gazette* gave him no special introduction, calling him

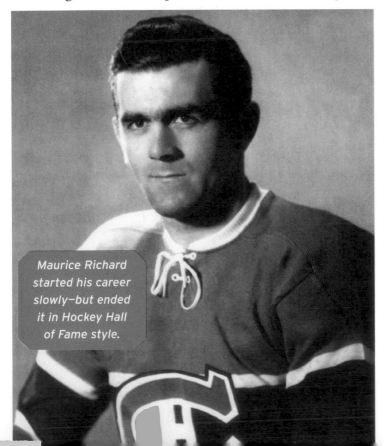

Maurice Richard started his career slowly—but ended it in Hockey Hall of Fame style.

"swift-skating" and noting that most of his previous three seasons had been marred by significant injury.

In 1939, with Verdun, he broke his leg in the first game and missed the entire season. A year later, he suffered a broken arm and missed more than half a season. His fragility, not his star skills, was the only talk he generated.

The Habs hosted the Bruins to open the 1942–43 season, and Richard was the only Montreal player making his NHL debut. On the other side, Bill Shill, Jackie Schmidt, and Don Gallinger were all playing in their first game for the B's.

A day later, though, Richard was the rising star. He played on the Ambulance Line (so named by coach Dick Irvin) with Tony Demers (who missed all of the previous season with his own broken leg) and Elmer Lach, and according to *Gazette* reporter Dink Carroll, "was a standout. He was going at top speed all night, carried the puck well, and outskated his checks."

Richard also assisted on the game's first goal, by Demers, just 36 seconds after the opening faceoff. The Habs went on to win, 3–2, much to the delight of the Forum fans. Less than two months later, however, Maurice broke his ankle in a game against those same Bruins and missed the rest of the season.

Just a Child

Bep Guidolin

BOSTON BRUINS // NOVEMBER 12, 1942

It was Kid Line versus Kid Line, but it was no contest. The Leafs' Jack McLean got all the ink the next day, but it was Bep Guidolin who set the record.

The Bruins were in Toronto to face the Leafs, but these were the war years and "normal" no longer existed. Many NHLers had left their teams to join the war efforts, and the Bruins had a particularly tough time finding quality replacements. Desperate, the Bruins signed talented teen Bep Guidolin to a contract.

What made this unique was that when Guidolin made his NHL debut the night of November 12, 1942, at Maple Leaf Gardens, he was 16 years, 338 days old. Appropriately, he wore number 16. He was the youngest player ever to skate in the NHL, and given Entry Draft rules of today's NHL he will likely remain so for the rest of time.

But on the other side of the ice was McLean. The 19-year-old was also making his NHL debut, for the Leafs, and he was sensational. He opened the scoring for Toronto in the second period and assisted on two more goals in the third, leading the Leafs to a 3–1 win.

McLean played on a Kid Line with youngsters Gaye Stewart and Bud Poile, while Guidolin played with Don Gallinger and Jack Shill. The Bruins babies were stymied, however, by goalie Turk Broda.

Boston general manager Art Ross was pleased with the play of his young sprouts. "A few more games, and they'll go places!" he enthused.

Twelve days later, in his second career game, Guidolin, indeed, scored. Despite his age, he played the rest of the season with Boston, counting seven goals and 22 points in 42 games. Not bad at all for a mid-teenager. As a result, Guidolin holds all "youngest to" records, such as youngest to score a goal, record an assist, earn a penalty.

Bep Guidolin (No. 12) was only 16 when he played in the NHL, a record that will last forever.

Brothers O' Mine

Max, Doug, and Reg Bentley

CHICAGO BLACK HAWKS // DECEMBER 3, 1942

On the afternoon of December 3, 1942, Chicago Black Hawks coach Paul Thompson made a decision that created hockey history. He decided to move Bill Thoms from right wing back to defence and call up Reg Bentley to play on a line with brothers Max and Doug for a home game against the New York Rangers.

Max and Doug had played together more or less full time since 1939, but this was different: for the first time in NHL history, three brothers would play as a complete forward line.

Only 6,730 fans braved a fiercely cold night to come to the Stadium to witness this momentous event, and the brothers almost connected as a trio on a goal, which would have been more incredible. As it was, Doug Bentley scored in the third to give the Hawks breathing room, 3–1. The second assist was credited to Max Bentley, but the first went to Aud Tuten.

Although he was a pro for nearly two decades, Reg had an NHL career that lasted only about six weeks. He scored once in 11 games, but that goal is the one that dreams are made of.

On January 3, 1943, Reg scored on Jimmy Franks, in New York, with assists going to Max and Doug. This was the first time in NHL history that three brothers combined for a goal.

Reg played almost exclusively in the west before and after these 11 games. More famously, Max and Doug went on to have Hall of Fame careers, with Max winning the Stanley Cup three times with the Leafs in the late 1940s. But for a brief time in 1942–43, the three brothers made a little hockey history by playing together in the NHL.

The Bentley brothers–(l-r) Reg, Max, Doug.

From the Get Go

A player has exactly 15 seconds to do what Gus Bodnar did, and he must use those 15 seconds at the exact beginning of his NHL career, his first NHL game, his first NHL shift, the start of the game by the scoreclock.

Indeed, Gus Bodnar was out for the opening faceoff on a line with Elwin Morris and Bob Davidson, and just 15 seconds later, Bodnar had his first career goal. He beat the Rangers' Ken McAuley in a game at Maple Leaf Gardens before 11,654 wartime patrons. In the end, the game finished as a 5–2 win for the home side, and Bodnar was the clear star, scoring twice and adding an assist.

The *New York Times* called Bodnar a "20-year-old Army reject from Fort William," when describing his goal, a quick shot off a loose puck left by McAuley on the opening rush of the game.

Those three points put Bodnar in elite company. Only 61 players have scored twice or more in their debut and only 40 have tallied as many as three points.

Including that night nearly eight decades ago, some 7,863 players have made their NHL debuts, and none have matched him.

This game was extraordinary in itself from an NHL debut perspective because some 11 players from both teams were making their initial foray into the world's best league. For the Rangers, those players included Tom Dewar, Archie Fraser, Jack Mann, Jack McDonald, Don Raleigh, and McAuley. For the Leafs, newcomers included Bodnar, Morris, Red Carr, Eric Prentice, and Ross Johnstone.

Gus Bodnar's record for fastest first goal has stood the test of time.

Just a Sec

Bernie Ruelle

In order to understand how Bernie Ruelle got into the lineup for the Detroit Red Wings' season and home opener on October 31, 1943, an understanding of how contracts worked in the old days is necessary. Way back then, most players were signed for one season at a time and re-negotiated a new deal before the start of each opening night.

Of course, the owners held all the cards because a player couldn't simply go to another team if he didn't like his team's offer—he was "owned" by his team, more or less, in perpetuity. As well, players often didn't sign until days, sometimes hours, before the first game, figuring—usually incorrectly—that the longer they held out, the better chance they had of obtaining an optimal deal.

Detroit general manager Jack Adams was as tough as they came, and he brooked no dissent. But as game time approached in 1943, with the lowly New York Rangers in town, Adams could not get defenceman Cully Simon and forward Bill Jennings to sign on the proverbial dotted line. And so, Adams turned to the farm and brought in Rudy Zunich and Pat Egan to play spot duty on the blue line and Ruelle to take Jennings's spot up front.

The Red Wings jumped out to a 4–1 lead by the midway mark of the game, and although the Rangers scored a couple to make it 4–3, the Winged Wheelers added four in the final half of the third period to waltz to an 8–3 win.

Here's the kicker. Ruelle scored the game's final goal. Falling to the ice, he beat Ken McAuley from about 20 feet out. Time of the goal: 19:59.

That's right. One tick away from a 7–3 win and a mostly meaningless NHL debut, Ruelle instead made history by being the player who waited the longest in game one to score his first goal. He got into one more game a week later, a 6–4 win against Boston, but Ruelle didn't get his name on the scoresheet. He never played in the NHL after that.

And Jennings? He signed a contract right after Detroit's opening-night victory.

DETROIT (8)   NEW YORK (3)

Student Earns A+

Jean Marois

TORONTO MAPLE LEAFS // DECEMBER 18, 1943

Coach Hap Day was beside himself on the morning of December 18, 1943. His star netminder, Turk Broda, was enlisted in Canada's war efforts. His new regular goaltender, Benny Grant, was hurt. Chicago was in town for a date with the Leafs, and Day had a small list of not very satisfying goalies who could play for the team this night.

Jean Marois played in the NHL while still a high-school student.

At about 3 p.m. on Saturday afternoon, interim general manager Frank Selke, fulfilling the duties of Conn Smythe, himself off to war, settled on 19-year-old Jean ("Johnny") Marois, a student at St. Michael's College in Toronto, one of the top junior teams in the country and one of the Leafs' two feeder teams (along with the Marlies).

Marois was so nervous he let in one long shot early to Bill Mosienko, but the Leafs pounded Chicago's puckstopper Hec Highton, himself only 19, to the tune of eight goals, and the home side coasted to an 8–4 win. The Hawks actually led 4–2 in the second, but as the Leafs' offence improved, so, too, did Marois's confidence.

Marois was perhaps also a little rusty. He had been going to St. Mike's for eight years and hadn't played for the team for a week because of exams. He didn't make the trip across the border for the return game in Chicago on Sunday, and, incredibly, it would be another decade before he played another game in the NHL (with, ironically, the Black Hawks).

Master Hockey

Gordon Howe

The longest and in many ways most distinguished career in NHL history began modestly if not altogether innocuously at the Olympia in Detroit on October 16, 1946, the opening night of the 1946–47 season.

The Red Wings hosted the Maple Leafs in a game that featured the NHL debuts of no fewer than six players, three for the Maple Leafs (Garth Boesch, Howie Meeker, and Gus Mortson) and three for the Wings (Thain Simon, Cliff Simpson, and Mr. Hockey himself).

Of course on this night Howe was a long way from being called Mr. Hockey. He was but an 18-year-old with one year of pro hockey under his belt, that with Omaha in the USHL. In his rookie season in the NHL, he scored just seven goals in 15 games, but the first came midway through the second period of his debut.

The goal was not the highlight of the night, though, and came and went pretty quickly. It gave the Wings a brief 2–1 lead, but the Leafs came back and went ahead. Detroit tied the game with only 11 seconds remaining in the third in the most dramatic way. With goalie Harry Lumley on the bench (a rare strategy in 1946), Sid Abel beat Turk Broda with a long screen shot to tie the game, 3–3.

The other significant feature of this game was its roughness. The game included 12 penalties and four fights, the pure intensity of play explosive on virtually every shift.

Howe's goal came on a fine play that ended with a shot that fooled Turk Broda at 13:36 of the second. *The Detroit Free Press* wrote that, "Gordon Howe skated through the entire Leaf defence, exchanged passes with Brown and Abel, and tallied from 10 feet out."

By the time he retired in 1980, after his 32nd NHL season, Howe had played in more games, scored more goals, and recorded more points than any player in league history.

There was only one Gordie Howe, but he had humble beginnings.

Needle Skates into the Crease

Gil Mayer

TORONTO MAPLE LEAFS // DECEMBER 1, 1949

Conn Smythe had had enough! Turk Broda, just about the greatest goalie in the NHL during the 1940s, was performing with unnecessary girth, according to the Leafs' owner and general manager. By late November 1949, Turk weighed 197 pounds, which, in Smythe's estimation, was too much. He ordered the goalie to get down to 190 or lose his job.

Turk went to his west-end YMCA in Toronto to work off the poundage, but in the meantime, the Leafs had games to play and a net to guard. Enter slender 'tender Gil Mayer, all five-foot-six, 130 pounds of him, who had the opposite problem: he needed to gain weight!

Nevertheless, Mayer made his NHL debut the night of December 1, 1949, and surely he is the only goalie to make an entrance because the incumbent was deemed too fat! Injuries? Sure. Superstar in the making? Of course. Replacing tubby goalie? Hmmm . . .

The Turk's weight became a national obsession for a week or more. Joe Perlove, crack scribe for the *Toronto Star*, contacted the chief nutritionist at the Health and Welfare office in Ottawa, trying to get to the bottom of the dilemma. Opined Dr. L.B. Pett: "Too much weight is always related to eating habits," he offered, "and a person can't blame his parents, grandparents, or anyone else for his extra pounds."

So, when the Red Wings rolled in to Maple Leaf Gardens on the first day of December, the Leafs had 20-year-old Mayer—aptly nicknamed Needle—between the pipes.

Although he played well, Mayer and the Leafs lost to the Red Wings, 2–0, and all reports indicate Broda was down to 189 in due course (although he looked exactly the same). Smythe had got huge publicity across the country for benching Broda, but both knew the Leafs couldn't win without him.

Broda congratulated Mayer after his first game, and then Turk saw Detroit captain Sid Abel in the corridor and asked him if the Wings had a tough night.

Joked Abel, "It's always tougher when you're not around."

Turk Broda's weight was Gil Mayer's opportunity.

Doubleheader Dick

Dick Bittner

BOSTON BRUINS // FEBRUARY 11, 1950

Jack Gelineau, Boston's number-one goalie, had been out, missing two games with a groin injury. But he was back in net the night of February 11, 1950, an important home date with playoff implications against Detroit.

Gelineau was in pain, though, and his teammates hardly helped him out. The result was a 9–4 shellacking, and Montreal was in town for a game against the Bruins the very next night. Actually, Montreal was barely in town before the start of the game. A coal shortage cancelled the team's overnight train the previous evening, so the Habs had to take the day train, arriving at the Garden just before 8 p.m.

Across the hall, Boston coach Buck Boucher conferred with three goalies—Gelineau, Dick Bittner, and Lorne Chabot, Jr., trying to figure out who should play. The coach decided Gelineau's groin was too tender, and after watching Bittner and the Boston Olympics shut out the Atlantic City Sea Gulls, 4–0, in the afternoon game at the Garden, Boucher gave him the nod.

> Bittner stopped 18 of 21 shots for the Bruins, earning an important tie before the team embarked on a five-game road trip. Gelineau got better, and Bittner went back to the EHL, never to return to the NHL. A one-game wonder, a two-games-in-a-day warrior, and a hero for a night.

Dick Bittner played two games in a day, his NHL debut the second of a busy Sunday.

The Replacement

Lorne Davis

Lorne Davis played 95 NHL games over a nine-year career.

Lorne Davis

No Rocket? No Boom Boom? No problem.

The Montreal Canadiens limped into the Stadium in Chicago for a big Thursday night game, but they were without their top two players, Maurice Richard and Bernie Geoffrion.

Called up from the Buffalo Bisons of the AHL was Lorne Davis, a 21-year-old farmhand who was up for just the one game on an emergency basis. The youngster from Saskatchewan more than held his own.

Davis got his name on the scoresheet three times. The first came in the form of a boarding penalty early in the game, but nothing bad came from the infraction. Early in the second, he set up linemate Dick Gamble for a goal to give the visiting Habs a 2–0 lead.

Then, after the Hawks scored in the third to cut Montreal's lead to 3–1, Davis scored an insurance marker at 13:27.

Davis played but three games this season and 95 over the next decade with four teams (winning the Cup with Montreal in 1953). But his first game remains special, both because of the players he was replacing and the results he produced.

Playoff Debut Assists

// Jim McFadden, Detroit Red Wings
March 29, 1947

Of the 144 players in NHL history who made their NHL debut in the playoffs, only 14 have earned an assist. Jim McFadden, however, stands out. He is the only player in league history to record two points in his playoff debut (both assists).

And he did so while replacing Gordie Howe in the lineup.

McFadden made his debut on March 29, 1947, for Detroit, in Game 2 of the Red Wings' semi-finals series against the Maple Leafs. Toronto won the opener at the Gardens, 3–2 in overtime, but in Game 2 things were markedly different.

Put simply, Detroit's lineup was in tatters because of injuries. Goalie Harry Lumley was in hospital for groin surgery and had to be replaced by Red Almas, and Gerry Couture cracked a bone in his right hand in the first game and couldn't play. Howe, meanwhile, had bad knee pain and didn't think he was going to be able to dress for the second game.

General manager Jack Adams called up McFadden from Buffalo of the AHL to play right wing for Howe. Cliff Simpson and Fern Gauthier were also recalled from the team's practice squad, the latter to replace Couture on a line with Pat Lundy and Jim Conacher.

Detroit's Jim McFadden is the only player in NHL history to earn two points in his playoff debut.

In the end, though, Howe played, but so, too, did McFadden, taking the place instead of Al Dewsbury. McFadden had an immediate impact, forcing Jimmy Thompson to hold him on a rush and getting the penalty call early in the game. The Wings scored twice and never looked back, winning in a 9–1 romp.

"We were outskated, outplayed, out-pushed, out-fought, and out-anything else you can think of," said livid Leafs' owner Conn Smythe after the game.

McFadden set up a Billy Taylor goal early in the second period to make it 3–0 for the visitors, and he assisted again on a Ted Lindsay goal early in the third to make it 4–1. The Wings scored six unanswered goals in that final period. After the game, Adams roared into the dressing room and shook McFadden's hand vigourously. "You were great out there, Jim! You were great!" he enthused.

It was to get no better, though. The Leafs made adjustments and gathered their wits for Game 3, winning it and the next two by 4–1, 4–1, and 6–1 scores to eliminate the Wings. McFadden played in every game and didn't record another point after those initial two helpers, but statistically it remains the greatest playoff debut in NHL history.

// Dunc Fisher, New York Rangers
April 4, 1948

In what turned out to be the final game of the semi-finals series, the Detroit Red Wings beat the Rangers, 4–2, in New York, eliminating them from the Stanley Cup chase in six games. The Wings opened a four-goal lead by the midway point of the third period to wrap up the game, and Fisher got his assist on a Don Raleigh goal to make it 4–1.

Fisher was one of four players called up from New Haven for the game, along with Jack Lancien, Nick Mickoski, and Buck Davies.

// Sid McNabney, Montreal Canadiens
March 27, 1951

Every player's debut has something special about it, and in the case of Sid McNabney, his claim to fame is that his debut was the longest of all time. He and his Montreal Canadiens teammates needed four overtime periods to defeat Detroit at the Forum, 3–2, and, given the two teams' performances this season, it was an improbable victory at that.

The Red Wings finished first overall in the regular season with 101 points, a league record. Their record of 44-13-13 was miles ahead of third place Montreal, which had 65 points and a sub-.500 record of 25-30-15. Detroit, which had home-ice advantage in the series, of course, had lost only three of 35 games at the Olympia all year, including a 5-1-1 advantage against the Habs.

Adding to that, the Habs were missing four regulars—Elmer Lach (ankle), Ken Mosdell (torn groin), Bernie Geoffrion (knee), and Bobby Dawes (separated shoulder).

And so McNabney got the call from Buffalo of the American Hockey League after the Bisons were eliminated from the AHL playoffs. He set up Butch Bouchard for the 1–1 goal midway through the first period after Gordie Howe had scored just a minute earlier.

McNabney also incurred a hooking penalty early in the second, but there was no great price to pay as the Habs' penalty killers did a perfect job. Montreal went on to win the next game in three overtime periods and the series in six games, losing in the Cup Finals to the Maple Leafs.

In all, McNabney played five games in these playoffs, the only NHL appearances of his career.

// Wayne Hicks, Chicago Black Hawks
March 24, 1960

Without Bobby Hull (throat injury) and Stan Mikita (broken jaw), the Chicago Black Hawks were no match for Montreal in the opening game of the 1960 Stanley Cup

semi-finals. Even still, the Habs managed only to sneak out a 4–3 series win as a stubborn Hawks team did everything but upset the four-time defending Cup champions.

Wayne Hicks, who had played with Sault Ste. Marie in the EPHL, got into his first NHL game in place of Mikita and helped orchestrate a late rally. Trailing, 4–2, he and Pierre Pilote made a nice passing play to set up Ron Murphy for a goal at 18:17, but the Hawks couldn't get the tying puck past Jacques Plante.

Hicks never played again in these playoffs but did play another 115 games in the regular season over the next several years.

// Len Frig, Chicago Black Hawks
May 3, 1973

Whereas players make their debuts in the regular season because a coach wants to give them a chance or see what they're like, the playoffs are a different matter. It's so frequently tied to team performance or injuries, and injuries are more common in the playoffs because of the increased intensity.

And so it was during the Chicago-Montreal Stanley Cup Finals of 1973. Not only had the Habs won the first two games by comfortable scores of 8–3 and 4–1, the Hawks were hurting: Stan Mikita had a bad finger; Doug Jarrett a cracked rib; Keith Magnuson a broken jaw.

As a result, coach Billy Reay recalled Len Frig and Dave Kryskow from Dallas, the team's Central Hockey League affiliate. Frig, a big and strong defenceman, was slated to take Magnuson's spot, and Kryskow ended up not playing in Game 3.

It was a game to remember, almost one of the greatest comebacks in sports history—but not. Instead, Frig turned out to be something of a hero.

The Hawks could do no wrong on this night for the longest time. They built a 4–0 lead after 20 minutes, and Frig helped to add to the tally early in the second. Mikita, who ended up playing, found Frig in the high slot and got him the puck. Frig took a quick shot, and John Marks re-directed the puck past a helpless Ken Dryden.

That made it 5–0, and no one then could have imagined that seemingly meaningless goal would turn out to be the game winner. Montreal got a goal, then another, and another, and a fourth. The 5–4 game in the third now got more than a little too close for the Hawks' comfort, but they held off the Canadiens, scored two late goals into the empty net, and won 7–4.

And the 23-year-old Frig not only got into his first game, a playoff game no less, he assisted on the winning goal.

Player	Team	Date	Score	Round	Game	Time of assist
Jim McFadden	DET	March 29, 1947	9-1	SF	Game 2	2:10 2nd/5:27 3rd
Dunc Fisher	NYR	April 4, 1948	2-4	SF	Game 6	12:49 3rd
Sid McNabney	MTL	March 27, 1951	3-2	SF	Game 1	13:23 1st
Wayne Hicks	CHI	March 24, 1960	3-4	SF	Game 1	18:17 3rd
Len Frig	CHI	May 3, 1973	7-4	F	Game 3	2:08 2nd
Dave Salvian	NYI	April 7, 1977	2-1	Pre	Game 2	13:56 1st
Rick Paterson	CHI	April 22, 1979	1-3	QF	Game 4	7:05 2nd
George McPhee	NYR	April 5, 1983	5-3	DSF	Game 1	18:44 2nd
Cliff Ronning	STL	April 9, 1986	2-1	DSF	Game 1	4:53 2nd
Tony Amonte	NYR	April 11, 1991	4-5	DSF	Game 5	10:35 1st
Steve Junker	NYI	May 12, 1993	7-5	DF	Game 6	7:19 1st
Jarome Iginla	CGY	April 21, 1996	5-7	CQF	Game 3	1:27 3rd
Marcel Goc	SJ	April 15, 2004	3-1	CQF	Game 5	9:34 2nd
Mark Stone	OTT	April 21, 2012	2-0	CQF	Game 5	9:18 1st

// Dave Salvian, New York Islanders
April 7, 1977

See page 144

// Rick Paterson, Chicago Black Hawks
April 22, 1979

Bob Verdi, distinguished writer of the *Chicago Tribune*, was in no mood for compliments and kind words on April 22, 1979, the night Rick Paterson made his big-league debut.

The Hawks lost that night to the New York Islanders, 3–1, concluding a four-game sweep of the Stanley Cup quarter-finals. That one goal was the Hawks' first in more than 180 minutes of game action, and that loss was the team's record-setting 16th playoff loss in a row.

So, even though Paterson assisted on the team's lone goal, Verdi could manage only to say that "[Mike] Walton's goal, assisted by Rick Paterson, a minor league graduate who exhibited signs of hope, merely cut the Islander advantage to 2–1."

And that was it. Paterson's debut came and went as quickly as the Hawks' season.

// George McPhee, New York Rangers
April 5, 1983

The Rangers beat the Flyers, 5–3, in Game 1 of the best-of-five preliminary round series in the 1983 playoffs, and McPhee made his contribution to the win.

The 24-year-old got into the game as a replacement for the injured Don Maloney (arthritic right knee) and played on a line with Ed Johnstone and Mike Allison. McPhee set up the team's fifth goal in the second period, holding the puck until the perfect moment before feeding Johnstone, who scored.

// Cliff Ronning, St. Louis Blues
April 9, 1986

Drafted 134th overall in 1984 by St. Louis, Cliff Ronning wasn't supposed to make it, and if he ever did, it would be for nothing more than a cup of coffee. He was too small.

But the year after the Draft, 1984–85, he scored a preposterous 197 points with the New Westminster Bruins, and he impressed coach Dave King so much that King invited the pint-sized player to skate for Canada's National Team in preparation for the 1988 Olympics in Calgary.

Ronning accepted, and for a year and a half he was on the team, but in between he managed to play a few games in the NHL. In fact, Ronning dressed for the

Blues for the series opener of the division semi-finals against Minnesota, on April 9, 1986. Joining him was National Team teammate Brian Benning, and they got to Minneapolis after a 32-hour trip from the Soviet Union a few days previous. To complicate matters, visa problems ensured the 20-year-old Ronning got in only one practice with the team before the playoffs started.

All the same, he helped St. Louis win the game, 2–1, on the road. It wasn't necessarily a play to tell the grandkids about, but it got the Blues on the board all the same. Early in the second period, Ronning dumped the puck into the Minnesota corner. Mark Hunter dug the puck out and got it in front to Lee Norwood, and his quick shot beat Don Beaupre. It was Norwood's first career playoff goal.

The North Stars tied it up later in the period, but a short-handed goal from Doug Gilmour gave the visiting Blues the series lead on the road.

And the tiny Ronning not fit for the NHL? He lasted 18 years and skated in 1,137 regular-season games.

// Tony Amonte, New York Rangers
April 11, 1991

Dino Ciccarelli gave the visiting Washington Capitals a key 5–4 win in overtime of Game 5 of the division semi-finals in Madison Square Garden, dimming the bright performance of a Rangers rookie line consisting of Amonte (one assist), Steve Rice (goal, assist), and Corey Millen (goal, assist). Amonte's assist came on Millen's goal midway through the first period, giving the Rangers a short-lived 1–0 lead.

// Steve Junker, New York Islanders
May 12, 1993

Game 6 of the 1993 Prince of Wales Conference Finals is where Steve Junker made his NHL debut, and it came because Patrick Flatley suffered a knee injury in Game 5. Junker did his bit in the crucial 7–5 win by assisting on a Derek King goal eight minutes into the game that put the Islanders up, 2–1.

// Jarome Iginla, Calgary Flames
April 21, 1996

It is just a matter of time before we can add Jarome Iginla's name to the very short list of Hockey Hall of Fame members whose first NHL game came in the playoffs. The just-retired Iginla isn't yet Hall of Fame eligible, but the minute he is, he'll be inducted.

And, indeed, he seemed to be destined for greatness from an early age. Even at 16, he was a Memorial Cup champion with the Kamloops Blazers, in 1994. At 17, he was a repeat winner. That summer, 1995, the Dallas Stars drafted him 11th overall, and midway through the 1995–96 season he helped Canada win gold at the World Junior Championship.

Iginla was named the tournament's Best Forward, but in a rare situation he was traded in the NHL while at Canada's pre-tournament training camp with the juniors. From a distance, he learned that he and Corey Millen were traded by the Stars to the Calgary Flames for Joe Nieuwendyk.

The Blazers were upset in the WHL playoffs, but the Flames immediately signed Iginla to an NHL contract. In the opening round of the playoffs, the Flames faced Chicago, but the Hawks won the first two games at the Stadium.

Back in Calgary for a must-win Game 3, Iginla was inserted into the lineup and played on the first line with Theo Fleury and German Titov. It was a game Iginla will remember for the rest of his life, not just because it was his first game, not just because he recorded his first point, but also because it was almost the greatest comeback in Stanley Cup history. Almost.

Unfortunately, it was the Hawks who jumped out to a stunning 5–0 lead early in the second period, but Fleury got one back later in the period to make it 5–1. Fleury got his second early in the third, assisted by Iginla, and the Flames got two more to make it a 5–4 game.

That was as close as they got. Chicago pulled away with two late goals to win, 7–5. The next game saw Iginla score his first career goal, but the Hawks won that game as well, 2–1, in triple overtime, to eliminate the Flames. But by this time, "Iggy" had given the Flames something to look forward to for the next decade and more.

// Marcel Goc, San Jose Sharks
April 15, 2004

Like Len Frig, Marcel Goc not only made his NHL entrance in the playoffs, he assisted on the winning goal. The bonus was that it was also the series winner, San Jose eliminating St. Louis in five games after a 3–1 win on April 15, 2004.

With the game tied 1–1 midway through the middle period, Goc checked Christian Backman in the St. Louis end, and the puck went right to Mark Smith. Smith snapped a quick shot past Chris Osgood to give the Sharks a lead they never relinquished.

Goc played only 5:23 this night but also appeared in four more games in these playoffs, later scoring his first career goal. The Sharks lost in the Conference Finals to Calgary, but Goc went on to have a fine NHL career.

Mark Stone had an impressive debut in Ottawa,
helping the Sens beat the Rangers, 2-0.

// Mark Stone, Ottawa Senators
April 21, 2012

The 2011–12 season was a good one for Mark Stone. Drafted a lowly 178th overall by Ottawa in 2010, the 19-year-old averaged nearly two points a game with Brandon in the WHL, was the leading scorer for Canada at the World Junior Championship (winning a bronze medal), and was called up to the Senators for the 2012 playoffs.

And then, in the second game of the opening round in the chase for the Stanley Cup against the New York Rangers, Daniel Alfredsson suffered a concussion and was lost for the series. After the teams split the first four games, Ottawa coach Paul MacLean had become frustrated with Jason Spezza.

Spezza was supposed to be one of the team's scorers, and with "Alfie" out the team needed his goal production all the more. But through four games, Spezza had no goals and looked a little lost.

What did MacLean do? He put Stone in Game 5 and played him alongside the struggling Spezza. The result? Stone set up Spezza for the opening goal—the game-winning goal, no less—at 9:18 of the first period. The Sens won, 2–0, and Stone has a great memory.

He played only 8:43 in the game, almost half of it on the power play, but he got the job done. It was his only game of these playoffs.

Inauspicious Beginning

Jacques Plante

MONTREAL CANADIENS // NOVEMBER 1, 1952

"We may be able to make a deal for another goalkeeper if Plante doesn't measure up."

Wow, were those words, improbably uttered by an unnamed spokesman of the Montreal Canadiens, preposterously off the mark, or what?

The date was November 1, 1952, and the Habs' starting goalie Gerry McNeil was recovering in hospital after surgery on a fractured cheekbone suffered two days previous in Toronto. The Habs called up the 23-year-old Plante from the Montreal Royals of Quebec's senior league.

Unfortunately—or perhaps, fortunately—no one cared about who was playing goal. The city was consumed by only one thing. Rocket Richard had 324 career goals, tied with Nels Stewart as the all-time leaders, and it was expected the Rocket would stand alone atop this hallowed scoring list after this home game against the Rangers.

Stewart, in fact, came out to centre ice before the game to shake Richard's hand and wish him the best, but it was to no avail. The Habs skated to a dominating 4–1 win, but Richard was held scoreless.

Plante was excellent in turning aside 19 of 20 shots, but one of his famous idiosyncrasies did not make its way to the NHL with his pads and glove. Plante was well known for wearing a toque in goal, but coach Dick Irvin pointedly told him that that kind of thing wasn't done at the NHL level, so Plante played the game not only bare-faced but also bare-headed.

> The Canadiens won the game and Plante played well, and over the long haul he did, indeed, "measure up," winning the Stanley Cup six times in 11 years with the Habs.

Jacques Plante wasn't always the sure-thing superstar. His first game was fraught with uncertainty.

Dream of Dreams

Al Hill may have had five points in his NHL debut and Auston Matthews may have popped in four beautiful goals, but no one in NHL history has the kind of first-game memories to compare to Wayne Hillman.

Among the 7,863 NHLers, his story stands alone as the most special first game ever.

To look at the roster for the 1960–61 Chicago Black Hawks is to see a snapshot of the Hockey Hall of Fame: goaltender Glenn Hall; defenceman Pierre Pilote; forwards Bobby Hull and Stan Mikita. Although the Hawks hadn't won the Stanley Cup since 1938, this was a team built to win.

Chicago (75 points) finished well behind Montreal (92) and Toronto (90) in the regular-season standings, but the team played above its weight class in the playoffs, shocking the Canadiens in six games before taking on Detroit in the Cup Finals.

The win over Montreal was nothing short of historic because the Habs had won the Cup five years in a row (1955–60) and were again overwhelming favourites. The turning points in that series came in Games 3 and 5. In the former, Murray Balfour scored his second goal of the night midway through the third overtime period to give the Hawks a 2–1 win and a 2–1 series lead.

In Game 5, in Montreal, Hall shut out the mighty Habs, 3–0, sending the series back to the Windy City for a pivotal sixth game. Hall shut the Habs out again, another 3–0 score, sending the Hawks to the Cup Finals for the first time since 1944 and eliminating the vaunted Canadiens.

On the other side, Detroit eliminated the Leafs in five games in another upset, setting the stage for an all-American finale, the first since 1950. Oddly, this finals was scheduled such that every game alternated between cities, and each of the first five games was won by the home side, Chicago at the Stadium in Games 1, 3, and 5, and the Red Wings at the Olympia in Games 2 and 4.

For Game 6, though, on April 16, 1961, Hawks coach Rudy Pilous had some decisions to make. The win in Game 5, crucial as it was, came at a price. Murray Balfour broke his left arm after crashing into the goal post and was out of the lineup, as was defenceman Dollard St. Laurent, who suffered a knee injury.

Wayne Hillman (white shirt, far right of Cup) won the glorious trophy after playing only one NHL shift!

Wayne Hicks, Chico Maki, and Wayne Hillman were three young players who had spent the season with the farm team in Buffalo, but once their season was over they joined the Hawks as insurance. Maki had already made his NHL debut in Game 1 of the finals, getting only a few shifts, and Hicks had made a brief appearance in the 1960 playoffs. Hillman had yet to skate on NHL ice.

Hicks and Maki were right wingers, and one was sure to replace Balfour on a line with Hull and Red Hay for Game 6. The winger who didn't play on that top line was likely to skate alongside Ron Murphy and Tod Sloan because the third member of that line, Eric Nesterenko, took a pounding the previous game and wasn't 100 percent. Hillman, a defenceman, filled in for St. Laurent.

In the end, it was Hicks and Hillman who got the call to play. Neither saw much ice time. In fact, Hillman played only one shift, late in the game, with the score 5–1. Detroit scored the only goal of the first, but Chicago got one early and late in the second and sprinkled three more goals throughout the third. They won the Cup by that score, and with the win, a most extraordinary moment in hockey history was made.

Wayne Hillman became the first—and to this day, the only—player to win the Stanley Cup the night he played in his first NHL game. And, he got his name on the Cup for one shift's worth of effort!

Stanley Cup Finals Debuts

Although Wayne Hillman has the distinction of making the most memorable Stanley Cup Finals debut in league history, there have been a total of 20 players who played their first games in the ultimate series. Amazingly, the last of those came more than 30 years ago, and in the last nearly 60 years there have been but four. As the stakes have gotten higher, it appears coaches are more and more reluctant to put an unknown quantity into the most critical of situations.

On only two other occasions has a player made his debut in the Cup-winning game, but both of those were in losing situations. Leroy Goldsworthy started his career the night of March 29, 1929, for the New York Rangers, but Boston won the game, 2–1, taking home the Cup with a two-game sweep in the best-of-three finals.

Four years later, Buzz Boll made his debut with the Leafs—April 13, 1933—but the Rangers won in overtime, 1–0, to sweep the Leafs in four straight games.

Of the 20 Cup Finals debut players, only one, Len Frig, recorded a point. Frig made his debut with Chicago in Game 3, on May 3, 1973, and earned a single assist in a 7–3 win over Montreal, but the Habs won the Cup in six games.

The only other stats associated with these debuts are penalties. Lee Fogolin, Ab McDonald, and Esa Tikkanen all incurred a minor penalty, and Kelly Buchberger got into a fight and drew a five-minute major.

Interestingly, of these 20 players, Frig played the most games in the final series during his debut—four. Eight players appeared in only one game and another eight

in two, but Frig got into Game 3 of the finals with the Hawks and played in the remainder of the series, something none of the others did. He scored in his third game, a wild 8–7 Hawks victory.

And then there is Paul Goodman's singular achievement. He is the only goalie in NHL history to make his debut during the Stanley Cup Finals (see story on page 32).

Kelly Buchberger (No. 16) was the last NHLer to make his debut in the Stanley Cup finals—in 1987.

Players Who Made Their NHL Debut in the Stanley Cup Finals

Player (Team)	Date	Score	Game	Cup Result
Leroy Goldsworthy (NYR)	March 29, 1929	Boston 2 at Rangers 1	Game 2 of 2	Lost
Buzz Boll (TOR)	April 13, 1933	Rangers 1 at Toronto 0 (OT)	Game 4 of 4	Lost
Paul Goodman (CHI)	April 7, 1938	Chicago 1 at Toronto 5	Game 2 of 4	Won
Don Metz (TOR)	April 13, 1939	Boston 2 at Toronto 0	Game 4 of 5	Lost
Gaye Stewart (TOR)	April 14, 1942	Detroit 3 at Toronto 9	Game 5 of 7	Won
Gerry Couture (DET)	April 12, 1945	Detroit 0 at Toronto 1	Game 3 of 7	Lost
Lee Fogolin (DET)	April 11, 1948	Toronto 2 at Detroit 0	Game 3 of 4	Lost
Fred Glover (DET)	April 8, 1949	Toronto 3 at Detroit 2 (OT)	Game 1 of 4	Lost
Gerry Reid (DET)	April 10, 1949	Toronto 3 at Detroit 1	Game 2 of 4	Lost
Doug McKay (DET)	April 15, 1950	Detroit 4 at Rangers 0	Game 3 of 7	Won
Eddie Mazur (MTL)	April 19, 1951	Toronto 3 at Montreal 2 (OT)	Game 4 of 5	Lost
Stan Long (MTL)	April 13, 1952	Montreal 0 at Detroit 3	Game 3 of 4	Lost
Ab McDonald (MTL)	April 13, 1958	Montreal 3 at Boston 0	Game 3 of 6	Won
Bill Hicke (MTL)	April 11, 1959	Toronto 1 at Montreal 3	Game 2 of 5	Won
Chico Maki (CHI)	April 6, 1961	Detroit 2 at Chicago 3	Game 1 of 6	Won
Wayne Hillman (CHI)	April 16, 1961	Chicago 5 at Detroit 1	Game 6 of 6	Won
Len Frig (CHI)	May 3, 1973	Montreal 4 at Chicago 7	Game 3 of 6	Lost
Esa Tikkanen (EDM)	May 23, 1985	Edmonton 3 at Philadelphia 1	Game 2 of 5	Won
Brett Hull (CGY)	May 20, 1986	Calgary 3 at Montreal 5	Game 3 of 5	Lost
Kelly Buchberger (EDM)	May 17, 1987	Philadelphia 2 at Edmonton 4	Game 1 of 7	Won

Hall of Famer Playoff Debuts

One thing is clear. If you're an aspiring player and think you'll be so good that one day you'll be in the Hockey Hall of Fame, you're best not to play your first NHL game in the playoffs. Only four such players have gone on to be inducted: Brett Hull, Jarome Iginla (pending), Mike Modano, Joe Mullen.

// Joe Mullen, St. Louis Blues
April 11, 1980

It was a small note, but the start of a big career. The *St. Louis Post-Dispatch* announced that Joe Mullen had been recalled from Salt Lake City, the Blues CHL affiliate, in the hopes that he'd play that night against Chicago. Mullen led the CHL in scoring during the regular season and starred in the team's first playoff game, scoring three goals.

The Blues were desperate. Their first-round series with the Black Hawks was a best-of-five, and they lost the first two games by scores of 3–2 and 5–1. They needed more goals. They needed to play better in their own end. And they needed to do those things now or face a summer come too soon.

Chicago roared out to a 2–0 lead, though, and coasted to a 4–1 win. Mullen's debut was over almost before it began.

// Brett Hull, Calgary Flames
May 20, 1986

The 1986 Stanley Cup Finals was a case of close but no cigar for the Calgary Flames. Facing the Montreal Canadiens in the best-of-seven, they also faced a rookie goalie named Patrick Roy who had been instrumental in leading the Habs' surprise trek to the Cup.

The Flames had home-ice advantage, and they used it to good effect in the opener, winning, 5–2. Game 2 wasn't quite the same, though, as they lost in overtime, 3–2. Worse, coach Bob Johnson was worried his team was suffering from a serious case of fatigue. They had played 20 playoff games in 41 days (many of those back-to-back), a gruelling stretch that 21st century players don't have to endure.

Johnson had Brett Hull, son of Bobby, on his playoff roster, but Hull had yet to get in a game. He joined the NHL team after his NCAA season had ended at the University of Minnesota-Duluth, where he scored 52 goals in 42 games as a sophomore.

"I'd like to get some fresh blood in there," Johnson said in advance of Game 3, in Montreal. "I know one thing: Brett Hull can come in and maybe score a goal for us. Plus, he weighs 211 pounds. He can play physically if it becomes a physical game."

Johnson didn't put just Hull in the lineup—he put in five new faces: Hull, Yves Courteau, Perry Berezan, defenceman Terry Johnson, and goalie Reggie Lemelin (who came in late in the first period to replace a beleaguered Mike Vernon).

Hull came as advertised. He had a great scoring chance on his first shift, hitting the post on a wicked shot from the faceoff circle on a power play. In fact, he was dangerous all night long, even if he didn't register a point.

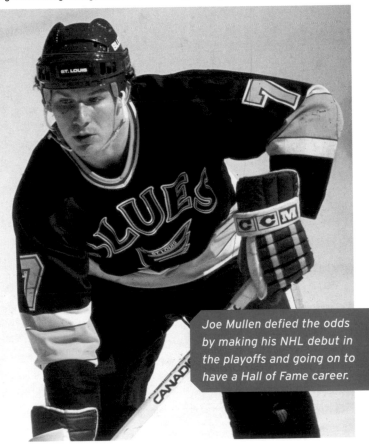

Joe Mullen defied the odds by making his NHL debut in the playoffs and going on to have a Hall of Fame career.

"I was just so nervous going out there," he admitted. "I was so glad something good happened on my first shift. After that, I thought I played pretty well. I had some chances."

Offered assistant coach Pierre Page: "You watch Hull, and you watch Mullen. Who was better? I say Hull. He was a factor every time he was on the ice."

Johnson concurred. "I thought Hull was a threat on the ice. He made things happen. Hull showed us he can play in this company. He may be our third right winger on Thursday night."

Hull did play in Game 4, another loss, but Johnson had him back up in the press box for Game 5, when the Habs won the Cup. The "Golden Brett" needed another year before he made the NHL full-time, and after that he became one of the greatest goalscorers in the long history of the NHL.

// Mike Modano, Minnesota North Stars
April 6, 1989

One Norris Division semi-finals featured the Minnesota North Stars and St. Louis Blues. The Blues had home-ice advantage and won the first game, 4–3, in overtime. North Stars coach Pierre Page decided to make several lineup changes for the second game in two nights, inserting Mike Modano, Steve Gotaas, and Ville Siren into the lineup.

The 18-year-old Modano was the most notable inclusion. He was the team's first overall draft choice the previous summer, only the second American so honoured (after Brian Lawton, 1983). He played the 1988–89 season with the Prince Albert Raiders in the WHL, and at season's end joined the North Stars.

Modano's presence, however, didn't alter the series in Minnesota's favour. The Blues won again, 4–3, and again the winning goal came in overtime. Modano played only one more game that spring and made the team at training camp the following September.

Jarome Iginla, Calgary Flames
// April 21, 1996

The Western Conference quarter-finals included a Chicago-Calgary matchup, and after two games the Hawks were in the driver's seat, having won both games in Chicago and confounding Flames coach Pierre Page.

Coming home for Game 3, Page had to do something. Just before game time, the team signed Jarome Iginla, and Page immediately bumped him to the top line and scratched Pavel Torgayev.

"There were a couple of veterans in the room before the game, calming me down, saying, 'It's just another game.' I had a hard time believing that," Iginla related after.

Iginla had flown in from Kamloops, where the Blazers had just been eliminated from the WHL playoffs, arriving at the Saddledome only an hour and a half before the opening faceoff. And he got on the plane only an hour after signing his first pro contract, one that would pay him $850,000 in each of his first three seasons (plus bonuses).

"I came off the plane, and they told me I would be playing," Iginla continued. "They didn't tell me the night before. I think they wanted me to save my nerves. If they had told me, I wouldn't have been able to sleep."

Playing on the first line as a centreman, between German Titov and Theo Fleury, Iginla fit right in. He had three shots on goal, won more faceoffs than he lost, and registered an assist on a Fleury goal early in the third period.

"I had some chances that I should have scored on," he said, downplaying his strong game.

Coach Pierre Page was more enthusiastic. "We put him in the frying pan right away. I thought he handled himself pretty well. I thought he gave us a real boost. He played like an experienced guy."

Jarome Iginla's career started in the playoffs and finished in the Hall of Fame.

Tre Kronor Pioneer

Ulf Sterner

The Boston-New York game of January 27, 1965, at Madison Square Garden, was historic because Ulf Sterner played his first NHL game. It was also a huge contrast of expectations and reputation, for Sterner was as famous to fans in Europe—as a superstar forward—as he was a complete unknown to NHL spectators.

Sterner was born in Deje, a tiny village of fewer than 2,000 souls in the south of Sweden. The 23-year-old was the first European player—born and trained—to make it to the NHL. But, despite his youth, he was no inexperienced rookie. He had already played in two Olympics (1960, 1964) and three World Championships (including an historic gold in 1962). He scored once against Canada in a 5–3 win in the '62 Worlds, a game famous to this day as the first time Sweden defeated Canada in international competition going back to 1920. (Up to that point, Sweden had had an 0-20 record against Canada at the Olympics and Worlds.)

Sterner also notched a hat trick at the 1963 Worlds against Canada in a 4–1 win, thus putting himself on the NHL radar. The Rangers signed him to a contract for the 1964–65 season, assigning him to St. Paul of the CHL. After scoring 12 goals in 16 games, he was promoted to Baltimore of the AHL, where he again acquitted himself well.

New York duly called him up to Broadway, and in late January he made history. Unfortunately, he didn't get on the scoresheet in that debut, but he did manage two shots on goal while wearing No. 5. Goalie Eddie Johnston stopped both shots, but the Rangers won the game, 5–2.

Alas, Sterner failed to do much else in the next three games—all losses. He was sent back to the AHL, and at season's end he decided to return to Sweden to focus on league play at home and international play with Tre Kronor.

In the end, it worked out well for him. He played in nine World Championships and two Olympics and was inducted into the IIHF Hall of Fame in 2001.

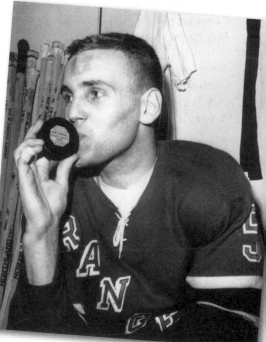

Sweden's Ulf Sterner was the first European player to appear in an NHL game.

The Day the Game Changed

Bobby Orr

BOSTON BRUINS // OCTOBER 19, 1966

"I'll do my best," Bobby Orr said after practice in preparation for the season opener the following night. "I just hope I can live up to expectations, if people don't expect too much."

Ahem.

The Bruins defeated Detroit, 6–2, at the Garden, in game one of the 1966–67 season, game one of the new NHL which now included Number Four. In truth, all of the talk was about Orr after the game.

Summed up *Boston Globe* reporter Tom Fitzgerald: "There was a brilliant debut by defenceman Bobby Orr, the 18-year-old super-boy who more than fulfilled the demanding assignment by living up to all of his extravagant notices."

Fitzgerald continued: "Bobby demonstrated that the critics who doubted his defensive savvy were dead wrong. He played the position like a veteran; was very tough in dislodging opponents around the net; blocked shots; and made adept plays in moving the puck from his own end."

Orr created the goal that gave Boston a 2–0 lead early in the second period. His low point shot on a power play was tipped in by Wayne Connelly, after which followed a deafening ovation that lasted more than a minute for the rookie.

Of course, playing Detroit in the 1960s meant playing Gordie Howe, and reporters flocked to the Detroit dressing room for an opinion from the man starting his record 21st NHL season.

"He'll do, for sure," Howe purposefully understated. "He anticipates well. He makes good passes, and I guess he does just about what you'd expect of a good defenceman."

When asked to compare his own debut to Orr's, he quipped: "There was one big difference. Detroit gave me $250 for signing. What did they give him? $50,000?"

"I'm glad it went the way it did," Orr said. "I'm glad we won. That's the big thing."

The game was never the same after Bobby Orr (No. 4) arrived in the NHL in 1966.

Double Debuts in the Crease

Only eight times in NHL history have two goaltenders made their debuts in the same game. On five occasions they opposed each other, and three times the pair played for the same team. Not surprisingly, it wasn't until after expansion in 1967 that this happened for the first time.

// Doug Favell, Philadelphia Flyers
Wayne Rutledge, Los Angeles Kings
October 14, 1967

The not so venerable Long Beach Arena was home to the Los Angeles Kings during their first season of play, and in their second game ever, they hosted the equally new Philadelphia Flyers.

The Kings had won their first game and Philly had lost theirs, and in the nets were two youngsters who had never seen an NHL sheet of ice previously—Doug Favell of the Flyers and Wayne Rutledge of the Kings.

Rutledge, 25, was replacing the legendary Terry Sawchuk, who suffered an injury in practice the previous day.

The 22-year-old Favell was by far the busier of the two this night, facing 38 shots to Rutledge's 16, and the Kings skated to a 4–2 win even though they trailed 2–0 early thanks to some weak goaltending from Rutledge.

"I was nervous. You bet I was," he easily admitted after the game. "It was a bad start, but a good finish. I'll take all of those I can get. I'm surprised no one could hear my knees knocking when I came out, but the team really worked for me, and it wasn't so bad after those first few minutes."

// Jim Stewart, Boston Bruins
Marco Baron, Boston Bruins
January 10, 1980

Returning home after a six-game road trip, the Boston Bruins were going with Gilles Gilbert in goal this night against St. Louis and Marco Baron as his backup. Number-one man Gerry Cheevers was still out with a sore right knee, so Baron, called up from Grand Rapids, got to enjoy a bit of time with an NHL team.

Wayne Rutledge stares down Gordie Howe in the goalie's debut.

But when Gilbert woke up this morning, he felt sick as a dog, so the Bruins called up Jim Stewart, a 22-year-old playing for Utica in the EHL, and he got the start ahead of Baron. Call it a hunch on the part of coach Fred Creighton, but it was a hunch gone awry.

Stewart surrendered five goals on just nine shots and was replaced for the start of the second by Baron, who got into his first game in a most roundabout way. He was much better, and so was the team in front of him, but Mike Liut at the other end was excellent and the Blues won, 7–2.

"I was kind of excited," Stewart said of his callup, "but I didn't think I was going to play. I felt great in the pre-game warmups, and I didn't think I was nervous, but I must have been. Nothing went right from the first shot on. I couldn't stop a basketball. Three of their goals went through my legs, and twice I moved too quickly. It was some kind of a shock to be here."

FLYERS
GOAL: Favell. DEFENSE: Watson,
Van Impe, Miszuk, Gauthier, Hanna.
FORWARDS: Hoekstra, Sutherland,
Rochefort, Angotti, Blackburn, Selby,
Hannigan, Peters, Hicks, Kennedy.
LOS ANGELES
GOAL: Rutledge. DEFENSE: Wall,
White, J. Amadio, Rolfe.
FORWARDS: Labossiere, Smith, Gray,
Hughes, R. Lemieux, MacDonald, Ir-
vine, Campbell, Joyall, Flett, Kilrea.
FLYERS   2 0 0—2
Los Angeles   0 1 3—4
FIRST PERIOD
1. FLYERS, Sutherland (unassisted),
0:42; 2. FLYERS, Hoekstra (Rochefort,
Gauthier), 9:08. Penalties: Hannigan
(high-sticking) and Flett (high-stick-
ing), 2:48; Gauthier (high-sticking),
4:17; Hughes (cross-checking), 10:07;
Miszuk (interference), 15:19; Watson
(holding), 19:48.
SECOND PERIOD
3. LOS ANGELES, Kilrea (Lemieux,
Irvine), 3:20. Penalties: Miszuk (cross
checking), 0:15; Van Impe (high sticking), 6:10; LaBossiere (elbowing), 6:10;
White (holding), 10:54; Hicks (high
sticking), 12:40; Lemieux (cross checking), 12:40; Van Impe (holding), 14:27.
THIRD PERIOD
4. LOS ANGELES, Wall (Flett,
Campbell), 3:26; 5. LOS ANGELES,
LaBossiere (B. Smith, Rolfe), 13:18;
6. LOS ANGELES, Kilrea (unassisted),
19:44. Penalties: Hannigan (elbowing),
4:45; LaBossiere (charging), 4:57; Van Impe
Rolfe (charging), 4:57; LaBossiere (hooking),
(tripping), 6:17; LaBossiere (hooking),
16:32.

// Karl Friesen, New Jersey Devils
Chris Terreri, New Jersey Devils
October 18, 1986

True, both Friesen and Terreri got into their first NHL game, but their experiences were markedly different. The opposition was the Pittsburgh Penguins, a team that had started the season with five straight wins and with Mario Lemieux playing like a man possessed.

Friesen got the start, and he witnessed No. 66 in his prime. Lemieux earned five assists, three to linemate Terry Ruskowski for an improbable hat trick by a player hardly known for his scoring touch, and the Penguins chased Friesen midway through the third period with the score 8–3.

Terreri came in and stopped six shots in 9:38 of play, the Penguins having eased up with the game solidly in hand. Terreri went winless in seven games this season, playing mostly in the AHL, and Friesen was winless in four before moving to Germany to play.

// Frederic Chabot, Montreal Canadiens
Matt DelGuidice, Boston Bruins
January 31, 1991

It was one of the oddest games in NHL debut history, a game almost pulled from the exhibition schedule and plopped down in the middle of the regular season. Montreal was in Boston for a Thursday night game, and Andre Racicot was in goal for Montreal in place of an injured Patrick Roy.

Andy Moog was in the blue ice for the Bruins, having slowly but surely wrested the starter's duties from Reggie Lemelin. The Habs were debilitated by injuries and were without Petr Svoboda, Eric Desjardins, Brian Skrudland, Denis Savard, Lyle Odelein, and Mathieu Schneider.

But the healthy Bruins could only split four goals with the short-handed Habs in the opening period. Boston, however, got the only goal of the second and added two more early in the third to take a commanding 5-2 lead. That fifth goal by Dave Poulin came at 10:03.

At this time, Montreal coach Pat Burns pulled Racicot in favour of newcomer Frederic Chabot. In a fit of pique, Boston coach Mike Milbury did the same, pulling Moog and inserting rookie Matt DelGuidice. The "rookie-off" produced no more goals. Chabot stopped all five shots he faced and DelGuidice stopped the seven he faced.

Both goalies made their NHL debuts as substitutes, and both played the exact same game time—9:57. Very strange, indeed.

Andrew Raycroft shared his debut glory with Maxime Ouellet.

// Andrew Raycroft, Boston Bruins
Maxime Ouellet, Philadelphia Flyers
October 7, 2000

Two goalies got into their first NHL games for differing reasons on this night. The Bruins came out firing on all cylinders, scoring early and building a 3–0 lead over the Flyers by the midway point of the opening period. Flyers goalie Brian Boucher had a tough time, surrendering five goals by the early part of the third period and prompting coach Craig Ramsay to take Boucher out and insert Ouellet.

Oullet stopped all six shots he faced in the final 16 minutes. Meanwhile, when the Bruins scored their fifth goal to take a commanding 5–1 lead, the game was more or less decided. Byron Dafoe, who had started in goal for the Bruins, exacerbated a groin injury and soon after took himself out of the game for precautionary reasons. That allowed Andrew Raycroft to see his first NHL action, and he blocked the only four shots he faced in 11:30 of playing time.

// Yann Danis, Montreal Canadiens
Michael Garnett, Atlanta Thrashers
October 12, 2005

The Montreal Canadiens skated into Atlanta and beat the Thrashers, 2–0. Yann Danis became part of that rare and exclusive group of goalies to earn a shutout in his first game. In his case, he stopped all 32 shots for the win, only the 18th time such a feat had been achieved in NHL history. Of those 18 first-game shutouts, three have been by Canadiens (Bob Perreault in 1955 and Wayne Thomas in 1973).

"All I was thinking about was trying to get the win," Danis said. "I was nervous when I started. I had butterflies, but I made the first two or three saves, and I was okay."

At the other end, Mike Dunham started for the Thrashers but midway through the opening period, with the score 1–0, he injured his groin and was forced to leave. Enter Michael Garnett, who was virtually the equal to Danis all night, giving up but one goal on 30 shots in his first game.

// Mike Condon, Montreal Canadiens
Matt O'Connor, Ottawa Senators
October 11, 2015

Ottawa's home opener to start the 2015–16 season was . . . different. Matt O'Connor was tabbed as the Senators' *third* goalie behind clear number one Craig Anderson and injured backup Andrew Hammond. But coach Dave Cameron made the perplexing decision to start O'Connor in the team's first game because the rookie had had such an impressive training camp.

On the other side of centre ice, Michel Terrien gave his rookie goalie Mike Condon the Saturday night start so that a well-rested Carey Price could play on Sunday.

O'Connor was a terrific story at this time. Undrafted, he played three years at Boston University, attracting evermore attention as his NCAA career unfolded. Ironically, after his third year, there was a bidding war among several NHL teams, and he settled with Ottawa.

It was all downhill from there. Montreal won the game, 3–1, and Condon won the battle of the rookies. He allowed a second-period goal to Jean-Gabriel Pageau, the only shot of 21 he failed to save.

Montreal's Yann Danis earned a shutout in his first game.

O'Connor played well enough. "I think I battled and showed some perseverance," the 23-year-old said. "It's really motivating when you have management and coaches believe in your ability. And I feel very motivated to keep building off the month I've had."

But Matt O'Connor never played in the NHL again.

// Collin Delia, Chicago Blackhawks
Scott Foster, Chicago Blackhawks
March 29, 2018

On March 29, 2018, Chicago goalie Anton Forsberg suffered an injury during the morning skate that rendered him incapacitated for that night's home game against Winnipeg. No problem. Coach Joel Quenneville tabbed intended backup Collin Delia as the starter. This would be his first NHL game. Cool.

But there was another problem. Two days earlier the Hawks had sent J-F Berube to Rockford (where Delia had come from), so as of noon on game day the team had only one goalie. They turned to a local puckstopper named Scott Foster. The 36-year-old had played NCAA hockey in the early 2000s but was now, like so many, a shinny-playing beer-leaguer with a full-time office job.

Of course, it was a thrill for Foster to sign a one-day contract and get dressed with the Hawks. He sported number 90, took shots in the warmup, and parked himself at the end of the bench for a front row seat to an NHL game. Also cool.

Patrick Kane got the home side going with an early goal, and the Hawks were ahead by a 6–2 count early in the third period. And then Delia got injured. With 14:01 still to play, Foster had to put on his final pieces of equipment and skate onto the ice and play.

Over the course of those tense 14 minutes, he stopped all seven shots, each save inspiring a roar from the United Center crowd. When he made a sensational save on Paul Stastny, the place exploded.

"The initial shock happened when I had to dress," Foster explained after the game. "You just kind of black out after that."

Dylan Sikura also played in his first game, earning two assists. Defenceman Brent Seabrook played in his 1,000th career game, and Delia got the win. Nobody remembers those details. All that stands out is the personable Foster living the dream of every shinny player not good enough to make The Show. For 14 minutes, he was good enough.

Caught in the Middle

Robbie Irons

ST. LOUIS BLUES // NOVEMBER 13, 1968

When the NHL expanded from six to 12 teams in the fall of 1967, it afforded dozens of minor-league players a chance to skate in the NHL. It also meant six new teams needed coaches, and that's how the legendary Scotty Bowman got his first shot, with St. Louis.

Bowman, smart as they come, knew he needed great goaltending if his new team were to be a contender every night, so he convinced two legends—Jacques Plante and Glenn Hall—to sign. He also sweetened the deal by telling them they'd more or less split the playing time, and when they weren't playing they could watch the game in a suit rather than dress as the backup and take shots during the warmup.

Cut to the night of November 13, 1968, at Madison Square Garden. The Blues were playing the Rangers during a lengthy and successful road trip, and it was Hall's turn to start. More importantly, after 14 years in the league and countless cuts to his face, Hall decided he would wear a mask for the first time. He had used one in practice for years but never in a game.

Was it intended or accidental, was it subliminal or suggestive or subconscious? Whatever the answer, something happened early in the game that had never happened to Hall previously. After just 2:01 of play, referee Vern Buffey gave Noel Picard a penalty for delay of game.

Incensed, Hall accosted the referee, earning a misconduct. Not remorseful, he continued to lambaste Buffey and nudged him in the process, earning a game misconduct. These were the first such penalties of Hall's career, but it put Bowman in a bind.

He was forced to put Robbie Irons in goal right away. A farmhand from Kansas City of the CHL, Irons was given a quick instruction by Bowman before leaving the bench—get injured during the warmup. Seriously? Yes. Get injured. Or say as much.

Sure enough, when Irons went out to take a few practice shots (as was allowed in the day), he feigned an injury. Bowman then told Buffey that he'd have to bring in Jacques Plante, who had scurried down from his seat and was already in the dressing room getting ready. Buffey agreed, but play had to resume in the meantime.

And so, after stopping one shot in 2:59 of play, Irons was out and Plante in. Incredibly, Irons, 21, had a 14-year pro career, but he never again played in the NHL.

First Shift, First Shot, First Goal

Perhaps the ultimate NHL debut is the one in which a player steps onto the ice and, on his first shift, with his first shot on goal, scores. Easy peasy. There have been a surprising number of these goals, but still, of the 7,863 NHLers in league history, they are a rare occurrence.

// Bob Barlow, Minnesota North Stars
October 11, 1969

There are precious few feel-good stories as special as Barlow's. Yes, he scored on his first shot on his first shift in his first NHL game, but there is so much more to his career.

On this night in 1969, the 34-year-old Barlow could look back on a night he had anticipated all his life. Like many players, he started in junior—in his case with the Barrie Flyers. After that it was the minors. Over the course of 15 years he played in the AHL and WHL and even a bit of senior hockey in northern Ontario.

But with expansion in 1967, there were new opportunities, and two years later the North Stars called up the veteran to play against Philadelphia. Just 68 seconds

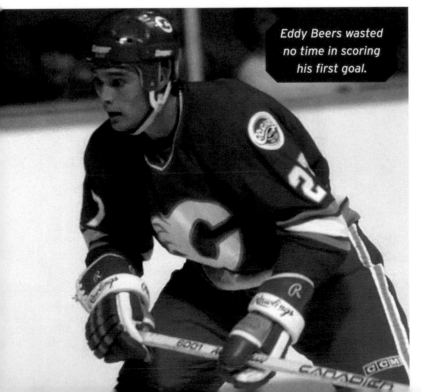

Eddy Beers wasted no time in scoring his first goal.

after the opening faceoff, he beat Bernie Parent with a shot to give the Stars an early 1–0 lead. Incredibly, the goal held up thanks to shutout goaltending from Cesare Maniago, so Barlow's first quick goal was also the game winner.

"It was the most important goal of my life," Barlow said. "I've waited a long, long time for that one."

Indeed, he had scored more than 300 goals in the minors before this first in the NHL. "I saw it go in and could only think, 'Get that puck!'" he continued. "I would have dived over the boards to get it."

// Rick Kessel, Pittsburgh Penguins
March 21, 1970

Chicago beat the Penguins, 5–3, but Kessel made history just 2:19 into the game when he picked up the rebound off a Glen Sather shot and beat Gerry Desjardins with his own shot.

// Mike Allison, New York Rangers
October 9, 1980

It's always nice to connect one of the greatest players ever to another player's accomplishment, and it's ironic that one of the game's finest goalscorers—Phil Esposito—was responsible for setting up Allison's early goal. But that's what happened. It was Allison in the slot (Espo's office) who took the pass and backhanded a quick shot past Rogie Vachon just 2:44 into the game for his first goal on his first shift and shot.

// Eddy Beers, Calgary Flames
March 17, 1982

It was a special night for Beers, but it came during a 9–4 rout by the Los Angeles Kings. He wasted no time in giving the Flames the early lead when he took a pass from Mel Bridgman, made a great move on goalie Mario Lessard, and lifted the puck into the open goal at 1:45.

// Kevin Stevens, Pittsburgh Penguins
March 1, 1988

There was no shortage of drama as Stevens made his debut. For starters, the Penguins had lost six games in a row and were in last place in the Patrick Division, outside a playoff spot with less than a month to go in the regular season.

Denis Hamel of Buffalo scored after just 129 seconds of play.

Stevens was fresh off the Olympics in Calgary, where he had played with the U.S. team that finished a disappointing seventh. The visitors in his NHL debut were the lowly Minnesota North Stars, and although Stevens scored on his first shift-shot-game, he did so at 4:29 to make it 3–0. He later added an assist on a Mario Lemieux power-play goal in the third as the Pens cruised to an important 8–3 win.

// Rob Ray, Buffalo Sabres
October 21, 1989

A most improbable entry on this list, Ray was a fighter his entire career. Over the course of 15 years and 900 regular-season games, Ray scored a paltry 41 goals while incurring a whopping 3,207 penalty minutes. Yet midway through the first period of a Buffalo-Pittsburgh matchup that marked his debut, he scored his first of those 41 career goals on his first shot and shift. Incredible.

// Denis Hamel, Buffalo Sabres
January 6, 2000

Recalled from Rochester of the AHL earlier in the day, Hamel got the Sabres off on the right foot, knocking in the rebound of an Alexei Zhitnik shot at 2:09 to stake the team to a 1–0 lead. By the end of the night, though, this little piece of history was forgotten as the Devils rallied and won easily, 6–3.

// Yannick Lehoux, Phoenix Coyotes
November 8, 2005

Lehoux's path to the NHL was truly a long and winding road, but his NHL debut was all the sweeter for it. Drafted 86th overall by Los Angeles in 2000, he never played

for the Kings. Instead, he finished junior and then played for four years in the AHL without a single chance to skate in the NHL. Despite being a decent scorer with the Manchester Monarchs, he ended up in a contract impasse and decided he'd go to Europe. Switzerland, to be precise.

After being there for only a few weeks, the Kings summoned him, and life took another turn. He got on a plane, but upon arriving at LAX he was greeted by his mother who told him that during his flight the Phoenix Coyotes had claimed him off waivers.

The rule was tricky. Because he was playing in Europe, and because the Kings hadn't signed him prior to the start of the NHL regular season, he had to clear waivers to join L.A. That didn't happen, so he flew to Phoenix where coach Wayne Gretzky got him into the lineup for a Tuesday night game in Minnesota. ("Coach Wayne Gretzky," by the way, still doesn't sound quite right.)

No sooner was Lehoux skating in the NHL than he blasted a hard shot from the right circle past goalie Dwayne Roloson just 1:05 into the game to give the Coyotes an early 1–0 lead.

"It's great! I didn't expect to do that so fast," he enthused, before correcting himself. "At the same time, I've waited 23 years."

Phoenix went on to win the game, 4–2, but Lehoux managed only two career goals in 10 NHL games.

Tampa Bay's Nikita Kucherov (middle) started off hot and has never cooled down.

// Luke Gazdic, Edmonton Oilers
   October 1, 2013

What a great story to start a career. A low draft choice by the Dallas Stars in 2007, Gazdic kicked around in the minors for years. A "tough guy," he was finally put on waivers by the Stars two days before the start of the 2013–14 season, and the Oilers took a chance on him, putting him on their opening night roster for a home game against the Winnipeg Jets.

Two minutes into the game, on his first shift, there was a faceoff in the Jets end. The puck came to Gazdic, and near the end red line he just fired a weak back-hand on goal. The puck hit something in front and beat Ondrej Pavelec at 2:21. The official announcement for the goal was Gazdic—but it was later credited to Mike Brown!

Further video evidence, though, showed that the Jets' Jim Slater redirected the puck, so Gazdic got credit once again. Will Acton, who won the faceoff, got the only assist. It was also his first NHL game (and point).

// Nikita Kucherov, Tampa Bay Lightning
   November 25, 2013

Not only did Kucherov waste no time in scoring his first career goal, it turned out to be the game winner as well.

It was a night to celebrate, starting with a pre-game ceremony for Tampa Bay captain Martin St. Louis, who was honoured by the Lightning for playing in his 1,000th career game. Of course, that's a significant milestone for any player, but for St. Louis, who was never drafted, it was all the more special.

And then, the 20-year-old Kucherov, who was called up from Syracuse of the AHL, scored just 2:02 into the game to stake the team to a 1–0 lead. It proved to be the only goal the Lightning would need. He took a pass from Ted Purcell and wired a shot past Henrik Lundqvist in the New York Rangers' goal. A thing of beauty, to be sure.

Mattias Janmark (left) had a great first shift with Dallas, scoring a goal on his first shot.

"I was just in the right spot at the right time," he said. "Teddy made a good pass to me, so I just needed to shoot the puck on net. I didn't see it go in. I just saw [teammate Alex] Killorn with his hands up. I was just so happy to score a goal. It's like a dream come true."

// Mattias Janmark, Dallas Stars
October 8, 2015

Dallas beat the visiting Pittsburgh Penguins, 3–0, and it was Janmark's early goal that set the tone for the Stars this night. Drafted 79th overall in 2013, he made the team out of training camp two years later, and this night was both the home and season opener.

Although it was Janmark who put the puck in the net, it was Ales Hemsky who made it all happen. Coming out of his end on a turnover, he tore down the right wing and waited for Janmark to go to the goal. Hemsky made a perfect pass, and Janmark redirected it past Marc-Andre Fleury at 1:39 of the first period. It was a pretty goal.

// Dan Carr, Montreal Canadiens
December 5, 2015

A time of increasing popularity for NHL general managers is late March when the NCAA college season is finished and undrafted players become available for signing at no cost beyond the contract. This group of players represents late bloomers. They weren't good enough to be drafted at 18 or 19 but developed significantly during their (usually) four years of college, becoming coveted prospects.

Into this category can be placed Dan Carr, who was scooped up by Montreal after his 2013–14 season at Union College was over. He then played a year and a half in the AHL and made his debut for the Habs in Carolina early in the 2015–16 season.

Even better, he scored 2:44 into the game on a wraparound, fooling Cam Ward. The 'Canes rallied, though, winning the game, 3–2, and spoiling Carr's celebratory mood.

"It really sucks. That about says it all," he offered after the loss.

// Jake Guentzel, Pittsburgh Penguins
November 21, 2016

Called up from Wilkes-Barre because Pittsburgh coach Steve Sullivan liked his offensive skills, Jake Guentzel practised in the morning with eventual linemates Evgeni Malkin and Phil Kessel in preparation for a home game that night against the New York Rangers.

"When you play with those two, it's pretty fun," the rookie said after the preparatory skate. "I think it's everyone's dream to get to this level, so when you have the chance, it's going to be fun and I'm going to enjoy it."

Did he or didn't he?

A small group of players who scored in their first game might have scored on their first shot and first shift but confirming the event hasn't been possible. This small list includes Dave Cressman, Mark Hunter (probably), Charlie Conacher, Les Costello, and Harry Howell.

He heeded his own advice and scored on his first shot and then a little later on his third. The first came just 1:02 into the game when his quick wrister beat Antti Raanta under the left pad to stake the home side to a 1–0 lead. A dozen minutes later, he made it 2–0 by knocking in a rebound, but that was to be the only scoring he and his team would do this night. The Rangers scored five unanswered goals to win, 5–2.

Dan Carr needed only 2:44 of game time to score his first goal.

Playing with Phil Kessel (left) and Evgeni Malkin (right), Jake Guentzel scored the first time he stepped onto the ice.

// Max Comtois, Anaheim Ducks
October 3, 2018

It was a season in reverse for Comtois, a second-round draft choice of Anaheim in 2017. He made the NHL team in training camp and was in the lineup for the season opener, a road game in San Jose. In the first minute of play, on his first shift, he was sprung free by a clever little pass in centre ice by Adam Henrique. Comtois went in on goal and beat goalie Martin Jones with the team's first shot of the game. Time of the goal was just 49 seconds, one of the fastest first goals ever.

"Wouldn't believe it if you had said that to me before the game," Comtois enthused later. "It was a good play by [Henrique] to poke the puck to me, and I found a way to put it in the back of the net. I'm really happy to get this one out of the way. It's good for the confidence."

Comtois had seven points in the team's first 10 games, but after suffering an injury he was sent to the AHL's farm team in San Diego and a few games after that back down to junior, in Drummondville, where he spent the rest of the year.

Other players to score on their first shift and shot:

Gus Bodnar, Toronto Maple Leafs
October 30, 1943

See page 36

Norm Armstrong, Toronto Maple Leafs
December 15, 1962

See page 126

Danny Gare, Buffalo Sabres
October 10, 1974

See pages 74–75

Dave Christian, Winnipeg Jets
March 2, 1980

See page 92

Mario Lemieux, Pittsburgh Penguins
October 11, 1984

See page 106

Ted Speers, Detroit Red Wings
March 3, 1986

See page 75

Trevor Stienburg, Quebec Nordiques
April 2, 1986

See page 75

Alexander Mogilny, Buffalo Sabres
October 5, 1989

See pages 112–113

Mikko Lehtonen, Nashville Predators
October 7, 2006

See page 133

Czech Date

Jaroslav Jirik

ST. LOUIS BLUES // MARCH 22, 1970

Symbolically, it was one of the most important dates in NHL history. Nearly 20 years before the famous release of Sergei Pryakhin that allowed him to become the first Soviet-trained player to make it to the NHL, the Czechoslovakian government granted 30-year-old Jaroslav Jirik the right to pursue a career in North America.

Jirik was signed by St. Louis Blues scout Cliff Fletcher in 1969. Fletcher was in Europe and actually got three signatures, the other players being Josef Horesovsky and Jan Havel. The Czechs later refused the latter two the chance to travel but relented with Jirik.

Jirik was nothing short of a superstar in Europe. At the club level, he was a high-scoring forward with Kladno (and later Brno), and internationally he had played in three Olympics (1960, 1964, 1968) and seven World Championships over the previous decade.

Fletcher assigned Jirik to the Kansas City Blues of the CHL so he could get used to the North American game, and Jirik did just fine. He had 19 goals and 35 points in 53 games, and late in the season earned a three-game callup to the Blues.

Coach Scotty Bowman was away scouting, so injured defenceman Al Arbour took over behind the bench for two games in late March 1970. Arbour's lineup was light after the loss of three players—Tim Ecclestone, Larry Keenan, and Ab McDonald. Arbour then recalled Jirik and Norm Dennis from the CHL to fill in, but their first game was a 1–0 loss in Chicago.

Jirik conceded after the game the adjustment was more than he had bargained for. "This is a lot harder than Kansas City," he agreed. "They play their position more in the NHL, and the game is much faster. They also handle the puck much better."

Jaroslav Jirik was the first Czech in the NHL.

Butt It Has Its Place in History

Moose Dupont

NEW YORK RANGERS // FEBRUARY 28, 1971

The new Vancouver Canucks rolled in to Madison Square Garden on the last day of February 1971, and new to the Rangers' lineup was tough guy Andre "Moose" Dupont.

Playing with Omaha, he was leading the Central Hockey League in penalty minutes at the time, and the Rangers needed a defenceman desperately because Brad Park, Rod Seiling, and Ab DeMarco were all injured.

Writing in the *New York Daily News*, Lynn Hudson had this to say of Dupont's debut:

> "Dupont is known as a hitter with not great finesse, and the crowd yelled expectantly each time he took the ice. Dupont lived up to his reputation as a penalty-box occupant, being seated for butt-ending, a rather rarely called infraction, shortly after taking the ice."

He later took a hooking penalty, thus prompting Hudson to summarize, "Dupont did not look like the answer to the Rangers' urgent shortage of defencemen."

Dupont's debut is noteworthy for one trivial reason. Of all NHLers to make their debut since 1917, he is the one and only to incur that "rarely called" butt-ending penalty.

Moose Dupont holds a truly trivial record in NHL debut history.

Can't Be Beat

Ken Dryden

MONTREAL CANADIENS // MARCH 14, 1971

It was late in the season and diminutive goaler Rogatien Vachon was tired. He had played 15 games in a row, so coach Al MacNeil went to the bullpen, giving six-foot-four McGill law student Ken Dryden the start.

Dryden had attended the Habs' training camp the previous September and acquitted himself very well, playing two exhibition games against Chicago and Boston and looking comfortable in doing so. As a result, the Habs assigned him to the Montreal Voyageurs part-time while he attended classes.

Of course, this Montreal team had plenty of skill, so it wasn't surprising to see the team win handily, 5–1, over Pittsburgh, at the Forum. It was 3–0 before John Stewart scored for the Penguins late in the second, their only goal of the night.

"Maybe some goalies say they don't think of shutouts, but I do," Dryden confessed. "Trouble is, it's just when you start patting yourself on the back you get beaten."

Interestingly, this was Stewart's first career goal (in his seventh career game). Although shots were 36-36, Dryden was quick to point out he had a pretty easy night. "They had very few really good shots," he admitted after. "Sure, I made a couple of reasonably difficult saves, but I was warmed up

to them after easier ones on the same shifts."

As things turned out, Vachon got more of a break than he anticipated. Dryden played the remaining six games of the regular season and every game in the playoffs, leading the Habs to a stunning Stanley Cup. Famously, Dryden became the first player to win the Conn Smythe Trophy before the Calder Trophy. The next year, he was the clear number-one goalie. Vachon played one game before being traded to Los Angeles.

The rest, as they say, is history.

The incomparable Ken Dryden made an impression every time he guarded the goal.

The Flower Begins to Bloom

Guy Lafleur

MONTREAL CANADIENS // OCTOBER 9, 1971

The start of the 1971–72 season was an historic one for the Montreal Canadiens. They hired Scotty Bowman to be their coach; they named Henri Richard captain because Jean Beliveau had retired; and, they had a rookie named Guy Lafleur in the lineup.

At first the team wanted Lafleur to wear No. 4, but he refused to take Beliveau's iconic number. He chose 10, hoping to make a new number his own. On the day of the game, the *Montreal Gazette* published a special feature on the team, and Lafleur was the last player mentioned!

"It's sheer folly to suggest, as some people do, that young Lafleur is going to make Montreal forget the great Jean Beliveau. But in taking over Big Jean's spot at centre, the 20-year-old junior sensation already looms as a shining star in the NHL. He has speed, a quick shot and lays down passes accurately from forehand or backhand. He has great hockey savvy and unlike most rookies realizes the importance of defence in the NHL."

The home opener, against the Rangers, started with a ceremony to retire Beliveau's No. 4, but the game itself was something of a mish-mash for the Habs.

Goalie Ken Dryden, playing his first full season after winning the Conn Smythe Trophy the previous spring, was nervous, and Montreal had to rally for a 4–4 tie.

Lafleur got his first career point late in the second period, assisting on a goal by Yvan Cournoyer, but "The Flower" wasn't spectacular in his first game.

"I'm disappointed with my performance," Lafleur said. "I felt the pressure, of course. I missed a few passes because . . . well, I guess I was concentrating too much on rushing the net. Everything is so much faster here than in junior. Everybody moves a lot quicker. It takes a while to get used to it. I can see that now. All it means is that I've got to work a lot harder. It won't take long."

Guy Lafleur didn't have a great first game, but he made up for it over a sensational career.

Oldest Debut—The Great Debate

Lester Patrick
(New York Rangers, March 20, 1927)
vs.
Connie Madigan
(St. Louis Blues, February 1, 1973)

The NHL has long held that the oldest rookie in league history is Connie Madigan. He was 38 years old when he played in his first NHL game, in 1973, and the career minor leaguer lasted all of 20 games before being sent back down to the Blues farm team.

But the simple truth is that Lester Patrick was nearly five years older than Madigan when he played a few shifts on the blue line for the Rangers on March 20, 1927. The NHL's argument is that Patrick's appearance was a one-off whereas Madigan's was the start of something more ambitious.

Amazingly, though, Patrick played one more time just 18 days after his initial appearance, and he played goal.

In Game 2 of the Stanley Cup Finals, the Rangers were in Montreal to play the Maroons. Midway through the game, New York's starting goalie Lorne Chabot suffered an eye injury after being hit by a shot. There was no way he could continue.

Patrick, the team's general manager and coach, donned the pads and played the rest of the game, allowing only one goal and leading the Blueshirts to a stunning 2–1 overtime win.

In pre-war days, when a goalie incurred a penalty, he had to serve the two minutes himself, and a defenceman on the penalized team played goal in his place. Patrick, however, is the only player to play in the NHL as a skater and a goalie who was not filling in for a penalized goalie.

Regardless, the simple fact is that the oldest player to make his first NHL appearance was Patrick.

Connie Madigan was 38 when he made his NHL debut.

// Lester Patrick, New York Rangers
   March 20, 1927
   age 43 years, 80 days

From various accounts it appears that Patrick played but one shift, and a short one at that because he incurred a penalty soon after stepping onto the ice.

The esteemed Seabury Lawrence, writing in the *New York Times*, captured only this glimpse of Patrick: "Lester Patrick, manager of the Rangers, came on at defense for Johnson, his first game of the year, but he was soon benched for tripping."

"Lester Patrick, old-time star now managing the Rangers, played defence for a few minutes." –*Montreal Gazette*

"Lester Patrick, veteran western player and now manager of the Rangers, qualified himself for the play-offs by playing defence for a few moments." –*Toronto Star*

// Connie Madigan, St. Louis Blues
   February 1, 1973
   age 38 years, 120 days

It was a busy few days for Connie Madigan. On January 31, 1973, he was acquired by the St. Louis Blues from the Portland Buckaroos of the WHL for the loan of forward Andre Aubrey for the season and an undisclosed sum of cash. Madigan, a 38-year-old minor-league veteran, was then assigned to Denver, the Blues WHL affiliate.

Just one day later, he was recalled from the minors to play his first NHL game, against Vancouver. Finally, in his 17th season of pro hockey, he would become an NHLer.

"I've always had as my goal to play in the National League," he said. "Even after waiting all these years, it was still quite a thrill playing in my first game. I'm just glad to be here, although I've always thought I should have been here sooner."

A solidly built defenceman, he took a regular shift and the team won handily, 5–1, all goals coming in the first period. Madigan stayed with the Blues for 20 games in all, played three more years in the minors, and retired, his NHL dreams having come true.

Lester Patrick played defence and goal long after his pre-NHL playing days were supposed to be over.

Christmas Debuts

Gerry O'Flaherty might well go down as the last NHL player to make his debut on Christmas Day. He did so in 1971, after which the league stopped asking its players to sacrifice family for just another day at the rink.

Over the years only 23 mostly little-known players started their careers on the day of presents and turkey and Santa Claus.

Player, Team, Year	G/ Mins	A/ GA	P	PIM/ Decision
Frank Brophy, Quebec Bulldogs, 1919	0	0	0	0
George Carey, Quebec Bulldogs, 1919	2	0	2	0
Ed Carpenter, Quebec Bulldogs, 1919	0	0	0	0
Howard McNamara, Montreal Canadiens, 1919	1	0	1	0
George McNaughton, Quebec Bulldogs, 1919	0	0	0	0
Don Smith, Montreal Canadiens, 1919	1	0	1	0
Charles Stewart, Boston Bruins, 1924	60:00	5		L
Frank Steele, Detroit Falcons, 1930	0	0	0	0
Gord Pettinger, New York Rangers, 1932	0	0	0	0
Irv Frew, Montreal Maroons, 1933	0	0	0	2
Bingo Kampman, Toronto Maple Leafs, 1937	0	0	0	4
Harry Frost, Boston Bruins, 1938	0	0	0	0
Art Herchenratter, Detroit Red Wings, 1940	0	0	0	0
Bob Whitelaw, Detroit Red Wings, 1940	0	0	0	0
Frank Mailley, Montreal Canadiens, 1942	0	0	0	0
Henry Dyck, New York Rangers, 1943	0	0	0	0
Mel Read, New York Rangers, 1946	0	0	0	0
Bing Juckes, New York Rangers, 1947	0	0	0	0
Tod Sloan, Toronto Maple Leafs, 1947	0	0	0	0
Bert Olmstead, Chicago Black Hawks, 1948	0	0	0	0
Ron Howell, New York Rangers, 1954	0	0	0	0
Glen Sather, Boston Bruins, 1966	0	0	0	0
Gerry O'Flaherty, Toronto Maple Leafs, 1971	0	0	0	0

Tod Sloan is part of a rare group of players to start his career on Christmas night.

NOTES

// The only players to score a debut goal on Christmas were George Carey, Howard McNamara, and Don Smith, all in 1919.

// The only goalie to make his debut on this date was Boston's Charles Stewart, who allowed five goals in a 5–0 loss to Montreal.

// Glen Sather and Bert Olmstead started on this day and ended up in the Hockey Hall of Fame, the former as a Builder (and Cup-champion coach), the latter as a Player.

// The New York Rangers have five names on this list of 23, most of any team.

The Pioneer

Borje Salming wasn't the first Swede to play in the NHL. That distinction goes to Ulf Sterner. He wasn't the first to survive a full season. That was Thommie Bergman, in Detroit.

But he was the first European player to become a superstar, the first to play a full season of physical hockey, dominate play, and show the NHL that hockey in Europe was world class.

It all started at Maple Leaf Gardens on October 10, 1973.

Red Kelly was the coach, and the Leafs had nine new faces in the lineup for their first game of the season, a home tilt against former coach Punch Imlach and the Buffalo Sabres.

Salming had been spotted playing in Sweden when Team Canada played two exhibition games during their transition from Canada to Moscow in the Summit Series, and he and forward Inge Hammarstrom were signed by the Leafs a year later. It was an unprecedented move, literally taking two Swedes from their national league and expecting them to translate their skills to the NHL game.

Indeed, Hammarstrom had troubles doing so, but Salming thrived. Kelly partnered him with another youngster, Ian Turnbull, and they were the best tandem for the team during the pre-season.

In that first game, a 7–4 win over the Sabres, Salming was sensational and was named the game's first star.

Wrote Frank Orr in the *Toronto Star*: "In the past, NHL people often questioned the intestinal qualities of Swedish players. Nothing in Salming's play indicated a lack in that area. He's not a robust bodychecker, but he took his man out of the play solidly, blocked shots adroitly, and rushed well."

The next night was even more telling. The Leafs travelled to Philadelphia to play the gooning Flyers, and the Broad Street Bullies made it their priority to go after Salming. Dave Schultz slashed him; Salming slashed back. Schultz dropped his gloves; so did Salming. In the third period, Ed van Impe earned a five-minute spearing penalty. The Leafs lost, 2–0, but Salming proved he was here to stay.

"He looks like a really good one if he can stand up to the rugged going in this league," said Bobby Clarke, one of the nastiest players of the day. "Everyone will try him until he proves he won't back off."

Almost, Gus!

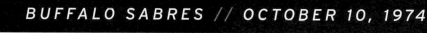

Danny Gare

BUFFALO SABRES // OCTOBER 10, 1974

Danny Gare came within three seconds of perhaps the most difficult record to beat.

Three decades after Gus Bodnar's record-fast first goal, Danny Gare came close to equalling the rare record, but fell just short.

Gare started the team's season opener at the Aud on a line with Craig Ramsay and Don Luce, and just 18 seconds after the opening faceoff, Gare had put the puck past goalie Gilles Gilbert. He took a shot by the side of the net, beat Bobby Orr to the rebound, and scored. It was a sign of things to come as the Sabres ran roughshod over the Bruins, winning 9–5 in Don Cherry's debut behind the Boston bench.

"I'll never forget it. Ever," Gare said later. "The crowd got on its feet and was going nuts. Orr got the puck out of the net, took his stick, and broke it right over the crossbar. 'Rammer' [Craig Ramsay] got the puck. I'm still so pumped and excited. I'm jumping up and down. Everything is happening so fast. So I go back and sit down on the bench and 'Rammer' hands me the puck, and I'm looking at it and I just said to myself, 'Well, maybe I belong.'"

"It's one of those moments in your career, in your life," he continued. "First game, you score and it's 18 seconds in. It was a big night for us. We built a lot of momentum and confidence as a team right away, and we went all the way to the Stanley Cup final."

1. Gus Bodnar / 15 seconds,
Toronto Maple Leafs, October 30, 1943

See page 36

2. Danny Gare / 18 seconds,
Buffalo Sabres, October 10, 1974

3. Alexander Mogilny / 20 seconds,
Buffalo Sabres, October 5, 1989

See page 112–113

4. Trevor Steinburg / 32 seconds,
Quebec Nordiques, April 2, 1986

5. Al Hill / 36 seconds,
Philadelphia Flyers, February 14, 1977

See page 78

6. Max Comtois / 49 seconds,
Anaheim Ducks, October 3, 2018

See page 65

7. Ted Speers / 55 seconds,
Detroit Red Wings, March 3, 1986

8. Brock McGinn / 55 seconds,
Carolina Hurricanes, October 16, 2015

// Trevor Stienburg, Quebec Nordiques
April 2, 1986 / 32 seconds

Playing on a line with Dale Hunter and Risto Siltanen, Stienburg was called up from the London Knights for two games at the end of the 1985–86 season. This line started the game, and 32 seconds later Stienburg had beaten Alain Chevrier of New Jersey with a shot. The Devils recovered and won, 6–5.

In all, Stienburg played 71 regular-season games (and one more in the playoffs) and scored eight goals, but none more memorable than his first.

// Ted Speers, Detroit Red Wings
March 3, 1986 / 55 seconds

On the afternoon of March 3, 1986, Ted Speers and Bob Probert were recalled from the Detroit farm team in Adirondack. It was the third recall for Probert, who saw NHL action both previous times, and the second for Speers, who didn't play the last time the Wings brought him up (January 11).

The occasion was a home game against division rivals Minnesota North Stars who were in third place in the Norris Division with 65 points. Detroit was solidly in last place with only 31 points.

As soon as Speers found out he'd be playing, he alerted his father, Dee, and brother, Jerry, who were living in Baltimore. Coach Brad Park then chimed in with a deal. "I told him, if his family got here in time, I'd start him."

Sure enough, they did, and Park was true to his word, sending Speers out for the opening faceoff alongside centreman Ron Duguay and left winger John Ogrodnick. Just 55 seconds later, Speers had his first goal.

Ogrodnick fired the puck in deep and chased after it, and Minnesota goalie Don Beaupre also chased after it. Ogrodnick got there first and poked it towards the goal. Speers had slipped on the play but was still moving to the net and got a touch on the puck before it went in.

"I think it was going to go in anyway, but I just wanted to make sure," he sheepishly admitted after. No hard feelings, though.

"Good for him. He was really tickled," Ogrodnick said

// Brock McGinn, Carolina Hurricanes
October 16, 2015 / 55 seconds

First shift, first goal. The night was October 16, 2015, McGinn and his Carolina Hurricanes were in Detroit to face the Red Wings early in the 2015–16 season. McGinn controlled the puck outside the Detroit blue line off a turnover and skated in down the left side on a two-on-one with Kris Versteeg.

Red Wings defenceman Niklas Kronwall, though, took the passing lane away and McGinn took the shot. Jimmy Howard made the save, but McGinn snapped the rebound in for the early 1–0 lead. The 'Canes went on to win, 5–3, their first of the season after three losses.

McGinn had been the last cut during training camp and was called up from the farm team in Charlotte two days earlier. He later assisted on an Eric Staal goal and was named the game's second star, making for a memorable debut from start to finish.

Easiest Goals Ever

Shy of an own goal for which the last player on the attacking team to touch the puck gets credit, the easiest way to score a goal is into the empty net. No goalie? You can't beat that. Yet only twice has a player scored a goal in his first NHL game by popping it into an empty net.

// Charlie Simmer, California Golden Seals
December 27, 1974

By any measure, the California Golden Seals were a miserable franchise during their precious few years of existence. They lost consistently and drew flies to their home games, and it was a team players longed to leave. But Simmer was drafted 39th overall by the Seals in 1974, so that is where his career began.

He had proved in junior that he could score, and in later years when he played on the famed Triple Crown Line in Los Angeles with Marcel Dionne and Dave Taylor he scored like a superstar. His beginnings were more humble, though. He made his NHL debut at home against Bobby Orr, Phil Esposito, and the rest of the Bruins.

The Seals were an anomaly this season. To date their road record was a pitiful 1-17-2 but at home they were 6-5-4. After a very impressive 5–2 win over the Bruins, they were 7-5-4.

Simmer got an assist on a critical goal from Dave Hrechkosy in the second period that gave the home side a 3–1 lead, but the teams later exchanged goals such that with time winding down it was 4–2. Coach Don Cherry removed goalie Ross Brooks for the extra attacker, and that's when Simmer scored his first goal. The time was 18:47, and he became the first NHLer ever to score his first career goal in his first game into the vacant cage.

// Lindy Ruff, Buffalo Sabres
October 11, 1979

It was Scotty Bowman's first game as coach of the Sabres, and the team's first of the 1979–80 season. Ruff had made the team out of training camp and was in the lineup after being drafted by the Sabres that summer.

Buffalo rallied from down 4–3 in the second period to score the game's final three goals to win, 6–4. Last of those was Ruff's empty netter. With Washington goalie Wayne Stephenson on the bench and the Caps pressing for a goal, Ruff got the puck and fired it the length of the ice, hitting the bull's eye.

"It's a good feeling to win that first game, especially at home," Bowman said. "We deserved to win."

And Ruff added his name to NHL debut history as just the second player ever to get his first goal in his first game via the empty net.

Charlie Simmer was a star forward with the L.A. Kings' Triple Crown Line, but he started his career with the California Golden Seals.

The First Lion Roars

Matti Hagman

BOSTON BRUINS // OCTOBER 7, 1976

Technically, there were three Finns to play in the NHL before Matti Hagman, but they were Finnish only by birth certificate and not by upbringing. Al Pudas, Pentti Lund, and Juha Widing all were born in Finland and went on to play in the NHL, but they had all moved to Canada at a very young age and were Canadian in every other way.

Matti Hagman was different, though. Born in Helsinki in 1955, he was a native Finn through and through, playing his minor hockey at home before turning pro in his teens with HIFK.

Hagman played in his first World Championship in 1975 while still only 19, and the Boston Bruins took notice. They selected him 104th overall in the 1975 Amateur Draft at a time when Europeans were simply not on the radar of most NHL teams. But the incredible play of Swedish defenceman Borje Salming with the Maple Leafs gave some scouts pause.

The Bruins were further interested after Hagman's terrific 1975–76 season. He played at the 1976 Olympics, in Innsbruck, and then in August and September he was a star with Suomi at the inaugural Canada Cup. Soon after the end of that tournament, Boston signed Hagman to an NHL contract, and he was in coach Don Cherry's lineup to open the 1976–77 season, becoming the first Finnish-trained player to make the league.

Although the Bruins won the home game against Minnesota, 6–2, only 9,221 were in attendance at the Garden in Boston. This was a loud and clear response to the fact that the team had allowed Bobby Orr to sign with Chicago. The greatest player in the game's history left to play for another team, and fans were appalled.

Rick Middleton was the star player for the Bruins this night, scoring a hat trick, and Hagman was held without a point. In all, the talented Finn played 237 regular-season games over four seasons, paving the way for future stars including Esa Tikkanen and Jari Kurri in the early 1980s.

Matti Hagman was the first of many Finns to make it in the NHL.

Greatest Debut of All Time

Al Hill

PHILADELPHIA FLYERS // FEBRUARY 14, 1977

It is, quite simply, the greatest NHL debut in league history, in part because of the points total, in part because of its improbability. Almost 7,900 players and 60,000 games, and what Hill achieved on Valentine's Day 1977, a home game for the Philadelphia Flyers against St. Louis, is what goes down in history.

> First, a summary of his special night. He recorded five points. He had two goals on two shots. He had three points in the first period, something only six other players have ever done. He also incurred a fighting major, making him the only player to record a Gordie Howe hat trick in his debut.

And he did all of this in game one, under the cloak not only of anonymity but total obscurity.

Said coach Fred Shero after the game: "I didn't know we had the guy. They just told me he was tough. I said, 'Bring him up.'"

Jay Greenberg of *The (Philadelphia) Evening Bulletin* wrote in his game recap: "We are still checking police records to see if any NHL players vanished over the last few years under mysterious circumstances. Is this a mass hysteric amnesia? Is Al Hill from Mars?"

What's even more amazing about this night is that Hill wasn't even a prospect of great value. He had been playing with the Springfield Indians of the AHL and was by no means setting the league ablaze. But the Flyers had run into injury troubles. Regulars Paul Holmgren and Harvey Bennett were out, so the Stanley Cup finalists of the previous spring were using this opportunity to see some new faces.

Bob Ritchie got into a game, and then Drew Callander, and on the morning of this game, management decided it was time to test Hill. But with so little notice, he had to make his way straight from his home to the arena. No time to check into an hotel, he arrived at the Spectrum at 5:30 p.m., dressed, and scored the game's first goal only 36 seconds after the opening faceoff. His long slapshot went between the pads of Blues goalie Yves Belanger, and that's how the night went for Hill.

Midway through the period, Hill tipped in a Reggie Leach shot for goal number two, and before the period ended Hill made a nice pass to Leach for a third goal. Three points in the first 17 minutes of Hill's NHL career.

Early in the second period, Hill got into a fight with Bob McMillan, and soon after returning to the ice he notched point number four. He used his size to knock a Blues player off the puck and passed to Bobby Clarke, who fed Mel Bridgman for the goal.

Hill crunched Rod Seiling in the third to set up Clarke for another goal, completing his five-point night. Despite his heroics, the game was still close.

"I was shaking before the game, through it, and I'm still shaking. This might be a dream," Hill told reporters after the game.

Of course, all good things must come to pass. The big left winger played three more games without doing much and was demoted. He was recalled for four games in March—again, nothing. He had one final assist on the final day of the regular season and didn't appear in the playoffs.

Al Hill (No. 37) scores a goal in the greatest debut in league history.

Hill had two goals, five points, and a Gordie Howe hat trick in his first game.

The Sutter Family

No family has sent as many players to the NHL as the Sutters, from tiny Viking, Alberta. Six of seven children of Louis and Grace made the NHL. Only Gary decided to stay home and work the family farm.

The six Sutters were Brian, Brent, Darryl, Duane, and twins Ron and Rich. Each of these players has sons, three of whom have gone on to play in the NHL and all of whom were drafted by NHL teams.

Brandon (Brent's son), Brett (Darryl's son), and Brody (Duane's son) have already played in the NHL. Shaun (Brian's son) was drafted 102nd overall by Calgary in 1998 but never played in the NHL.

Neither did Lukas, Rich's son. He was drafted twice, first by the Winnipeg Jets in 2012 (39th overall) and then, after not signing, two years later with the New York Islanders (200th overall). Riley (Ron's son) was selected 93rd overall by the Washington Capitals in 2018 and appears to be on track to make the NHL.

In all, that makes nine Sutters so far, and a tenth likely on the way.

The Sutter family is nobility in hockey circles.

Brian Sutter, St. Louis Blues / December 4, 1976

Called up from Kansas City of the CHL earlier in the day, Brian had a quiet debut at home in a 1–0 loss to the Atlanta Flames. His name didn't get on the game summary in any form, but he split this season between the two teams and was a full-time NHLer starting the following year.

Duane Sutter, New York Islanders / November 30, 1979

If you waltzed into Edmonton in 1979 and matched Wayne Gretzky's prodigious offence, you'd done something pretty special. That's what Duane did on this date. The 19-year-old was called up from junior in Lethbridge the day before the game and scored two goals and an assist, although the Oilers won the game, 5–3.

"I should be happy, I guess," he said after. His first shot was tipped in by Bryan Trottier late in the first period, and then he scored two of his own later in the second. "The boy played a fine game," said Islanders legendary coach Al Arbour.

Gretzky had a goal and two assists and was named the first star of the game, and Sutter was named second star.

Darryl Sutter, Chicago Black Hawks / December 13, 1979

Called up from the farm—the hockey farm, not the family farm—in New Brunswick, Darryl played his first game under unpleasant circumstances. The 5–2 road loss in Buffalo this night represented the Hawks' eighth game without a win, and the Sabres' victory was their team-record ninth in a row. Sutter played only eight NHL games this season before becoming a regular in 1980–81.

Brent Sutter, New York Islanders / February 25, 1981

Lady Luck smiled on Brent Sutter towards the end of February 1981. The New York Islanders were in town on the 25th to play Calgary, and Brent, who played junior hockey in nearby Lethbridge, planned on driving to the game to say hello to his brother, Duane, a member of the Islanders who was injured and not playing.

Brent, though, was drafted by those same Islanders 17th overall the previous year, and the team as a whole was limping into Alberta for the game. Mike Bossy was out with a thumb injury; John Tonelli had a bruised shoulder; Bryan Trottier had a knee injury; and, defenceman Denis Potvin was still out with a leg problem.

Coach Al Arbour called Brent and told him to bring his equipment—he'd be playing. Although Brent earned an assist in the game, it was a memorable debut for all the wrong reasons. The hometown Flames crushed the Islanders, 11–4.

Ron Sutter, Philadelphia Flyers / November 28, 1982

Back-to-back games on the west coast proved helpful to Ron Sutter's NHL debut. Although the Philadelphia Flyers won the first game, in Los Angeles, by a 4–0 score, they lost Paul Evans, who suffered a knee injury. Ron was called up from Lethbridge on an emergency basis and played in his first NHL game the next night, in Vancouver. The game ended in a 5–5 tie, but he didn't figure in the scoring.

Rich Sutter, Pittsburgh Penguins / January 1, 1983

Just five weeks after twin Ron made his first NHL start, Rich did the same, becoming the sixth Sutter brother to play in the NHL. All were now active in the league at the same time, a most extraordinary family feat.

Brandon Sutter, Carolina Hurricanes / October 10, 2008

Brent's son, Brandon, was the first child of an Original Six Sutter to play in the NHL, just seven years after the last of the first brothers retired (Ron). Drafted a lofty 11th overall by Carolina in 2007, Brandon made the 'Canes out of training camp a year later. He earned an assist on a Dan LaCouture goal early in the third period, which turned out to be the winning goal in a 6–4 win over Florida.

Brett Sutter, Calgary Flames / December 23, 2008

Curtis Glencross was injured, so Calgary coach Mike Keenan needed someone for a home game against Anaheim. In stepped Brandon, the eighth Sutter to get to the NHL. He was already back in Viking on the farm, expecting a little holiday over Christmas, but those plans changed quickly. The fact that his father, Darryl, was team GM didn't matter.

"It's not based on anything but merit," Keenan said. "He's earned it," said Dad the general manager. Brett proved critics wrong, at least for a night, which was extra special because he had left his equipment back in Quad-City and had to buy some new things while using skates and a few other items from his days in Red Deer, which he had kept at home.

Brett scored his first career goal early in the third to tie the game, 2–2. It was the first of three goals in a row that propelled the Flames to a 4–3 win. As it turned out, he didn't score another goal in the NHL for five years.

Brody Sutter, Carolina Hurricanes / October 16, 2014

The 23-year-old Brody, Sutter number nine, played less than six minutes in the game during a 2014–15 season in which he played mostly with Charlotte in the AHL. He didn't figure in the scoring, a 2–1 road loss in a shootout to the New York Rangers.

Scoring in a Period

Every player wants to score a goal in his NHL debut. Failing that, he wants at least to get an assist. Two points would be amazing. Three, rare company.

Now, what about three points in a *period* of your first game? That list consists of only seven names, and it's even smaller if you consider some asterisk-like exceptions.

Len Fontaine had three points in his first period of NHL hockey.

First Period

// Harry Hyland, Montreal Wanderers
December 19, 1917 (3 goals)

Of course, by the time Hyland played his first NHL game he was anything but a rookie. The 28-year-old had played every season of the NHA's existence (1909–1917) and won the Stanley Cup with the Wanderers in 1910. The first NHL game ever played saw Hyland's Wanderers squeak out a 10–9 win over Toronto. The first period featured eight goals, five to Montreal and three of those to Hyland. No first-game player matched this achievement for 62 years (see Real Cloutier story on page 83).

// Al Hill, Philadelphia Flyers
February 14, 1977 (2 goals, 1 assist)

No one knew much about the 21-year-old Al Hill before the game, but 36 seconds after the opening faceoff he had his first career goal in the bag. Eleven minutes later, he scored again, and he earned an assist on a Reggie Leach goal five and a half minutes after that. Three points in his first career 17 minutes.

// Len Fontaine, Detroit Red Wings
October 7, 1972 (1 goal, 2 assists)

After four years of toiling for Port Huron in the IHL, Len Fontaine, 24, finally made the grade and was in the Red Wings lineup for the first game of the 1972–73 season. He played 39 games with the Wings before being sent back down, and during that time he tallied 18 points, three in the first period of his first game.

He opened the scoring in New York, beating Ed Giacomin with a hard shot, his first career shot. Just 28 seconds later, he assisted on a Guy Charron goal, and at 15:39 he drew the second assist on a Red Berenson goal.

// Roland Eriksson, Minnesota North Stars
October 6, 1976 (3 assists)

Coming off an impressive performance with Sweden at the inaugural Canada Cup, the 22-year-old Roland Eriksson did everything he could to help his new team win, but despite his four assists, the Minnesota North Stars lost to the Rangers at Madison Square Garden, 6–5.

Eriksson collected three assists by the 12:36 mark of the opening period, helping three players score—Doug Hicks, Tim Young, Bill Goldsworthy. He assisted on

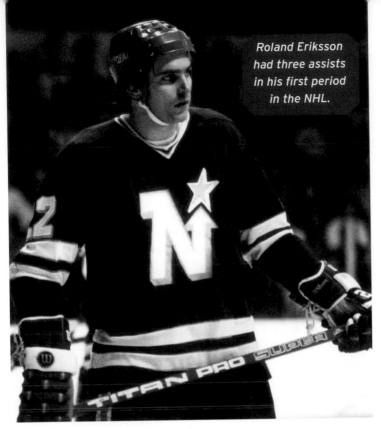

Roland Eriksson had three assists in his first period in the NHL.

another Young goal in the third period. Impressively, he and Earl "Dutch" Reibel are the only players to earn four assists in their NHL debuts.

Second Period

// Kent Nilsson, Atlanta Flames
October 10, 1979 (1 goal, 2 assists)

The Atlanta Flames visited Quebec for the first NHL game in Nordiques history, but it was the visitors who skated to a solid 5–3 win. Amazingly, this game produced two performances on this list of three points in a period (see Real Cloutier below). Twenty-three-year-old Kent Nilsson scored early to make it 2–0 Atlanta and later assisted on goals by Ivan Boldirev and Willi Plett.

// Vaclav Nedomansky, Detroit Red Wings
November 18, 1977 (3 assists)

Acquired in an historic trade with Birmingham of the WHA just days earlier, "Big Ned" made a spectacular NHL debut at age 33 after a career in Czechoslovakia and in the WHA that made this a much-anticipated moment in hockey history. Although Atlanta jumped into a 3–0 lead after one period, Nedomansky was great in the second, setting up three teammates for goals, two on the power play. The Flames prevailed, 4–3, but the dominant Czech had announced his NHL arrival in style.

Third Period

// Real Cloutier, Quebec Nordiques
October 10, 1979 (3 goals)

Outdoing Kent Nilsson's great play in the second period of the Atlanta-Quebec game, Real Cloutier, 23, saved his best for last, but it was too little, too late. A native Quebecker, he played junior with the Remparts and then with the Nordiques in the WHA from 1974 to 1979. His team trailed the Flames, 4–0, heading into the third period, but Cloutier scored three times in the period to make a game of it. Still, Atlanta won, 5–3.

Kent Nilsson had a goal and two assists in one period during his debut.

Share the Glory

Of all goalie debuts in NHL history, only once has a goalie shared a shutout. That historic game was played on Long Island on November 1, 1977, when veteran Billy Smith shared the spotlight with newcomer Goran Hogosta.

The game in question was played at home against the Atlanta Flames, and it was a laugher from the outset. Bob Nystrom scored 1:49 into the game, and by the end of the first period it was 5–0. Over the course of the game, Bryan Trottier had four goals and an assist, and linemate Mike Bossy had a goal and four assists.

The game extended the Islanders' unbeaten streak to seven and it came on coach Al Arbour's 45th birthday. So happy was he with the events of the night that with 8:35 left to play he put Hogosta in the game to replace Billy Smith. The Swede, a recent callup from the AHL farm team in Hershey, stopped all four shots and shared the shutout with Smith, who stopped the first 17 Flames attempts.

Hogosta had played one game for Sweden at the 1976 Canada Cup and a year later took Sweden to a silver medal at the World Championship. The Islanders signed him that June, and a month into the 1977–78 season he made his NHL debut in historic fashion.

The only other NHL games he played were with Quebec two years later.

In his debut, goalie Goran Hogosta shared a shutout with veteran Billy Smith.

The Penultimate Price

Vaclav Nedomansky

DETROIT RED WINGS // NOVEMBER 18, 1977

For a small boy growing up in communist Czechoslovakia in the 1950s or '60s, the idea of playing in the NHL was as far-fetched as flying to the moon.

Nedomansky started his pro career with Slovan Bratislava in 1963, and over the course of the next 11 seasons he averaged nearly a goal a game. He made a greater contribution, though, to the national team. Between 1965 and 1974, he appeared in every international tournament for the Czechs, including two Olympics and nine World Championships.

Oddly, it was at the 1969 Worlds that the Czechs had their greatest moment. The year previous, the Soviets had invaded Czechoslovakia and stripped its citizens of many basic rights, creating an anger that cannot be properly put into words. At the 1969 World Championship, the Czechs beat their enemies twice, 2–0 and 4–3.

Then, in 1972, the Czechs and Soviets tied 3–3 midway through the tournament and later the Czechs won, 3–2. These results provided the margin of victory, giving the Czechs an emotional, and politically charged, gold medal.

Perhaps Nedomansky's greatest performance, however, came at the 1974 Worlds. He led the Czechs to a massive 7–2 win over the Soviets, CCCP's worst loss ever, and "Ned" was named the tournament's Best Forward by the IIHF.

That July, Nedomansky obtained a travel visa from the Czech government to take a family vacation to Berne, Switzerland. Once they got there, he contacted the Toronto Toros, signed a five-year, $750,000 contract, and then obtained visas to travel to Canada. He left everything behind.

Although he proved equally special a player in the WHA, Nedomansky was unhappy after the team moved to Birmingham, and he struggled as badly on the ice as the team did at the gate. Early in his fourth year in the WHA, he was traded to the Detroit Red Wings, the first ever trade between the rival leagues.

The next day, November 18, 1977, Nedomansky made his NHL debut in St. Louis. He was 33 years old, a legend in a country he could never return to and now a rookie of sorts. The Wings played their worst game of the young season, losing easily to the Blues, 5–3, but Nedomansky assisted on all three goals, all in the second period.

Nedomansky was, finally and rightfully, inducted into the Hockey Hall of Fame in 2019.

After 60

Dave "the Hammer" Schultz is so connected to the Philadelphia Flyers' gooning days under coach Fred Shero that it's tough to remember he also played with Los Angeles, Pittsburgh, and Buffalo after his Philly days were over.

In 1978–79, he skated for the Penguins, but one day in late November, back spasms looked like they'd force him to the press box. The Penguins called up their top farmhand, right winger Mike Meeker, from Binghamton, for a game against the fighting Flyers on November 25, 1978. Meeker had been the team's leading scorer and was the Penguins top selection at the Amateur Draft 1978, 25th overall that year.

Schultz managed to get in shape by game time, but Meeker also played his first career game as well. It was another sordid affair with a total of 12 fighting majors assessed by referee Bruce Hood, including two to Schultz and one to Meeker.

Schultz earned a minor with former teammate Moose Dupont early in the game, and got into a fight with Behn Wilson in the second, and later Dupont again before the period was over.

It was ironic, in some sense, because over the summer the Flyers cleaned house and traded three regulars—Orest Kindrachuk, Ross Lonsberry, and Tom Bladon—to the Penguins for a first-round draft choice. The Flyers selected Wilson.

Meeker, meanwhile, fought Rick MacLeish after the game was over, thus becoming the only player in league history to earn stats in his first game after the game was actually over. MacLeish was one of the few skilled players on Philadelphia, but on this occasion he dropped the gloves against the more pugilistically savvy Meeker.

Meeker had one shot on goal during the 3–1 loss, but he incurred five penalty minutes at the 20:00 mark of the third period.

Meeker's career lasted but four games. He played the next night in Toronto before being demoted, and was recalled again in April 1979, playing against the Flames on April 1 and St. Louis two days later. He didn't register a point, and his only stats were those five minutes from his first game.

A back injury derailed his career, but Meeker went into fish farming on Manitoulin Island in Ontario and is now one of the largest producers, accounting for some 2.5 million pounds of fish a year at his aquaculture farm.

The Great One

Wayne Gretzky

EDMONTON OILERS // OCTOBER 10, 1979

The start of the 1979–80 NHL season was historic in many ways, chief among them because it was the night Wayne Gretzky played his first NHL game.

Gretzky played for the Edmonton Oilers, of course, one of four teams from the World Hockey Association that were joining the NHL this fall (along with the Quebec Nordiques, Hartford Whalers, and Winnipeg Jets).

In his two previous seasons of hockey, the teenage Gretzky had accomplished so much it is fair to say no player had ever entered the NHL with greater expectations. Not Morenz, not Richard, nor Howe, not even Orr.

In 1976–77, as a 16- and 17-year-old, Gretzky tore apart the OHL. As a 17- and 18-year-old, he did the same in the WHA. But everyone said things would be different once he hit the big time. The NHL downplayed the quality of play in the WHA to the point that it refused to acknowledge that league's scoring stats and refused to admit that the pirate league was of comparable quality.

Paradoxically, the NHL also said players coming from the WHA would not be considered rookies, and as such were ineligible for the Calder Trophy. This made no sense on two fronts. First, it considered all players from 1917–18 to be rookies, even though most played in the NHA the previous season.

Second, the NHL always maintained that players from other leagues (i.e., the minors or Europe) would qualify for the Calder Trophy because no other league was comparable to the one and only NHL. So, on the one hand, the WHA was inferior because the NHL said so, but on the other hand it was on a par with the NHL because incoming players weren't considered rookies.

Wayne Gretzky was but 18 when he joined the NHL in 1979.

No matter. Gretzky and the Oilers were in Chicago for their first game of the 1979–80 season, and history was about to be re-written. Said Gretzky on the flight to the Windy City, thrilled at the chance ahead: "You've got to be a man to play hockey, but you have to have a lot of boy in you."

It was a game of emotion that's difficult to understand. Glen Sather, 34, was the coach, and alongside Gretzky was 19-year-old Mark Messier. In all, 12 Oilers had never played in the NHL, and every player on the team was nervous for varying reasons.

"I've never been that nervous before a game in my life," Gretzky admitted after his debut.

To no one's surprise, the Oilers trailed 2–0 just 2:23 into the first period, but they slowly worked themselves into the game. Kevin Lowe got his team's first ever NHL goal, on a power play, one assist going to Gretzky, and Dave Hunter tied the game a short time later.

The Hawks pulled ahead and went on to win, 4–2, but all in all it was a good start for Gretzky and the Oilers. The game gave No. 99 his first point, and the league was about to undergo a scoring change for the next 20 years thanks to the Great One.

No. 99 was both the greatest scorer and passer the league has ever known.

Gretzky Helps Others

In addition to registering an assist in his first NHL game, Wayne Gretzky helped eight other players earn their first NHL point in debuts.

// Brett Callighen, Edmonton Oilers
Kevin Lowe, Edmonton Oilers
October 10, 1979

Edmonton's first ever NHL goal came on a power play. Gretzky passed the puck to Callighen, who got it back to Kevin Lowe at the point. His shot went all the way, beating Tony Esposito at 9:49 of the first period.

// Jari Kurri, Edmonton Oilers
October 10, 1980

Exactly one year after making his own NHL debut, Gretzky helped new teammate Jari Kurri record a point in his first game. No. 99 scored on the power play late in the second period of a 7–4 loss to Quebec, Kurri drawing one of the assists. Kurri, of course, would later join Gretzky in the Hockey Hall of Fame.

// Jim Playfair, Edmonton Oilers
November 19, 1983

It was perhaps the only public relations misstep Wayne Gretzky ever made, but there was more truth than falsity in his comments. After the Oilers demolished the visiting New Jersey Devils, 13–4, Gretzky famously called the Devils a Mickey Mouse franchise.

The full quote reads as follows: "It got to the point where it wasn't funny. I mean, we didn't have Semenko, Linseman, Messier. If we'd had them, we might have scored 20. It's not a question of New Jersey not working. It's a question of talent. They better stop running a Mickey Mouse operation and start putting somebody on the ice. That franchise has been looking that way for nine years. It's not funny. It's disappointing."

And in this throttling came defenceman Jim Playfair, playing his first career game. On a night when Gretzky had three goals and five assists, Jari Kurri scored midway through the third to make it 10–4. Gretzky had one assist and Playfair, his first career point, the other.

Memorable? You better believe it.

// Raimo Summanen, Edmonton Oilers
March 27, 1984

The Oilers hammered the Flames, 9–2, in Calgary, and Raimo Summanen, making his debut, was in heady company during the height of the Oilers' dominance. Late in the first period, Jari Kurri scored his 52nd goal of the season. Wayne Gretzky got his 115th point of the season on the first assist, and Summanen, with his first point ever, got the second helper.

// David Goverde, Los Angeles Kings
December 26, 1991

David Goverde is part of a very special group of goalies to earn an assist in their NHL debuts. What makes his even more special is he helped Wayne Gretzky score. The Kings beat the visiting San Jose Sharks, 5–3, and Gretzky scored the fifth goal into an empty net. Goverde was excellent in goal, got the win, an assist, and a place in history.

// Bob Jay, Los Angeles Kings
October 24, 1993

It was early in the season, but Gretzky scored his seventh of the year with assists to Mike Donnelly and Bob Jay. The goal gave the visiting Kings a 2–1 lead, but the Rangers came back and won, 3–2.

// Vitali Yachmenev, Los Angeles Kings
October 7, 1995

It was Larry Robinson's first game as a head coach with the Kings, and Wayne Gretzky and Company gave him the perfect introduction—a victory at home. No. 99 set up Yachmenev for a goal early in the first period against goalie Stephane Fiset of the Avs, and Yachmenev later scored again. The final score was 4–2 Kings.

A third-round draft choice by the Kings in 1994 (59th overall), Yachmenev, 20, developed in the OHL with the North Bay Centennials before joining the Kings this season.

He was put on a line with 99 and Dmitri Khristich, and the trio connected on a power play early in the first period to stake the Kings to an early 2–0 lead. Yachmenev also scored the go-ahead and game-winning goal in the third, also assisted by Gretzky.

Greatest League Debut Nights

Three nights in league history tower above all others for NHL debuts: December 19, 1917, October 10, 1979, and October 5, 2005.

// December 19, 1917

The NHL started as a four-team league consisting of the Toronto Arenas, Ottawa Senators, Montreal Canadiens, and Montreal Wanderers. Since this was the first night of play, every player was, technically, playing in his first NHL game, although most of the 36 first-timers had had long careers in the NHA and wouldn't be considered rookies by today's standards.

// October 10, 1979

With the introduction of four WHA teams, the NHL grew from 17 to 21 teams. On this night, the opening of the 1979–80 season, some 45 players across the league played in their first game. Many had already played in the WHA. The list includes:

Atlanta Flames (3): Kent Nilsson, Pekka Rautakallio, Paul Reinhart
Chicago Black Hawks (2): Rich Preston, Terry Ruskowski
Detroit Red Wings (3): Mike Foligno, Glenn Hicks, Dennis Sobchuk
Edmonton Oilers (10): Brett Callighen, Ron Chipperfield, Peter Driscoll, Wayne Gretzky, Dave Hunter, Kevin Lowe, B.J. MacDonald, Mark Messier, Dave Semenko, Risto Siltanen
Los Angeles Kings (3): Steve Carlson, Mark Hardy, Dean Hopkins
New York Rangers (1): Doug Sulliman
Quebec Nordiques (9): Gilles Bilodeau, Curt Brackenbury, Real Cloutier, Bob Fitchner, Michel Goulet, Jamie Hislop, Pierre Lacroix, Gary Lariviere, Wally Weir
Toronto Maple Leafs (3): Laurie Boschman, Greg Hotham, Mark Kirton
Winnipeg Jets (11): Mike Amodeo, Scott Campbell, Willy Lindstrom, Morris Lukowich, Jimmy Mann, Peter Marsh, Barry Melrose, Craig Norwich, Lars-Erik Sjoberg, Peter Sullivan, Ron Wilson

The only team in action this night that did not have a new face was the Pittsburgh Penguins.

Laurie Boschman was part of NHL history on his debut night.

// October 5, 2005

The start of the 2005–06 season didn't see the addition of new teams, but nevertheless on this night another 45 players skated in their first NHL game. This high number can be attributed to three factors.

One: the 2004–05 season was lost entirely because of the lockout, meaning that rookies from that year and this new one were more or less crammed into one cohort.

Two: wanting to make a splashy return, the NHL scheduled 15 games, every team in action on one night.

Three: given that the NHL was now 30 teams, it didn't take much to reach 45 on one night, provided (as above) that there were enough games scheduled.

Indeed, no team had more than three newcomers, and only three of 30 (Edmonton, Montreal, Vancouver) didn't have at least one:

Mighty Ducks of Anaheim (2): Ryan Getzlaf, Corey Perry

Atlanta Thrashers (2): Braydon Coburn, Jim Slater

Boston Bruins (2): Andrew Alberts, Kevin Dallman

Buffalo Sabres (1): Tomas Vanek

Calgary Flames (1): Dion Phaneuf

Carolina Hurricanes (2): Niklas Nordgren, Cam Ward

Chicago Blackhawks (3): Rene Bourque, Duncan Keith, Brent Seabrook

Colorado Avalanche (1): Wojtek Wolski

Columbus Blue Jackets (2): Jaroslav Balastik, Gilbert Brule

Dallas Stars (1): Jussi Jokinen

Detroit Red Wings (2): Johan Franzen, Brett Lebda

Florida Panthers (1): Rostislav Olesz

Los Angeles Kings (1): George Parros

Minnesota Wild (2): Derek Boogaard, Matt Foy

Nashville Predators (1): Ryan Suter

New Jersey Devils (1): Zach Parise

New York Islanders (3): Chris Campoli, Robert Nilsson, Petteri Nokelainen

New York Rangers (1): Ryan Hollweg

Ottawa Senators (3): Brandon Bochenski, Brian McGratton, Andrej Meszaros

Philadelphia Flyers (2): Jeff Carter, Mike Richards

Phoenix Coyotes (1): Keith Ballard

Pittsburgh Penguins (2): Sidney Crosby, Max Talbot

San Jose Sharks (1): Ryane Clowe

St. Louis Blues (3): Jeff Hoggan, Jay McClement, Andy Roach

Tampa Bay Lightning (1): Timo Helbling

Toronto Maple Leafs (2): Alexander Steen, Andy Wozniewski

Washington Capitals (1): Alexander Ovechkin

Andy Wozniewski was part of the NHL's greatest debut night in 2005.

Miracle Man

Dave Christian

WINNIPEG JETS // MARCH 2, 1980

Just a couple of weeks after helping the U.S. National Team win an Olympic gold—the Miracle on Ice—Dave Christian traded his amateur togs for the professional sweater of the Winnipeg Jets.

He was one of many from that American team now scattering across the NHL, making good use of their fame to get a chance at glory in the big league. Ken Morrow was now with the New York Islanders; Mark Johnson with Pittsburgh; Mike Ramsey with Buffalo; hero goalie Jim Craig with the Atlanta Flames; backup goalie Steve Janaszak and forward Steve Christoff with Minnesota.

The Jets had drafted Christian 40th overall in 1979, but he wanted to pursue his Olympic dreams first before considering the NHL. Good idea. He played his first game, in Winnipeg, on March 2, 1980, and he scored his first goal on his first shot only seven seconds into his first shift.

This should or could be an NHL record, but the NHL considers only the time from the start of the game of the player's debut, not his own first shift, which is why Rudy Migay's 15 seconds is considered the record.

Christian came out with the team's second shift for a faceoff in the Chicago end of the ice. He beat Tom Lysiak on the

draw. The puck went to Ross Cory who got it to Morris Lukowich, who took a shot on goal. Mike Veisor made the save, but Christian knocked in the rebound just seven seconds after that faceoff to start his career.

Nevertheless, if you count the time between a player stepping on the ice to play his first game (which is the NHL definition of "game played" after all) to the time he put the puck in the net, no one in league history has done it faster than Dave Christian.

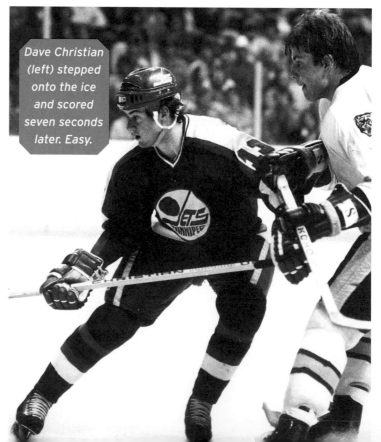

Dave Christian (left) stepped onto the ice and scored seven seconds later. Easy.

He Who Helps Others

Peter Stastny

QUEBEC NORDIQUES // OCTOBER 9, 1980

Everyone knows Wayne Gretzky is the scoring king, the superstar who recorded more assists in his career than anyone else's total points. But many people don't know that in the 1980s, when Gretzky was at the very height of his powers, the player who was second in scoring for that entire decade was Peter Stastny.

Stastny defected from Czechoslovakia and was a star for many years with the Quebec Nordiques, first alongside brother Anton and a year later another brother, Marian. Peter duly recorded an assist in his first career NHL game, on October 9, 1980, but then he went on and helped a record ten other players earn points in their NHL debuts. Not even Gretzky managed to do that.

1. Dave Pichette, Quebec Nordiques / December 7, 1980

Early in December 1980, the Leafs and Nordiques played back-to-back games on the weekend. In the first game, in Toronto, the Leafs skated to a 5–2 win, but Quebec coach Michel Bergeron was none too pleased with how the Leafs took liberties with his team.

As a result, Dave Pichette and Terry Johnson were called up from Hershey for the rematch in Quebec City on Sunday night, a game that ended up taking three and a half hours to play and produced 164 penalty minutes. Pichette wasn't part of the fisticuffs, but he did earn two assists in his first career game, a 4–4 tie. The first came off a Michel Goulet goal, the other assist going to Peter Stastny. Pichette's second assist came off a Stastny goal.

2. Gaston Therrien, Quebec Nordiques / January 21, 1981

It didn't take long for Stastny to help Gaston Therrien add his name to the scoresheet. Stastny scored just 4:04 into the game against Buffalo thanks to assists from brother Anton and Therrien.

3. Marian Stastny, Quebec Nordiques / October 6, 1981

Marian was the third of the three Stastny brothers to defect to Canada, making his NHL debut with Peter and Anton at the start of the 1981–82 season. Of course, it couldn't have been more special to record his first career point than on a goal by Peter, with a second assist to Anton. This was the first of many the brothers scored together with the Nordiques.

4. Bo Berglund, Quebec Nordiques / October 4, 1983

Berglund's first career goal came early in the second period in a home game against the Islanders. It tied the game, 2–2, and came off passes from Peter Stastny and Alain Cote. It was his only shot of the game in a 7–3 Nordiques victory.

5. Tommy Albelin, Quebec Nordiques / October 8, 1987

On a night when Peter Stastny earned four assists in a 5–1 road victory in Hartford, Albelin got his first career goal in the opening period after taking a pass from the aforementioned Stastny and firing a long screen shot that beat Mike Liut.

6. Ron Tugnutt, Quebec Nordiques December 29, 1987

Again, it's rare that a goalie earns an assist in his NHL debut, but Peter Stastny scored at 7:13 of the second period against Buffalo on a play that started with Tugnutt touching the puck and sending Stastny in on a breakaway. It was Stastny's 300th career goal. Tugnutt had been called up from the Fredericton Express the previous week and won his first game, 5–1, against Buffalo, stopping 29 of 30 shots to go with the assist.

7. Iiro Jarvi, Quebec Nordiques / October 6, 1988

Opening night of the 1988–89 season saw the Nordiques play a road game in Hartford, and Peter Stastny got the game's first goal at 3:13 with assists from veteran Goulet and newcomer Jarvi.

8. Darin Kimble, Quebec Nordiques / January 17, 1989

A "resident tough guy," as it were, Kimble had his name on the scoresheet in a few places the night he skated in his first NHL game. He got into a fight with Perry Anderson just 2:57 after the opening faceoff. Then, early in the

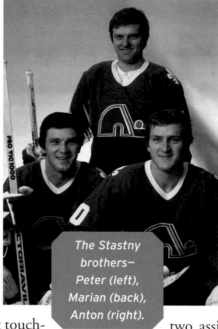

The Stastny brothers— Peter (left), Marian (back), Anton (right).

third, Jarvi and Stastny set him up for his first career goal. Later in the period he got into another fight, with David Maley. In all, one goal and 10 penalty minutes and a 7–4 Nordiques win over New Jersey.

9. Scott Niedermayer, New Jersey Devils / October 16, 1991

Late in the 1989–90 season, his 10th with Quebec, Peter Stastny was traded to the New Jersey Devils, where he played for three and a half years. And while no NHL debut goal was ever recorded by three future Hall of Famers (i.e., the goal and two assists), the game of October 16, 1991, was a rare example of two future inductees connecting on the same play.

In this case, it was a David Maley goal assisted by Scott Niedermayer and Stastny. Niedermayer was the first overall selection at the 1991 Entry Draft and was replacing Eric Weinrich on the blue line this night. At 18 years, 47 days old, he was the youngest player in Devils history. The goal started with a point shot by Niedermayer, a deflection by Stastny, and Maley getting the rebound.

10. Scott Pellerin, New Jersey Devils / December 6, 1992

Stastny connected with newcomer Scott Pellerin twice this night during a 7–3 Devils win in Buffalo. Stastny scored midway through the first, assists to Bill Guerin and Pellerin. Then, late in the third, on a power play, Pellerin scored his first NHL goal, assists to Stastny and Scott Stevens.

Relatively Speaking

Gordie, Howe About That!?
March 9, 1980

The feelings and emotions of playing that first NHL game are special for every player, and generally his first comment after the game is about how happy he is that his parents could make it to the game or how disappointing it was that they didn't make it.

Imagine now that the father didn't just make it to the game—he also played in it!

Of course, only one family can make that claim—Gordie Howe and his sons, Mark and Marty.

Gordie made his NHL debut on October 16, 1946, but he was in the lineup for the most incredible family achievement in NHL history. On October 11, 1979, the Hartford Whalers played a road game in Minnesota, and dressed for the Whalers was Gordie and his 23-year-old defenceman son, Mark. For the first time, a father and son played together.

Later in the season, on March 9, 1980, Gordie's other defenceman-son, Marty, was called up from Springfield to make his NHL debut, and both Gordie and Mark were also in the lineup. For the first time, a father and his *two* sons played in the same game!

In all, Gordie played with Mark and Marty seven times, four games late in the regular season (March 9, 12, 13, 19) and all three Whalers games in that year's playoffs (April 8, 9, 11).

At the other end of the spectrum are the Sullivan brothers. Frank and Peter were both sons of Frank Sr., who played hockey for Canada at the 1928 Olympics. Frank Jr., made his NHL debut with the Maple Leafs on March 11, 1950. Peter, however, didn't make his NHL debut until October 10, 1979, nearly three decades after his brother.

And then there are the history-making Hunter brothers, Dave, Dale, and Mark (see page 97). Of the more than 30 brothers of at least three, they are the only trio to each have recorded a point in their first NHL games.

More traditionally, there have been well over 150 father-son combinations in the NHL, but among those only seven times has both the father and the son recorded a point in their NHL debuts.

And of the hundreds of brothers who have played (more than 300 pairs), only 16 have both earned a point in their NHL debuts.

Gordie Howe (centre) and his two sons line up for a faceoff on March 9, 1980.

Father/son

Keith Acton, father	December 11, 1979, Montreal Canadiens—one assist
Will Acton, son	October 1, 2013, Edmonton Oilers—one assist
Lionel Conacher, father	November 26, 1925, Pittsburgh Pirates—one goal
Brian Conacher, son	November 18, 1951, Chicago Black Hawks—one assist
Dave Creighton, father	February 12, 1949, Boston Bruins—one goal, one assist
Adam Creighton, son	December 17, 1983, Buffalo Sabres—one assist
Bernie Geoffrion, father	December 16, 1950, Montreal Canadiens—one goal
Danny Geoffrion, son	October 23, 1979, Montreal Canadiens—one assist

Wayne Hicks, father	March 24, 1960, Chicago Black Hawks—one assist
Alex Hicks, son	November 15, 1995, Mighty Ducks of Anaheim—two goals, one assist
Al Palazzari, father	November 30, 1943, Boston Bruins—one goal
Doug Palazzari, son	October 9, 1974, St. Louis Blues—two goals
Brent Sutter, father	February 25, 1981, New York Islanders—one assist
Brandon Sutter, son	October 10, 2008, Carolina Hurricanes—one assist

Danny Geoffrion had the unenviable task of following in his father's footsteps in Montreal.

Brothers

Wayne Babych	October 11, 1978, St. Louis Blues—one assist
Dave Babych	October 10, 1980, Winnipeg Jets—one goal
Drew Callander	February 7, 1977, Philadelphia Flyers—one goal
Jock Callander	November 12, 1987, Pittsburgh Penguins—one goal
Odie Cleghorn	December 21, 1918, Montreal Canadiens—one goal
Sprague Cleghorn	December 21, 1918, Ottawa Senators—one goal, one assist
Lionel Conacher	November 26, 1925, Pittsburgh Pirates—one goal
Charlie Conacher	November 14, 1929, Toronto Maple Leafs—one goal
Bill Cook	November 16, 1926, New York Rangers—one goal
Bun Cook	November 16, 1926, New York Rangers—one assist
Bob Crawford	October 9, 1979, St. Louis Blues—one goal
Marc Crawford	October 6, 1981, Vancouver Canucks—one assist
Archie Fraser	October 30, 1943, New York Rangers—one assist
Harvey Fraser	November 1, 1944, Chicago Black Hawks—one goal, two assists
Peter Ihnacak	October 6, 1982, Toronto Maple Leafs—one assist
Miroslav Ihnacak	January 10, 1986, Toronto Maple Leafs—one goal
Dave Hunter	October 10, 1979, Edmonton Oilers—one goal
Dale Hunter	October 9, 1980, Quebec Nordiques—two assists
Mark Hunter	October 8, 1981, Montreal Canadiens—one goal
Stephan Lebeau	March 15, 1989, Montreal Canadiens—one goal
Patrick Lebeau	February 20, 1991, Montreal Canadiens—one goal
Dave Maloney	December 18, 1974, New York Rangers—one assist
Don Maloney	February 14, 1979, New York Rangers—one goal, one assist
Bob Miller	October 13, 1977, Boston Bruins—one assist
Paul Miller	November 20, 1981, Colorado Rockies—one assist
Scott Niedermayer	October 16, 1991, New Jersey Devils—one assist
Rob Niedermayer	October 6, 1993, Florida Panthers—one assist
Cal O'Reilly	February 28, 2009, Nashville Predators—one assist
Ryan O'Reilly	October 1, 2009, Colorado Avalanche—one assist

Peter Stastny	October 9, 1980, Quebec Nordiques—one assist
Marian Stastny	October 6, 1981, Quebec Nordiques—one assist
Duane Sutter	November 30, 1979, New York Islanders—two goals, one assist
Brent Sutter	February 25, 1981, New York Islanders—one assist
Blake Wesley	October 13, 1979, Philadelphia Flyers—one assist
Glen Wesley	October 8, 1987, Boston Bruins—one assist

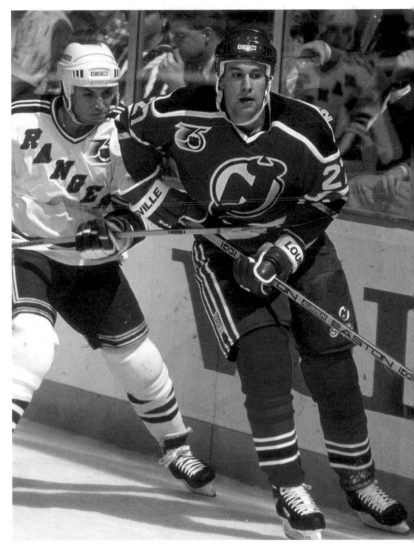

Scott Niedermayer (right) playing in his first game, October 16, 1991. His brother, Rob, made the NHL two years later.

Team Record Debuts

Eleven times has a team had as many as nine players in the lineup making their NHL debut on the same night, and each time it was the result of the team making its NHL debut as well.

The biggest debut night was, of course, the first night of play in the history of the NHL, December 19, 1917, but that discounts the fact that most players came from the NHA, precursor to the NHL.

On that night, the Montreal Wanderers had 10 "new" NHLers while Toronto, Ottawa, and the Canadiens had nine.

Three times in the 1920s, teams had 10 new players, again because these teams were joining the NHL: Boston, on December 1, 1924; the Rangers, on November 16, 1926; and the Detroit Cougars (soon to become the Red Wings), on November 18, 1926.

As one might expect, the next biggest era of NHL debuts occurred in the fall of 1979, when four WHA teams joined the NHL. The Winnipeg Jets hold the all-time record of 11 new players for their first game on October 10, 1979, and that date also saw 10 new NHLers dress for Edmonton and

nine for Quebec. One night later, the fourth WHA team, Hartford, had nine new players as well.

The Jets lost their first game, 4–2 to Pittsburgh, and the rookies that night included: Mike Amodeo, Scott Campbell, Willy Lindstrom, Morris Lukowich, Jimmy Mann, Peter Marsh, Barry Melrose, Craig Norwich, Lars-Erik Sjoberg, Peter Sullivan, and Ron Wilson.

Morris Lukowich was one of 11 Jets to make their debuts on October 10, 1979.

Lukowich and Sullivan scored the two Jets goals that night.

Interestingly, all WHA teams lost their first NHL games, and back in the 1920s, the Bruins and Rangers won their inaugural matches while the Cougars lost. On the first day of NHL play in 1917, the two Montreal teams won and Toronto and Ottawa lost.

Lars-Erik Sjoberg (holding the Avco Cup) was the first European captain in NHL history.

What a Help!

After two years with the Quebec Remparts in junior hockey, 18-year-old Michel Goulet jumped to the WHA and played the 1978–79 season with the Birmingham Bulls. But after that one season, the WHA merged with the NHL, and Goulet was drafted 20th overall by the Quebec Nordiques. He went on to score 548 goals and was later inducted into the Hockey Hall of Fame.

> Goulet played his first career NHL game on October 10, 1979, and didn't register a point. There's nothing exceptional in that. But what is amazing is that over the course of his career, he helped eight other players record a point in their first NHL games (seven by assisting on one of his goals).

1. Louis Sleigher, Quebec Nordiques / February 18, 1980

Goulet scored early in the second period to give the visiting Nordiques a 2–1 lead, Sleigher drawing the first assist. The Minnesota North Stars rallied for five unanswered goals and won easily, 6–2.

2. Dale Hunter, Quebec Nordiques / October 9, 1980

Hunter can thank Goulet not only for his first career point but his second as well. Hunter assisted on Goulet's goal to open the scoring in Calgary, and he assisted again in the third on the final goal of the game, which gave the Nordiques a 5–5 tie with the Flames.

3. Dave Pichette, Quebec Nordiques / December 7, 1980

Pichette also had two assists in his first NHL game, one on a Goulet goal and a second on a score from Peter Stastny. Stastny also had the other assist on the Goulet goal, making Pichette indebted to both men for his excellent debut in a 4–4 home tie with the Leafs.

4. Max Middendorf, Quebec Nordiques / December 13, 1986

Goulet scored just 41 seconds into the game, Middendorf assisting and joining a rare group of players to earn a point in the first minute of their career. The goal launched the Nords on their way to an easy 7–0 win over Buffalo.

5. Iiro Jarvi, Quebec Nordiques / October 6, 1988

Opening night of the 1988–89 season saw the Nordiques play a road game in Hartford, and Peter Stastny got the game's first goal at 3:13 with assists credited to Goulet and Jarvi.

6. Ryan McGill, Chicago Blackhawks / October 10, 1991

Late in the 1989–90 season, Goulet was traded to Chicago, where he played the final four and a half years of his career. In a game near the start of the 1991–92 season, at home to Vancouver, Goulet scored early in the second period to tie the game, 3–3. McGill got an assist on the play, his first career point.

7. Igor Kravchuk, Chicago Blackhawks / February 27, 1992

Four days removed from winning Olympic gold with the Unified Team in Albertville, France, Igor Kravchuk signed a three-year contract with Chicago for $700,000, a sum that didn't include the $90,000 the Hawks also paid the Red Army to release the 25-year-old to the NHL.

"I want to play NHL because here are many famous players," he said in halting English after the game.

That night, the Hawks hosted the Red Wings, and things only got better for the newest NHLer. Kravchuk scored the game-winning goal early in the third period, breaking a 2–2 tie. The play started when Goulet fought off Bob Probert to get the puck, and he passed it to Kravchuk. His low blast beat Tim Cheveldae, and Chicago went on to win, 4–2.

8. Milan Tichy, Chicago Blackhawks / December 31, 1992

Now towards the end of his career, Goulet was having a tough 1992–93 season with Chicago. He was a healthy scratch for several games and missed nine games with a groin injury, but he was somewhat healthy and back in the lineup for the team's New Year's Eve game against Tampa Bay.

Ever-proud, Goulet responded with a sensational night, scoring once and adding two assists to lead the Hawks to an easy 5–0 win over the Lightning. His goal was assisted by linemate Jeremy Roenick and defenceman Milan Tichy. Tichy and Adam Bennett were minor-league call-ups on the blue line to replace the injured Steve Smith and Igor Kravchuk.

Tichy, playing in his first career game, got the puck to Roenick behind the Tampa goal, and JR made a nice little pass to Goulet to the side. Goulet beat Pat Jablonski with the first shot to make it 1–0 early in the second period, much to the delight of Tichy.

Michel Goulet had a Hall of Fame career with the Quebec Nordiques.

Oh, no!

Saveless games

Every player is ecstatic to get into his first NHL game, but sometimes things just do not go as planned. On three occasions, a goalie has come into a game with a virgin record of 0-0-0 and a goals-against average of 0.00 and left with a GAA of . . . infinity!

The weird thing is that the goalies in this category of debuts ended up having excellent careers.

// Andy Moog, Edmonton Oilers
December 23, 1980

Ed Mio had wrested the starter's job from Ron Low in the Oilers' net, but as the team headed to Los Angeles they were mired in a seven-game losing streak on the road.

This was a symbolically important game as it pitted the second-year Oilers, featuring Wayne Gretzky, against Marcel Dionne and the Triple Crown Line, which was 1-2-3 in league scoring.

On this night, everything happened. Dionne had four assists, Simmer and Taylor had two goals each, and Gretzky had a hat trick. The Kings, though, hammered Edmonton, 7–4.

Mio, however, had a terrible night in every way. He was hit in the throat by a Dave Semenko shot during the warmup but managed to start. Then, he gave up four goals as the team fell behind, 4–2, by the early part of the third period. And then he took a bullet shot off the shoulder from Greg Terrion and had to leave the game.

Coach Glen Sather called on Moog to come in, at 5:37 of the third, but he lasted only 2:09 of playing time. Two minutes into his first game, he was staring down Mike Murphy on a breakaway. Murphy scored, and 14 seconds after that Sather put Mio back in.

Moog's first game ended after 129 seconds, one goal allowed, zero shots saved. He had been recalled from Wichita for the game and was in and out before he knew what had happened.

"It couldn't be any worse," he said. "They tell me it gets better from here. I hope so."

// Jean-Sebastien Aubin, Pittsburgh Penguins
October 21, 1998

Tom Barrasso pulled a groin muscle in Pittsburgh's previous game, thus prompting the recall of Jean-Sebastien Aubin from Kansas City of the IHL. The 21-year-old had been drafted 76th overall by the Penguins in 1995 and had been in junior and minor pro ever since.

A tiny crowd of 9,073 at the Ice Palace in Tampa took in this game, won 5–0 by the home side, and Peter Skudra was the starting goalie for the Pens. But the Lightning scored less than six minutes into the game. Tampa scored two more early in the second, prompting coach Kevin Constantine to pull Skudra at 8:03 of the middle period with the team down, 3–0.

Soon after, however, Rob Zamuner beat Aubin on the first shot faced by the goalie in his career, making it 4–0, and less than two minutes later Wendel Clark scored on shot number two. Those were the only two shots Aubin faced in 11:57 of game action, and Constantine reverted to Skudra for the third period. Aubin's save percentage was an even .000.

// Miikka Kiprusoff, San Jose Sharks
October 24, 2000

Playing their seventh game of the young season, the Sharks were in Raleigh for a game against Carolina. Evgeni Nabokov started the game, but early in the second period, with the score 1–0 for San Jose, Nabokov took a shot off his mask and was cut above the right eye. He had to leave for stitches, so in came Kiprusoff to play in his first NHL game.

Incredibly, he didn't face a shot for more than seven minutes, but the first one that came his way was one he couldn't stop. Martin Gelinas scored. Nabokov came back into the crease at 16:17 of the second, so the records show that Kiprusoff faced but one shot and allowed a goal.

Another and Another

Ron Loustel started the game on March 27, 1981, as an ambitious and thrilled 19-year-old. He finished the game as a 40-year-old on the verge of retirement. At least, that's what this unique NHL debut felt like for the teenager.

"My dream turned into a nightmare," he said after.

Drafted 107th overall by the Winnipeg Jets in 1980, Loustel played most of that upcoming 1980–81 season with the Saskatoon Blades of the WHL. But near the end of the year he was recalled on an emergency basis. The Jets were in need of a goalie for their home game against Vancouver, and Loustel was named the starter.

It was late in the season, and the Jets were a miserable outfit. They were dead last in the standings with a record of 9-53-12 and had a goals for/against differential of 229-365. Ouch.

Bad team, new goalie. It was a less than ideal situation.

The result was a 10–2 score for the Canucks. Oddly, the Jets actually led 1–0. Loustel was peppered with 51 shots and was all but abandoned by his elder teammates. Arv Olson, in the *Vancouver Sun*, described the Jets as, "the most pathetic excuse for a team in all of pro hockey."

Vancouver coach Harry Neale was sympathetic, saying, "The kid wasn't their problem. They could have had anybody in there, and they still would have lost by a big score."

Loustel was gutted by the third goal, a rolling puck that he tried to play but missed. It continued into the net, much to his embarrassment. "All I had to do was let the puck hit my stick," he said flatly after the game. "It's the worst goal I've let in, in my whole life. How embarrassing, before 14,000 fans. I'll never forget it."

Most Goals Allowed, NHL Debut:

12 . . . Frank Brophy, Quebec Bulldogs, December 25, 1919
10 . . . Ron Loustel, Winnipeg Jets, March 27, 1981
9 . . . Bert Lindsay, Montreal Wanderers, December 19, 1917
9 . . . Paul Harrison, Minnesota North Stars, October 11, 1975
8 . . . Doug Jackson, Chicago Black Hawks, November 22, 1947
8 . . . Paul Pageau, Los Angeles Kings, February 3, 1981
8 . . . Roberto Romano, Pittsburgh Penguins, January 13, 1983
8 . . . Karl Friesen, New Jersey Devils, October 18, 1986
8 . . . Jason Muzatti, Calgary Flames, October 16, 1993

Goalie Roberto Romano did not have a great debut, allowing eight goals.

Triple Gold Beginnings

Tomas Jonsson

NEW YORK ISLANDERS // OCTOBER 7, 1981

Tomas Jonsson was the 40th Swedish-born player to make the NHL when he played for the New York Islanders at the start of the 1981–82 season.

Jonsson was a star defenceman with Modo in Ornskoldsvik, the small, northern town in Sweden that has produced a disproportionate number of truly great players, including Anders Hedberg, Peter Forsberg, Markus Naslund, and the Sedin twins.

Several factors made his debut notable. First, the Islanders had won the Stanley Cup in 1980 and 1981, so Jonsson was joining a team at the very height of its powers. Second, Jonsson was the *only* new face on the Cup team, so expectations were high.

"I was a little nervous," he admitted of his first game. "There's a big difference playing in a real game instead of an exhibition game. Also, it takes a little time to adjust. There's a big difference playing in North America. The rink is smaller, which makes you have to think quicker and pass quicker and move quicker."

Partnered with the more defensive-minded Ken Morrow, Jonsson had a strong first game in a 4–1 victory over the Kings. He got the chance to play because of an injury to star blueliner Denis Potvin, but when Potvin returned it wasn't Jonsson who was demoted.

In fact, Jonsson helped the Isles win a third straight Cup, and in doing so he made a kind of history for being only the third European to get his name on the trophy (following teammates and Islanders-Swedes Anders Kallur and Stefan Persson).

Much later in his career, Jonsson was part of Tre Kronor's historic gold medal at the 1994 Olympics in Lillehammer, making him (and countrymen Mats Naslund and Hakan Loob) the first players ever to join the IIHF's Triple Gold Club (Stanley Cup, Olympic gold, World Championship gold [1991]).

The first three Swedes to win the Stanley Cup: (l-r) Tomas Jonsson, Stefan Persson, Anders Kallur.

M-I-C-K-E-Y M-O-U-S-E

Jim Playfair

EDMONTON OILERS // NOVEMBER 19, 1983

The Edmonton Oilers began a November 1983 weekend of back-to-back games with a 7–0 hammering of Buffalo. In that game, Mark Messier incurred a game-misconduct for being the third man in during a fight between Dave Lumley and Larry Playfair. Being his third such penalty of the season, Messier was suspended for the next game, against New Jersey.

Coincidentally, coach Glen Sather called up Playfair's younger brother Jim, a defenceman, to make his NHL debut because Charlie Huddy was out with back spasms.

Jim Playfair made his debut the night the Oilers pummelled the Devils, 13–4.

Jim had been traded the previous day in the WHL, going from the best team, Portland, to the worst, Kelowna, but he didn't get a chance to play for his new team before being summoned to play in his first NHL game.

It was one of the most famous games in NHL history. Wayne Gretzky had eight points; Jarri Kurri scored five goals; Willy Lindstrom scored a hat trick, but nobody seemed to notice; Jim Playfair scored his first career goal; and the Oilers demolished the Devils, 13–4.

Jim Playfair also got an assist, but as he said after, his goal was nothing to brag about: "My shot, on the goal, wasn't that hard, but I guess Chico Resch isn't a bad guy to score your first goal on."

Jim Playfair's unassisted goal midway through the third period made it 11–4 for the home side, but he'll likely remember the context of the goal as much as his shot for the rest of his life.

Greatest Debut Goal Ever

Mario Lemieux

PITTSBURGH PENGUINS // OCTOBER 11, 1984

Some players sneak up on you, show you something you didn't expect, play above their reputation, do something you didn't believe they could do.

Such was not the case with Mario Lemieux. In his final junior game with Laval in the Q, he scored 10 points, this during a season in which he averaged two goals and four points *per game*!

He was drafted first overall by Pittsburgh in 1984, when the Draft was held at the Montreal Forum, but because he was embroiled in a contract dispute with the team he did not meet with Penguins officials when his name was called. By the time training camp opened, though, he was under contract and clearly NHL ready.

But all the hype in the world couldn't have prepared fans for one of the greatest debuts ever. Less than three minutes into the game, he stole the puck from Ray Bourque at the Pens blue line.

Bourque was in his sixth year in the NHL, a superstar defenceman in the mold of Bobby Orr. All he tried to do was control the puck at the Pittsburgh line and chip it in, but Lemieux, on his first shift, simply plucked the puck from the blueliner.

Lemieux raced up ice as Bourque turned and gave chase, but no one was going to catch No. 66. He deked goalie Pete Peeters with ridiculous ease, and at 2:59, on his first shot, he had his first goal. It was a brilliant and electric goal and a Hall of Fame beginning to a Hall of Fame career.

"It took a lot of pressure away from me," Lemieux said in his then-halting English. "Now that's it. It's over, and I'll be more relaxed on the ice."

Late in the second, Lemieux got his first assist on a Warren Young goal, but it wasn't enough. Boston rallied for a 4–3 win.

Nevertheless, it was obvious the star of the night—and the star of the future—was Mario Lemieux.

Mario Lemieux scored arguably the greatest NHL debut goal.

Never Too Late

Esa Tikkanen
EDMONTON OILERS // MAY 23, 1985

It was never a case of "if" with Finnish forward Esa Tikkanen, only a matter of "when." But when he did make his NHL debut with Edmonton, on May 23, 1985, for Game 2 of the Stanley Cup Finals between the Oilers and Philadelphia Flyers, he set a record for the latest debut in league history (by calendar date).

Given the number of playoff games that have been played in June in recent years, May 23 doesn't seem particularly late. But given the pressures of playoff hockey, and the even greater pressures of Cup Finals hockey, one can understand a coach's reluctance to put a rookie in the lineup. Better to go with an experienced player from the minors.

In Tikkanen's case, though, the call-up capped a great 1985 season for the young Finn and climaxed a junior career that was impressive. In 1981–82, he made the extraordinary decision to play provincial junior hockey in Regina, Saskatchewan, something European juniors just didn't do at the time.

A year later, he returned to Finland and played at the World Junior Championship in 1983. That summer he was drafted 80th overall by Edmonton, a high selection at the time for a European.

Tikkanen also played at the 1984 and 1985 World Juniors, leading the tournament in assists (14) and points (20) in the latter. After his 1984–85 Finnish season ended, he joined the Oilers late in the playoffs after signing a contract on May 20. Just three days later, he got the call to play Game 2 of the finals, thanks to a terrible performance by the Oilers in the first game.

Playing Game 1 at the Spectrum in Philly, the Oilers were crushed, 4–1. Coach Glen Sather was furious. The Oilers won the Cup for the first time the previous year but weren't playing like champions. "There will definitely be lineup changes," he vowed after the game.

Sather followed through on his words, benching Dave Lumley, Jaroslav Pouzar, and Billy Carroll and inserting veterans Dave Semenko and Pat Hughes and rookie Tikkanen. Semenko and Hughes were brought in for their toughness, and neither played very much. Although he wasn't a major factor, Tikkanen played a regular shift, and the Oilers fought to an impressive 3–1 victory.

Tikkanen played in Games 3 and 4, both victories, but Sather went with a more experienced lineup for the clinching game. The Oilers pummelled the Flyers, 8–3, to win their second straight Cup, and Tikkanen, who had played but three career games, got his name on the Stanley Cup.

The Debut That Wasn't (or Was?)

Marc D'Amour

CALGARY FLAMES // OCTOBER 11, 1985

Of the 7,863 NHL debuts since 1917, none was like the one experienced by Marc D'Amour.

D'Amour was a goalie. Born in Sudbury in 1961, he played four years of junior with the Soo Greyhounds (1978–82). He was never drafted by an NHL team, so he signed with the Colorado Flames in the CHL. He played his way up to the IHL and AHL, eventually signing with the Calgary Flames and being assigned to their AHL farm team in Moncton.

D'Amour was called up to the NHL Flames for the home opener on October 11, 1985, against Winnipeg. Reggie Lemelin played the whole game, and D'Amour was the backup.

Marc D'Amour was credited with statistics before he ever played an NHL game.

It was an odd game. The visiting Jets could do no wrong in the early going, building a 3–0 lead 13 minutes after the opening faceoff. But the Flames struck for two quick goals midway through the second and then tied the game at 13:33.

Then all hell broke loose.

The fun began when Calgary's Tim Hunter high-sticked Jets goalie Brian Hayward. Hayward responded with a spear, and Dave Ellett jumped in to protect his goalie, earning a game misconduct. Then the benches emptied, which meant D'Amour came onto the ice as well. He ended up with a roughing minor and game misconduct, going to the dressing room despite never having been on ice during game action.

The NHL never credited D'Amour with a game played because he never was on ice during play, but how can a player who didn't play earn 12 minutes in penalties? If that were his only time in the NHL, he'd have a stats line that read 0-0-0 and 12 PIM.

Regardless, D'Amour is the only player in NHL history to accrue statistics in a game in which he didn't officially play. It's surely the oddest NHL debut ever.

Overshadowed

Risto Jalo

EDMONTON OILERS // MARCH 14, 1986

What if you play your first NHL game but nobody notices? Does it count? Yes, it does, of course, but Jalo had to feel that his special night was so overshadowed by so many great Oilers performances that it mattered not one iota whether he played, or even earned his first career point.

You see, the Oilers demolished the Detroit "Dead Things," as *Edmonton Journal* reporter Jim Matheson called the hapless Red Wings, by a 12–3 score.

Here's what happened. Paul Coffey tied Tom Bladon's record for points by a defenceman in a game with eight. This came on the strength of two goals and six assists—those six helpers also tying the record for most in a game.

Wayne Gretzky had a goal and four assists to reach 194 points for the season, on his way to another mind-boggling 200-point year. Mark Messier had a goal and three assists while Glenn Anderson had three goals and two assists. Anderson scored his 49th, 50th, and 51st goal of the season, and after hitting 50 late in the first period he fetched the puck out of the net as a landmark, hallmark souvenir.

That was a drag for Jalo, who assisted on that goal, his first career point. But he could hardly claim the black rubber ahead of Anderson, could he?

> Jalo holds a unique place in NHL history, though. In addition to this game he also played on March 18 and March 25, earning an assist in each game. These were the only games of his NHL career, making him the only player to play as many as three career games and score a point in each game.

Risto Jalo's debut was lost in the scoring exploits of his Edmonton teammates.

The Soviet Pioneer

Sergei Pryakhin

CALGARY FLAMES // MARCH 31, 1989

Sergei Pryakhin wasn't just a hockey player. He was a symbol, a focal point, a definable moment in history. Yes, he wore skates and a helmet and tried to put the puck in the net, but first and foremost he was Soviet, and he was the first player allowed by the Soviet government to leave the homeland to play in the NHL. This was monumental.

Of course, today the name Pryakhin is not famous beyond his first game, his presence in the league. He never became a superstar, which begs the question, why him?

"When we drafted Pryakhin, we tried to make an educated guess," explained Calgary Flames general manager Cliff Fletcher, who chose the Soviet player with the 252nd selection in the 1988 NHL Entry Draft. "We asked ourselves, 'Which player might the Soviets let go? What category of player?' We knew they wouldn't want their first player over here to fail. It had to be someone in that middle category, someone good enough to play in the NHL but interchangeable with other Soviet national team players. He had to have the physical attributes conducive to NHL play as well as the right attitude to live in North America. We made some discreet inquiries, and we came to our decision."

Dave King, Canada's National Team coach, had another view. He believed with the eroding Soviet economy that the country was desperate for money. It could use the handsome transfer fees for Pryakhin and a few others to buy equipment and upgrade facilities at home.

The Soviets sent a team to tour the NHL during the middle of the 1988–89 season, and Pryakhin was on it. It was then that he learned he'd be playing in Calgary later in the season. It made sense. At six-foot-three and 210 pounds, he had the size to handle the NHL. He was 25 years old, so he was in his prime. He had played at the historic 1987 Canada Cup and 1987 World Championship, so he had experience at the world-class level, and playing with the touring Soviet team gave him added experience on the smaller ice.

Playing on a line with Theo Fleury and Tim Hunter, Pryakhin formally made history at 2:29 of the opening period when he stepped onto the ice for the first time. Winnipeg captain Dale Hawerchuk crushed him with a nice welcome check, but Pryakhin got up and showed some puck-handling skills heading up ice. He played only five-on-five this night, and lost in the hoopla of his debut was Joe Mullen's 50th goal of the season, propelling the Flames to a 4–1 win before 20,002 at the Saddledome.

After the game, Pryakhin's stall was surrounded by reporters. "I didn't show everything I could do, but for the first time, it wasn't bad," he said through a translator. "I thought it would be more physical. In all honesty, yes I did. I expected the game would be somewhat faster."

Flames defenceman Al MacInnis probably said it best: "I feel sorry for him," he started. "He's kind of a guinea pig. No matter where he goes or where he plays, all eyes are going to be on him. I don't know if he realizes the amount of pressure that there is around him. He probably doesn't understand a lot."

The timing of this debut was odd, to say the least. There were only two games left in the regular season, and the Flames were Cup contenders. Pryakhin didn't get a point in those games and played only once in the playoffs. The Flames, meanwhile, won the Cup.

The following year, Pryakhin played only 20 games, scoring but two goals in an injury-plagued season. By 1991, he had retreated to Europe to finish out his career. He had made NHL history, and, of course, many more talented Soviet-era players were on their way. In terms of his own career, his time in the NHL was a bust, but in terms of hockey history, his first game was of huge importance.

Sergei Pryakhin was the first Soviet to be allowed to play in the NHL.

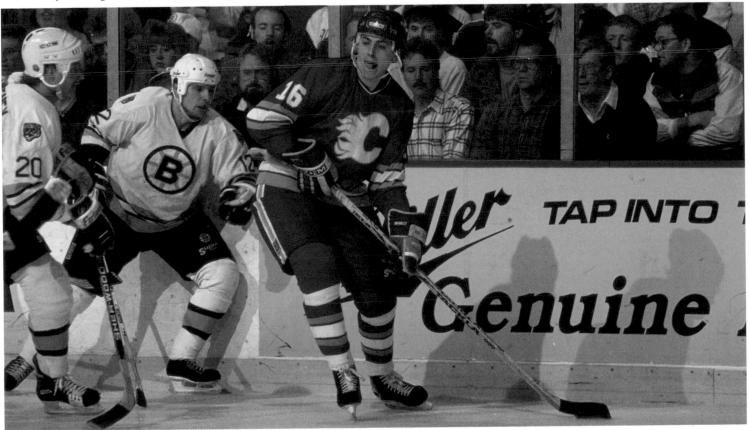

The First Soviet Superstar

Alexander Mogilny

BUFFALO SABRES // OCTOBER 5, 1989

The hockey world was a complex place in the late 1980s and early 1990s. In NHL terms, Sergei Pryakhin was only the start.

The NHL debut of Alexander Mogilny just a few months later was anything but ordinary. As a teen in the Soviet Union, he starred during the 1988-89 season, winning silver at the '88 World Juniors and just a few weeks later helping the team win gold at the Olympics in Calgary.

Mogilny played on a line with Pavel Bure and Sergei Fedorov that won gold at the '89 World Juniors, and at the World Championship that April in Stockholm, he defected to North America. He was the first to defect, a daring and dangerous move requiring plenty of help from the Sabres.

But by the start of the 1989–90 season, he was not alone.

Superstar defenceman Slava Fetisov, often called the Bobby Orr of Soviet hockey, soon followed. He and Sergei Starikov joined the New Jersey Devils. Igor Larionov and Vladimir Krutov joined Vancouver, and the third member of that great line, Sergei Makarov, joined Pryakhin in Calgary. Goalie Sergei Mylnikov, career backup to the great Tretiak, was signed by the Quebec Nordiques.

For all these players, starting a new life, representing the mysterious world of Soviet hockey, and playing a new style of the game were all of monumental importance. But only Mogilny was at the very start of his career, and it was his play more than any of the other Soviet players that was most scrutinized.

Noted for his speed and skill, Mogilny made an entrance into the NHL that was nothing short of sensational. He made the Sabres at training camp, of course, and was in the lineup for the team's first game at the Aud, October 5, 1989. He didn't disappoint.

Starting the game on a line with Pierre Turgeon and Dave Snuggerud, Mogilny scored just 20 seconds after the opening faceoff. It started with a routine dump-in by Mogilny, and Turgeon got to the puck first as it rolled around to the opposite corner. Turgeon got the puck behind the goal where Snuggerud and a Quebec player battled for possession. To the surprise of goalie Stephane Fiset, the puck somehow squirted out in front, and Mogilny had the easy

Alexander Mogilny made a brilliant first impression, scoring 20 seconds into his career.

tap-in to score. The Sabres went on to win the game, 4–3.

Mogilny finished the night with a game-high seven shots and established himself as one of the best young players in the world.

In 1988–89, Pryakhin was the only Soviet player in the NHL. In 1989–90, Mogilny's first year, there were 11, and by 1994–95 there were 59. Five years later, there were 71, enough for three teams. The Soviet/Russian invasion was under way.

Mogilny's first NHL goal in his first game on his first shot on his first shift was the third fastest of all time, but his very presence on ice had even more meaning than that 20-second quickie.

Goalies Facing Penalty Shots

Another exclusive—and modern—group of goaltenders is one featuring those who faced penalty shots during their NHL debuts. This list is but four names long—Bob Essensa, Jan Lasak, Marc-Andre Fleury, and Jimmy Howard. Two of the four (Lasak, Fleury) made the save.

// Bob Essensa, Winnipeg Jets
February 13, 1989

Playing for the Winnipeg Jets, Bob Essensa made a memorable debut in Detroit. He had played college at Michigan State and considered Joe Louis Arena his home building. On February 13, 1989, though, he was the opponent. Called up from Fort Wayne earlier in the day, he started for a Jets team that was reeling.

Coach Dan Maloney had been fired a week earlier, after a dismal 6–2 loss to these same Red Wings, and new bench boss Rick Bowness was looking for his first win. The start of the game was hardly promising. Dave Barr beat Essensa with Detroit's first shot of the game, just 25 seconds after the opening faceoff, and midway through the period, Steve Yzerman beat Essensa on a penalty shot.

The Jets, however, rallied to tie the game, and after five minutes of scoreless overtime, the game ended, 2–2. Essensa, though, became the first goalie in NHL history to face a penalty shot in his debut.

Jets defenceman Dave Ellett hauled down Yzerman at 10:30 of the opening period, thus creating the penalty shot. On that shot, Essensa came well out at the start, but as he backed in Stevie Y beat the goalie with a great shot over the glove. It was Yzerman's 52nd goal of the season, and it was one for the history books.

// Jan Lasak, Nashville Predators
April 9, 2002

On April 9, 2002, Nashville goalie Jan Lasak made his NHL debut in St. Louis. It was a memorable one. The Predators lost the game, 3–2, but Lasak became only the second goalie ever to face a penalty shot in his debut. He also stopped 39 of 42 shots and was brilliant from start to finish. He also incurred a minor penalty.

Bob Essensa got into his first game, and 10 minutes later faced Steve Yzerman on a penalty shot.

Jan Lasak faced a penalty shot, recorded an assist, and played brilliantly in his debut.

Pittsburgh's Marc-Andre Fleury stopped 46 shots, including a late penalty shot, in his debut.

// Jimmy Howard, Detroit Red Wings
November 28, 2005

The most recent goalie to face down a penalty shot in his NHL debut was Detroit's Jimmy Howard, on November 28, 2005.

Manny Legace had a bad knee and Chris Osgood had had some weak moments recently, so Detroit coach Mike Babcock decided to give the 21-year-old Howard a chance, calling the youngster up from Grand Rapids of the AHL.

"He's big, technically strong, [has good] rebound control," Babcock said the afternoon of Howard's big chance. "I think he has a bright future in hockey."

Howard had started the year with the Wings as backup to Legace while Osgood was recovering from a groin injury. But Legace and the team were playing so well, there was no chance for Babcock to get Howard into a game before demoting him.

The Red Wings were scheduled to play in Los Angeles, so Howard hustled onto a plane and got to the game on time. He stopped 22 of 24 shots, and Detroit won easily, 5–2. Joe Corvo scored on Howard on a penalty shot in the second period, but other than that the rookie goalie was excellent, earning a start in the team's next game as well.

Lasak faced down Keith Tkachuk in the latter half of the first period after the Blues forward was hooked from behind by Karlis Skrastins. Lasak kicked out Tkachuk's wrist shot to keep it a 1–1 game, and the Blues went on to win, 3–2.

Lasak got into the game thanks to an injury to Mike Dunham in the team's previous game. In a twist of 21st century times, Lasak had been playing with the Milwaukee Admirals in the AHL and went online to see how the Preds had done against Calgary. That's when he found out about Dunham's injury, and that's when he had a feeling he'd be recalled. He had a strong debut, but he also made history.

// Marc-Andre Fleury, Pittsburgh Penguins
October 10, 2003

It's hard to imagine now just how bad the atmosphere was around the Mellon Arena when Marc-Andre Fleury made his NHL debut, on October 10, 2003. Fleury was brilliant in his first game as the Pens were outclassed, losing to Los Angeles, 3–0, in the season opener. The final goal was into the empty net.

Fleury stopped 46 shots and was named the first star. Indeed, shots were 49–11 for the visitors, and had it not been for the heroics of the 18-year-old goalie, the score would have been downright lopsided.

Ironically, Fleury had a rocky start. The Pens got an early power play, but it was Eric Belanger who scored just 38 seconds into the game on a short-handed breakaway. Fleury was virtually letter-perfect the rest of the way.

Fleury faced Esa Pirnes on a penalty shot with just 2:20 left in the game. Pirnes skated straight in on goal and when he got to the top of the crease was about to shoot when Fleury deftly poke-checked the puck away. The crowd chanted, "Fleury! Fleury!"

Jimmy Howard won his first game for Detroit and had to deal with a penalty shot along the way.

Dream Becomes Nightmare

Andre Racicot

MONTREAL CANADIENS // DECEMBER 9, 1989

It was, unfortunately, a sign of things to come, and it was also the shortest goalie debut ever by a goalie starting in his first NHL game.

Yet, it should have been a dream come true. Goaltender Andre Racicot, a native of Rouyn-Noranda, Quebec, was drafted 83rd overall by Montreal in 1989. Perfect. His dream team. Racicot had just finished a unique four years in the QMJHL in which he played for four teams—Longueuil, Victoriaville, Hull, and Granby.

He played most of 1989–90 with the Habs AHL affiliate in Sherbrooke but got a call-up in early December when the Canadiens ran into injury problems. Backup Brian Hayward suffered a knee injury, opening a spot for a second goalie. Then, Patrick Roy was playing quite a bit and had played the night before in a wild 6–6 tie with Winnipeg.

The stage was set for the 20-year-old Racicot to make his NHL debut and give Roy a rest. It was a Saturday night at Maple Leaf Gardens. *Hockey Night in Canada*. It doesn't get better than this.

Except . . . the game didn't go as planned for Racicot. The first shot Racicot faced came off the stick of Tom Fergus. Goal. The second shot he faced was courtesy of Ed Olczyk. Goal. He then made save, save, save, but shot number six, from Vincent Damphousse also went in. Six shots, three goals in just 12:40 of playing time.

A livid Pat Burns pulled Racicot and was forced to put Roy in. The Leafs opened a 5–0 lead before coasting to a 7–4 win. Montreal, one of the best teams in the league, lost handily to one of the worst. Incredibly, though, it was Roy, giving up the fifth goal, who was saddled with the loss after the Habs staged a rally, and Racicot got a "no decision" out of the game.

"Hell, you can't blame him," Burns fumed after. "Two-on-ones, breakaways, the works."

"Red Light" Racicot had the shortest debut for a starting goalie in NHL history.

The Dominator

Dominik Hasek

CHICAGO BLACKHAWKS // NOVEMBER 6, 1990

Hasek was drafted by Chicago in 1983, 199th overall. It was a ridiculously low selection because, for all intents and purposes, it was a wasted pick. In 1983, Czechoslovakia was a communist country that never allowed its players to leave for the West. The Hawks used a low selection simply on the off-off-off chance that somehow, some way, he would be allowed to play in the NHL.

But world politics worked in favour of Eastern European hockey nations as the 1980s came to a close, and by the end of the decade players from the Soviet Union/Russia and Czechoslovakia/Czech Republic and Slovakia were being given permission to travel as they pleased. This turn of events brought Hasek to Chicago, and the Hawks assigned him to their farm team in Indianapolis to begin his pro career in North America.

Hasek spent most of his first year with the AHL's Ice, mostly because he didn't speak a word of English and needed some time to learn a bit. He also needed to work on handling the puck, a skill far more important in the NHL than in Europe.

He did, however, play a handful of games with the Hawks. The first of these came under stressful times. Coach Mike Keenan—"Iron Mike," as he was known—had a couple of pleasant problems. First, the Hawks had gotten off to a great start for the 1990–91 season.

As well, he had a starting goalie in Ed Belfour, who was clearly world class, and he had a great backup in Jacques Cloutier as well as a third goalie in Greg Millen. Then, in the minors, he had Hasek and the promising Jimmy Waite.

But, going into a game in Hartford on November 6, 1990, Keenan called up Hasek and left Cloutier and Millen at home, infuriating the veteran goalies who had done nothing wrong.

Speculation was that Keenan was giving Hasek some NHL exposure so that he could trade the Czech star, who was obviously going to be a starting goalie, just not in Chicago, not ahead of Belfour.

By the end of the night, Hasek had proved himself beyond doubt in a 1–1 tie that included five minutes of overtime.

"He was fantastic," enthused Keenan. "We got a point because of Hasek. He made a lot of key saves."

In all, Hasek stopped 28 of 29 shots, and the only Whalers player to beat him was Pat Verbeek.

Overtime Stats

Overtime has been a part of much of the league's history, but not all of it. In 1927–28, the league introduced a 10-minute period of sudden-death overtime, and year later that period was played in full (meaning any number of goals could be scored).

On November 21, 1942, overtime was eliminated because war-time restrictions on train travel forced the league to end games earlier to allow players to travel between cities and across the border.

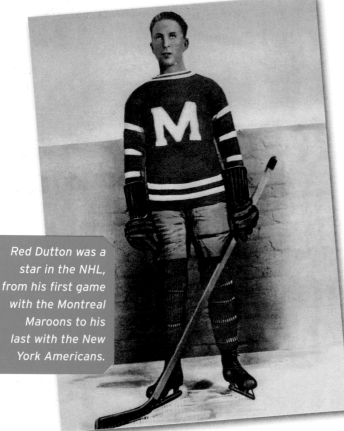

Red Dutton was a star in the NHL, from his first game with the Montreal Maroons to his last with the New York Americans.

Then, in 1983, a sudden-death overtime of five minutes was adopted, and in 2005 a shootout was added to the end of a game in case of a tie after 65 minutes.

In all those times, only two first-game players have scored goals in overtime. In 1941, Nick Knott scored for the Brooklyn Americans against Detroit, but the Red Wings also scored in that game, which ended 3–3.

The only other instance came in 1990, and it was an OT game-winning goal. Tim Sweeney's goal gave the Flames a 3–2 home win over Vancouver, earning Sweeney a place in NHL history as the only NHL player to score a game-winner in OT of his debut.

Goals in OT

Nick Knott, Brooklyn Americans / November 2, 1941

It was the second night of a new NHL season, and the Americans were at the Olympia in Detroit for their season opener. The Red Wings had defeated Montreal the previous night in their first game.

The Americans were bolstered by a loan-trade with Toronto. General manager Red Dutton had acquired Nick Knott, Peanuts O'Flaherty, Gus Marker, and Red Heron from the Leafs for Lorne Carr. Only Knott was playing in his first career game on this night, but it was the 21-year-old rookie who helped his new club earn a 3–3 tie with the Red Wings.

The Americans went up 2–0 in the second only to see the home side tie the game in the third to force a full 10-minute overtime. In that fourth period, Knott scored off a faceoff at 4:11, but just 73 seconds later John Stewart tied the game.

Tim Sweeney, Calgary Flames / October 4, 1990

Drafted 122nd overall by Calgary in 1985, Tim Sweeney had to wait five full seasons before seeing the NHL. The Flames took him as an 18-year-old high-school player, after which he played at Boston College for four years. From there he moved to pro and spent a year in Salt Lake in the IHL, but he was the Flames' leading goalscorer during the exhibition season in the fall of 1990, making the NHL team as a result.

Sweeney played well in his first game, but his timing couldn't have been better in the overtime. It was 2–2 after 60 minutes, but in the short fourth period defenceman Gary Suter took a pass from Doug Gilmour and fired a shot on goal. Kirk McLean made the save, but the puck trickled between his pads. Sweeney managed to swat the puck in while being checked, and at 1:07 of the OT he had scored the game winner.

Assists in OT

Red Dutton, Montreal Maroons / November 20, 1926

Playing in his first career game, Red Dutton made a tremendous impression on both the fans at the Forum and his teammates. In a game that saw the two Montreal teams, Canadiens and Maroons, play each other, Dutton helped the Maroons to victory in the first game of the intra-city rivalry this season.

According to the *Montreal Gazette* account, here's what he did in the overtime of a 1–1 game. "Little over four minutes of the extra session had been contested when Dutton cleared a Canadien rush in front of the Maroon goal. He started down the centre ice and, nearing the Canadien defence, swerved to the right. As he drew level with the Canadien defence pair, Dutton saw Nels Stewart flashing in on the left. The Canadien defencemen had been drawn to the right and Dutton whipped over a perfect pass to Stewart, who coasted for the merest fraction of a second with the puck at his stick and drove a bullet-like shot to the near corner of the net."

Maroons 2, Canadiens 1. Game over.

Alexei Zhitnik, Los Angeles Kings / October 6, 1992

It was a great start to defenceman Alexei Zhitnik's career. He earned two assists on the night, including one on the game-winning goal in overtime.

Barry Melrose was behind the bench, coaching the L.A. Kings for the first time. Wayne Gretzky was not playing in the season opener, recovering from a back injury. The Kings were in Calgary in what proved to be a tight game. The score was tied 2–2 after the first, 3–3 after the second, and 4–4 after the third.

Russian Alexei Zhitnik assisted on the game winner in overtime in his debut.

But late in the five-minute OT, Zhitnik got the puck to Jari Kurri, who found Tomas Sandstrom wide open on the left side. Sandstrom's first shot was brilliantly stopped by Mike Vernon, but Sandstrom followed up and potted his own rebound.

Drew Stafford, Buffalo Sabres / November 5, 2006

Stafford fed Daniel Briere for a goal at 3:57 of overtime, giving the visiting Sabres a 4–3 win over the Rangers in a Sunday afternoon game that started at 5 p.m. Stafford split this first season between the Sabres and the farm team in Rochester, but he was soon on his way to a lengthy NHL career.

Penalties in OT—Misconduct

Tie Domi, Toronto Maple Leafs / March 2, 1990

Well, Tie Domi made his NHL introduction memorable, incurring a remarkable 37 penalty minutes in a game in which he actually skated during play for about two minutes.

The game was Toronto at Detroit, and it was also Leafs coach Doug Carpenter versus Wings coach Jacques Demers. The two nearly came to blows by the players' benches, while on ice the players accrued a combined 272 penalty minutes by way of, among other infractions, 12 fighting majors and 13 misconducts.

Expecting a rough game, Demers had dressed policemen Joey Kocur and Chris McRae, and Carpenter countered with John Kordic and first-gamer Domi.

Domi and Kocur earned misconducts at 3:10 of the overtime, and half a minute later Steve Yzerman scored the winner to make it 3–2 Detroit.

Domi had earned a roughing penalty midway through the first period, and soon after returning to the ice he was slapped with a misconduct. In the second, he fought Kevin McLelland and was assessed a further misconduct.

Coach Demers was particularly critical of Domi, whom he said skated by the Wings bench making derogatory comments about the state of the Wings. Demers said these actions inspired the home side to rally from down 2–1 to win in OT.

"[Domi] challenges our bench, and he's smirking. Nineteen Toronto Maple Leafs play a physical game, show class, and one guy playing his first NHL game challenges our bench twice and makes fun of us," Demers fumed after.

Penalties in OT–Minor

Joe Simpson, New York Americans
December 2, 1925

It was the third game in franchise history and the first NHL game in Pittsburgh, at Duquesne Garden, but the visiting New York Americans spoiled the fun for the 8,000 fans, beating the local Pirates, 2–1, in overtime.

Bullet Joe Simpson, playing in his first career game, could have been the goat but luckily avoided that distinction thanks to Charlie Langlois. Simpson took a penalty early in overtime, but Langlois scored while the Americans were short-handed.

Cecil Browne, Chicago Black Hawks / November 15, 1927

Chicago visited Boston to play the Bruins in the season opener for both teams, and none other than Babe Ruth was in attendance for the game, which ended 1–1 after 60 minutes of regulation and another 10 minutes of overtime.

Browne incurred a slashing penalty in the OT, but no harm came of it.

Rick Tocchet, Philadelphia Flyers / October 11, 1984

Tocchet had a very fine career that lasted 18 seasons and 1,144 regular-season games, but his first was nothing to write home about. He didn't score, and he didn't earn an assist, but he did miss great chances in close and on a breakaway.

"It's the only game in my career where I've had so many blatant chances and missed them all," Tocchet lamented.

Worse, Tocchet incurred two penalties, including one in overtime that nearly cost his Flyers the game. As it was, the game ended 2–2, and he was exonerated.

Peter Zezel and Derrick Smith were also playing in their first game, and they both earned assists on Ilkka Sinisalo's goal to tie the score in the second period.

Shayne Stevenson, Boston Bruins / December 29, 1990

No one was happier to see this Boston-Minnesota game end in a 4–4 tie than rookie Shayne Stevenson. Called up from the AHL's Maine Mariners because of injuries and poor play by several incumbents, Stevenson took a regular shift, but in overtime he took a senseless slashing penalty, and the Stars almost scored on the ensuing power play.

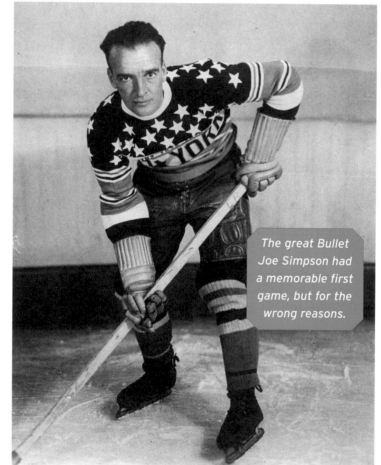

The great Bullet Joe Simpson had a memorable first game, but for the wrong reasons.

The Bruins had lost their previous game, in Winnipeg, 6–0, so coach Mike Milbury rattled the team by calling up centre Stevenson and right winger Peter Douris. Stevenson, the team's top draft choice in 1989, was leading Maine in scoring and came up also to replace the injured Dave Poulin.

Rob Niedermayer, Florida Panthers / October 6, 1993

Making his debut with the Panthers in Chicago, Rob Niedermayer had a good first game. He assisted on Scott Mellanby's goal to open the scoring midway through the first period, and he ended the night getting into a pushing-and-shoving match with Chris Chelios late in the overtime of a 4–4 game. They both got roughing minors, and Chelios earned a misconduct as well.

Todd Bertuzzi, New York Islanders / October 7, 1995

Bertuzzi had a "Gordie Howe minor hat trick" in his NHL debut, scoring a goal, earning an assist, and taking a minor penalty. The infraction came during regulation, and the penalty was an offsetting roughing penalty with Don Sweeney of Boston. The game ended 4–4, so no harm done and a memorable debut in every way.

Kelly Fairchild, Toronto Maple Leafs / March 20, 1996

A day that had "dream" written all over it finished in disappointment for Kelly Fairchild. The leading scorer for the Leafs farm team in St. John's, he was called up during the day on March 20, 1996, along with Brandon Convery, for an important game against Detroit that night.

This was Fairchild's first NHL game. After being drafted 152nd overall by Los Angeles in 1991, he went to the University of Wisconsin and worked his way into the NHL via the AHL.

The game was going well for Fairchild. He took a regular shift on the fourth line, and in the third period he set up Tie Domi for the go-ahead goal. An assist in his first game was just perfect for the 22-year-old. The Wings, however, tied the score later, necessitating overtime.

Early in the OT, Fairchild was penalized for obstruction/holding on Slava Kozlov, and late in the power play Darren McCarty scored. The Red Wings beat the Leafs for the fifth time in as many games, and the Leafs' playoff chances took a big hit.

"When [the referee] called it, I was kind of in disbelief. I was definitely upset," Fairchild said in the dressing room after the game. "But it was more upsetting when they scored."

Adam Munro, Chicago Blackhawks / March 1, 2004

One of nine rookies in the game for Chicago this night, goalie Adam Munro had a sensational NHL debut, stopping 33 of 35 shots and leading his team to a 2–2 tie with Nashville after five minutes of overtime.

Chicago goalie Adam Munro won his debut and earned a penalty after the game was over.

Munro earned a minor penalty at 5:00 of the OT (i.e., after the game was over) thanks to a group discussion after the final whistle that saw five players penalized. Both Munro and his counterpart, Tomas Vokoun, earned minors for leaving the crease, while Vokoun also earned additional minors for roughing and unsportsmanlike conduct.

Munro's rise in 2003–04 was impressive. He started with the Gwinnett Gladiators (ECHL), moved up to the Norfolk Admirals (AHL), and from there was recalled by the Hawks to replace Craig Anderson (who was demoted).

First Goal . . . Only Goal

Dream Number One is to play a game in the NHL. Dream Number Two is to score a goal in that debut. But only one player has done something so peculiar it defies logic—score *two* goals in his NHL debut . . . and then never score again!

// Ralph Barahona, Boston Bruins
February 3, 1991

It goes without saying that most aspiring NHLers do not consider the University of Wisconsin-Stevens Point as a launching pad to great hockey success. Yet somehow, after four years of obscurity there, forward Ralph Barahona earned an invitation to the Boston Bruins' training camp in the fall of 1990.

More incredible, he was the last cut at that camp, this nobody from nowhere. The Bruins sent him to the farm team in Maine, and well past the midway point in the season he was leading the Mariners in scoring.

Cue to the afternoon of February 2, 1991, when the Bruins were pasted by the Pittsburgh Penguins, 6–2, in Pittsburgh. The next day the teams were set to meet again, in Boston, so coach Mike Milbury recalled Barahona from Maine to play alongside former college teammates, Peter Douris and Andy Brickley.

The Bruins played a much stronger game at home and jumped into a 2–1 lead after the second, making it 4–1 early in the third. Barahona had been quiet up to that point, but midway through the third, playing on a line with Cam Neely, he scored. Neely had the puck behind the Penguins goal, Barahona jumped into the slot and took the pass. He wired a shot past Wendell Young to make it 5–1.

Five minutes later, Douris and Brickley combined to get him a second goal. Again Barahona went to the middle, this time taking a Douris pass and burying it. The Bruins won, 6–2, but after the game all the talk was about Barahona, where he came from, how he developed, what was in store for the 25-year-old.

That night and next day were likely the greatest moments in Barahona's career.

Two days later, he had an assist in Boston's 6–5 overtime win against Edmonton, and two days after that he was held without a point in the Bruins' 4–1 loss to Calgary. He played the rest of the year in the AHL with the Maine Mariners.

The next year, he was recalled for only three games, earning one assist, and thereafter his stats panel reads like a road map to obscurity.

Two goals in his NHL debut—and he never scored again. One of a kind.

First Goal . . . Only Goal

Art Ross, Montreal Wanderers

NHL Debut: December 19, 1917 / Toronto Arenas 9 at Montreal Wanderers 10
Goal: Ross (no assist), 2nd

He was one of the greatest players in hockey's early days and a future member of the Hockey Hall of Fame, so how is it that Art Ross was limited to one career NHL goal? Very simple. By the time the NHL played its first season, 1917–18, Ross was 30 years old and at the end of his playing days.

Boston's Ralph Barahona scored twice in his NHL debut—and never scored again.

Indeed, he was the playing-manager for the Wanderers this year. And this game that he scored in was the first NHL game ever played. He potted the game's 14th goal to give the home Wanderers an 8–6 lead over Toronto. Ross played only a few shifts to spell his regulars, and he appeared in only two more NHL games in his career.

No matter. He had been on Stanley Cup–winning teams in Kenora in 1907 and the Wanderers a year later and also played for the Ottawa Senators during a pro career that lasted a decade. Of course, he later became the longtime manager of the Boston Bruins.
// **Career Stats: 3-1-0-1-0 (GP-G-A-P-PIM)**

Howard McNamara, Montreal Canadiens

NHL Debut: December 25, 1919 / Montreal Canadiens 12 at Quebec Bulldogs 5
Goal: McNamara (Malone, Pitre), 14:20 1st

McNamara scored Montreal's fourth goal, late in the first period, during a run in which the Habs led 6–0 by the early part of the second. It was the first game of the season for both teams, and although McNamara was playing in his first NHL game he had previously played for the Canadiens during the days of the NHA. Although a founding member of the NHL in 1917, the Bulldogs took a two-year hiatus before playing games, this being the franchise's first ever.
// **Career Stats: 11-1-0-1-2**

Don Smith, Montreal Canadiens

NHL Debut: December 25, 1919 / Montreal Canadiens 12 at Quebec Bulldogs 5
Goal: Smith (unassisted) 19:50 3rd

Smith got the final goal of the game, and just before it ended. His goal merely piled on the total for the visiting Canadiens, who played a Quebec team that dressed only seven skaters.
// **Career Stats: 10-1-1-2-0**

Rolly Huard, Toronto Maple Leafs

NHL Debut: December 13, 1930 / Boston Bruins 7 at Toronto Maple Leafs 3
Goal: Huard (unassisted) 9:10 1st

One-game wonder. With injuries plaguing the Leafs, Conn Smythe created a make-shift second line of Huard (brought up from Buffalo of the International league), Herb Hamel (on loan from New Hamburg), and Roger Jenkins (recently acquired from Chicago). Huard scored the first goal of the game, beating Tiny Thompson with "a sneaker from the blue line" in the words of Lou Marsh, but by the end of the night it meant precious little except to the world of trivia.
// **Career Stats: 1-1-0-1-0**

John Albert scored in his first game, and never again (see story page 135).

Gord Kuhn, New York Americans

NHL Debut: February 19, 1933 / Ottawa Senators 1 at New York Americans 3
Goal: Kuhn (unassisted) 6:08 2nd

Called up from New Haven, "Doggie" Kuhn not only played in his first NHL game and scored his first goal—he got the game winner, and a sensational one at that.

After the Sens and Amerks traded goals in the first, Kuhn, according to the *Ottawa Evening Citizen*, "broke from the centre zone, worked his way between [Al] Shields and [Marty] Burke, regained his balance, and poked a quick shot between [Bill] Beveridge's legs."
// **Career Stats: 12-1-1-2-4**

Pete Leswick, New York Americans

NHL Debut: March 18, 1937 / Chicago Black Hawks 4 at New York Americans 9
Goal: Leswick (Hemmerling) 12:07 2nd

Leswick scored his goal midway through the game, giving the Amerks a comfortable 5–1 lead over Chicago. As it turned out, this was the game-winning goal, the only red-light shot of his three-game NHL career.
// Career Stats: 3-1-0-1-0

Hickey Nicholson, Chicago Black Hawks

NHL Debut: February 6, 1938 / Boston Bruins 7 at Chicago Black Hawks 2
Goal: Nicholson (Voss) 13:49 3rd

How bad were the injuries for the Hawks? So bad that coach Bill Stewart had to use three defencemen—Babe Siebert, Pudge MacKenzie, Roger Jenkins—as right wingers, leaving only three blueliners to play back. Ivan "Hickey" Nicholson was brought in by the team from the Kansas City Greyhounds as a "utility forward." He scored, to be sure, but it was late in the third and the score was already 5–0 Boston. His shot beat Tiny Thompson, a legend of the crease, and for that Hickey could be proud.
// Career Stats: 2-1-0-1-0

Herbie Foster, New York Rangers

NHL Debut: November 30, 1940 / Montreal Canadiens 1 at New York Rangers 6
Goal: Foster (Heller, Pike) 13:27 3rd

Called up from the Philadelphia Ramblers to replace the injured Alex Shibicky, Foster wasted no time in making a favourable impression on the 9,873 fans at Madison Square Garden this night. He scored midway through the third period to give the home side a commanding 5–1 lead over the basement-dwelling Canadiens, and the *New York Times* happily reported that, "Foster's speed caught the fancy of the crowd, and he was applauded to the rafters after his score."
// Career Stats: 5-1-0-1-5

Ken Stewart, Chicago Black Hawks

NHL Debut: January 11, 1942 / Detroit Red Wings 5 at Chicago Black Hawks 6
Goal: Stewart (D Bentley, March) 16:30 2nd

Doug Bentley took the shot, and Stewart banged home the rebound, beating Johnny Mowers with a quick shot. The goal, towards the end of the second period, gave Chicago a commanding 6–2 lead. It didn't seem particularly important at the time, but half an hour later it proved to be the game winner.
// Career Stats: 6-1-1-2-0

Shep Mayer, Toronto Maple Leafs

NHL Debut: October 31, 1942 / New York Rangers 2 at Toronto Maple Leafs 7
Goal: Mayer (Stewart, Poile) 14:39 2nd

Shep Mayer's name was on the scoresheet for every period of his first game. He took a penalty in the first period, scored a goal in the second, and drew an assist in the third. A week later, he earned an assist in his only other NHL appearance.
// Career Stats: 2-1-2-3-4

Bernie Ruelle, Detroit Red Wings

NHL Debut: October 31, 1943 / New York Rangers 3 at Detroit Red Wings 8
Goal: Ruelle (unassisted) 19:59 3rd

See page 37
// Career Stats: 2-1-0-1-0

George Grigor, Chicago Black Hawks

NHL Debut: January 6, 1944 / Chicago Black Hawks 1 at Toronto Maple Leafs 6
Goal: Grigor (unassisted) 10:29 2nd

Despondency had turned to cynicism in Chicago. Midway through a dismal 1943–44 season, fans and scribes were barely able to contain their contempt for a team that was already on the verge of missing out on the playoffs. Indeed, the Hawks lost their fifth in a row this night and their ninth in a row on the road, so the headline in the *Chicago Tribune* was sarcastic, not genuine, when it appeared: "Lone Chicago Goal Is Scored By An Amateur."

Mark Cundari played nearly 25 minutes in his debut, scoring his only career goal (see story page 135).

Lee Sweatt scored the game-winning goal for the Canucks in his first game, the only NHL goal he'd ever score (see story page 135).

George Grigor had been playing in the Toronto Mercantile League, but the Hawks got him into the lineup by reason of a lease-lend agreement that allowed a team to use a player for one night only. His unassisted goal midway through the second period merely made the score 4–1 for the Leafs. Grigor was used in a similar manner later that month, but he didn't score in a 4–3 Chicago win.
// Career Stats: 2-1-0-1-0

Gilles Dube, Montreal Canadiens

NHL Debut: October 13, 1949 / Chicago Black Hawks 0 at Montreal Canadiens 4
Goal: Dube (Reardon) 19:18 3rd

It's one thing to make the vaunted Montreal Canadiens as a 22-year-old rookie in training camp, but it's quite another to find yourself playing on the first line alongside Maurice Richard and Elmer Lach, two legends of the game. But that was the happy situation Dube found himself in as the 1949–50 NHL season opened at the Forum in Montreal.

Dube had hurt his shoulder in camp but declared himself ready for the first game. Good thing he did. He set up the Rocket for an insurance goal late in the third

period, and then later on a two-on-one with Richard, Dube took the shot, beating Frank Brimsek cleanly to give himself his first NHL goal. In 12 games that season, this was his only goal, and in two playoff games with Detroit in 1954, he was held without a point.
// Career Stats: 12-1-2-3-2/2-0-0-0-0

Odie Lowe, New York Rangers

NHL Debut: February 26, 1950 / Boston Bruins 3 at New York Rangers 4
Goal: Lowe (unassisted) 1:06 1st

It was an impressive debut for Lowe who, along with Don Smith, was recalled from the New York Rovers for the game because coach Lynn Patrick was without Edgar Laprade, Nick Mickoski, and Jackie McLeod.

Lowe and Smith started the game alongside veteran Alex Kaleta, and just 67 seconds later, Lowe had the first goal of his career—and the last. The goal came off a poor clearing by Boston goalie Jack Gelineau, who stopped Kaleta's shot but gave Lowe a great second chance, which he buried.

Lowe later assisted on Smith's goal in the second period, and these two points in his debut were the only two NHL points of his entire brief career.
// Career Stats: 4-1-1-2-0

Aggie Kukulowicz, New York Rangers

NHL Debut: January 7, 1953 / Chicago Black Hawks 6 at New York Rangers 4
Goal: Kukulowicz (Mickoski, Reise) 7:56 1st (pp)

Kukulowicz and Michel (Mike) Labadie were called up from the Quebec Citadelles for this mid-season game against Chicago. Kukulowicz put the Blueshirts ahead, 2–1, late in the opening period on a power play when he tipped in a point shot by Leo Reise.

Alas, it turned out to be the only one of his brief NHL career.
// Career Stats: 4-1-0-1-0

Les Kozak, Toronto Maple Leafs

NHL Debut: January 13, 1962 / Detroit Red Wings 3 at Toronto Maple Leafs 4
Goal: Kozak (Armstrong, Keon) 6:46 3rd

It's not often a player earns a promotion in almost audition-like circumstances, but Leafs coach Punch Imlach was in need of a skilled player, and he didn't have time to mess around with pleasantries. He was already down two star players in Red Kelly and Eddie Shack, but when Dick Duff went down with an ankle injury, Imlach could stand by no longer. He headed to Rochester to see the farmhands play, and

Hudson Fasching scored a sensational goal for Buffalo, his only one so far in 22 career games (see story page 136).

he gave this promise: "If I see someone who impresses me, he'll be in the lineup against Detroit Red Wings Saturday night."

Kozak responded with an inspired two-goal effort, and true to his word Imlach had Kozak in the lineup the next night. Even better, Kozak took a great pass from George Armstrong and one-timed a nice shot past legendary Terry Sawchuk. Not a bad memory to last a lifetime.
// Career Stats: 12-1-0-1-2

Norm "Red" Armstrong, Toronto Maple Leafs

NHL Debut: December 15, 1962 / Boston Bruins 2 at Toronto Maple Leafs 8
Goal: Armstrong (Pulford) 15:18 3rd

Recalled that day by Punch Imlach from the Sudbury Wolves (EPHL) to replace the injured Bob Nevin, Armstrong came from the Irish Block, an area northeast of Owen Sound originally settled by 41 Irish families in 1846.

A career minor leaguer, he was suggested to Imlach by Joe Crozier, who was coaching in Charlotte. Armstrong went to the Leafs' camp in 1962, but after being cut he signed with the Wolves. Imlach didn't use him in this game until late in the third period when the score was 6–1 for the Leafs. "Red" wasted no time in leaving his mark. He scored just 30 seconds after stepping onto the ice, taking a pass from Bob Pulford on a two-on-one. Armstrong's shot beat goalie Eddie Johnston.

Armstrong played seven games over the next month, never scoring after this initial outburst.
// Career Stats: 7-1-1-2-2

Ralph Keller, New York Rangers

NHL Debut: March 9, 1963 / New York Rangers 5 at Montreal Canadiens 2
Goal: Keller (Henry, Hebenton) 6:56 1st

Any first goal is special, of course, but a first—and only—goal scored on the great Jacques Plante is extra special. In a road win in Montreal? All the better. Keller's goal late in the first period—on his first career shot, no less—gave the visiting Rangers a 1–1 tie, and although teams were 2–2 after the second, the Blueshirts pulled away with three unanswered goals in the third.
// Career Stats: 3-1-0-1-6

Grant Erickson, Boston Bruins

NHL Debut: December 29, 1968 / Boston Bruins 3 at Detroit Red Wings 3
Goal: Erickson (Esposito, Hodge) 6:05 2nd

Usually when a player gets called up to play his first NHL game, he makes the heavens move to get to the team as quickly as possible. In Grant Erickson's case, though, that wasn't possible. He was playing in the Central league in Oklahoma when Bruins coach Harry Sinden requested his presence on a road trip that took the B's from St. Louis to Detroit.

Unfortunately, the weather caused havoc to Erickson's plans and it took him two days to join the team. He got there in time for the Red Wings game at the Olympia and didn't waste a moment in making an impact. Sinden didn't give him a shift until several minutes into the second period, but Erickson scored soon after stepping over the boards for the first time.

"I'm glad I got here!" he enthused after the game. The Red Wings burst out to a 3–0 lead, and Erickson's goal was his team's second en route to a comeback that tied the game. Playing alongside the great Phil Esposito and Ken Hodge, Erickson held his own when given the chance. "There was a good scramble," he said, describing his goal, "and after Phil shot, I was just able to rap in the rebound."
// Career Stats: 6-1-0-1-0

Morris Stefaniw, Atlanta Flames

NHL Debut: October 7, 1972 / Atlanta Flames 3 at New York Islanders 2
Goal: Stefaniw (Morrison) 12:48 1st (sh)

Not only was this the first game of the season, it was the first game for both the Atlanta Flames and the New York Islanders franchises. And although most players on the team were castoffs and reclaimed bodies from other teams, for Morris Stefaniw it was his first game.

Even better, he scored the first goal of the game on his first shot, and he became one of a very small group whose first NHL goal was also a short-handed goal. And of all players in this list who scored in their first NHL game and never again, Stefaniw is the only one to have a "shorty" to his name.

// **Career Stats: 13-1-1-2-2**

Lyle Bradley, California Golden Seals

NHL Debut: February 16, 1974 / California Golden Seals 3 at Pittsburgh Penguins 7
Goal: Bradley (J Johnston, McAneeley) 1:01 2nd (pp)

Bradley's introduction to the NHL was as wild as any. Seals owner Charles Finley had decided he'd had enough of owning the sad-sack team and sold it back to the league for $6.585 million. In a fit of pique, coach Fred Glover resigned on this day.

Defenceman Marshall Johnston then decided to retire as a player with the team and take over as coach. This all the while the team was in Pittsburgh expecting to play. Dressing only four defencemen and eleven forwards, Johnston's Seals were no match for the Penguins, but Bradley did score early in the second period to make it a 3–2 game for Pittsburgh. In six career games, this was his only goal.

// **Career Stats: 6-1-0-1-2**

Nelson Burton, Washington Capitals

NHL Debut: November 2, 1977 / Chicago Black Hawks 2 at Washington Capitals 2
Goal: Burton (Green, Collins) 13:45 1st

From the department of "sometimes when you least expect it" comes Burton's debut story. Playing for Hershey in the AHL, he had an infected left elbow and didn't make a road trip with the Bears. Lo and behold, the Caps needed another forward and called him up. That healed his elbow with great speed. He then opened the scoring.

The left winger got the puck back to Rick Green at the point, and the defenceman blasted a shot at Tony Esposito. Tony O made the save, but Burton pounced on the rebound. He continued his forward motion right into the goal to fish the historic puck out of the cage.

// **Career Stats: 8-1-0-1-21**

Bob Crawford, St. Louis Blues

NHL Debut: October 9, 1979 / St. Louis Blues 5 at Vancouver Canucks 2
Goal: Crawford (Dunlop, Brownschidle) 8:26 1st

The optimism was palpable. As the 1979–80 season got under way, with four WHA teams joining the NHL, star forward Brian Sutter promised his St. Louis Blues would win 30 games. It was a modest prediction but better than what most had

anticipated. And part of the reason for hope was that 20-year-old right winger Bob Crawford had made the team out of training camp.

Said coach Barclay Plager: "The biggest surprise, of course, has been Bobby Crawford. He started out looking great the first day of camp and we kept waiting for him to slow down, but he hasn't yet." Crawford didn't disappoint in the home opener, scoring the team's first goal of the new season midway through the first period. He lifted the puck over a sprawling Glen Hanlon in the Vancouver net, and the Blues went on to an impressive win. Despite his training camp, though, and this dreamlike start to the season, Crawford never scored a goal in the NHL ever again.

// **Career Stats: 16-1-3-4-6**

Brian Hill, Hartford Whalers

NHL Debut: December 26, 1979 / Philadelphia Flyers 4 at Hartford Whalers 4
Goal: Hill (Fotiu, Carroll) 7:00 3rd

Called up from Springfield on Christmas Day, Hill joined the Whalers for a home game on Boxing Day. He scored the tying goal in the third period, but that tie game also meant the Flyers' extraordinary unbeaten streak was now at 31 games.

Hill was stationed at the top of the crease when he took a pass from Billy Carroll and put the puck past Phil Myre. "I couldn't believe it was in," an elated Hill said after. "It's just something you dream about." True, but 19 games later, he still had only that one goal to brag about.

// **Career Stats: 19-1-1-2-4**

Pat Daley, Winnipeg Jets

NHL Debut: January 13, 1980 / Los Angeles Kings 3 at Winnipeg Jets 5
Goal: Daley (Sullivan, Melrose) 2:53 1st

The Jets were not a good team, but on this night they scored a big home win against Los Angeles. The 20-year-old Daley, fresh from a call-up from the minors, got things started with an early goal off a scramble, with Ron Grahame down and unable to get to the loose puck. It was Daley's first career shift, about 15 seconds in, and his first career shot. In 12 NHL games, it also proved to be his only goal.

"Any kid in Canada would like to do what I just did," he beamed. "To step out in front of 13,000 people and score a goal on your first shift. Everything just lit up for me. My dream had come true."

// **Career Stats: 12-1-0-1-13**

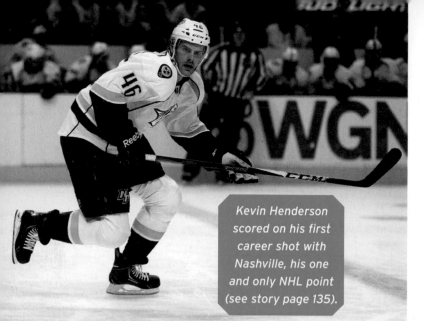

Kevin Henderson scored on his first career shot with Nashville, his one and only NHL point (see story page 135).

Gary Dillon, Colorado Rockies

NHL Debut: October 11, 1980 / Calgary Flames 2 at Colorado Rockies 6
Goal: Dillon (Berry, Quenneville) 8:06 1st

Bill Clement opened the scoring for Calgary at 7:03 of the first period, but just 63 seconds later Dillon, a call-up from Fort Worth of the CHL, tied the game and sent the Rockies on their way to victory.
// Career Stats: 13-1-1-2-29

Randy MacGregor, Hartford Whalers

NHL Debut: November 12, 1981 / Hartford Whalers 3 at Philadelphia Flyers 5
Goal: MacGregor (Miller, McIlhargey) 3:30 3rd

Numbers rarely tell the whole story, and, boy, that's the case with Randy MacGregor. The stats show he scored a goal, but it was no end-to-end rush to tell the grandkids about. He got into the lineup the night of November 12, 1981, because Rick Meagher had an infected left elbow and couldn't play. The 28-year-old MacGregor was recalled from the farm team in Binghamton.

The Flyers jumped into a 3–1 lead after two periods, and then MacGregor went to work. Here's how he scored, according to Terry Price, writing a game recap for the *Hartford Courant*: "The Whalers clawed back to within a goal when Randy MacGregor, playing in his first NHL game, scored at 3:30 of the third period. MacGregor scored when he accidentally slid into the Philadelphia cage with the puck pinned under the seat of his pants."

There you have it. He added an assist later in the game on a Blaine Stoughton goal. He also took a hooking penalty midway through the second, which led to a Paul Holmgren power-play goal. MacGregor played two nights later, then never saw a sheet of NHL ice again.
// Career Stats: 2-1-1-2-2

Dan Poulin, Minnesota North Stars

NHL Debut: December 12, 1981 /
Chicago Black Hawks 3 at Minnesota North Stars 6
Goal: Poulin (Barrett, Christoff) 6:02 1st

There was much to be distracted about on this day for North Stars fans because general manager Lou Nanne fully expected to acquire Darryl Sittler from the Leafs in a trade. "We're very close to a deal," he boasted, before adding, "I've given them a list of players whom I'm willing to trade."

Of course, the deal never materialized, but when the puck dropped to play a game that night against Chicago, Dan Poulin was in the lineup. Called up from the Nashville South Stars of the Central league because of a rash of injuries, he scored the game's first goal on his first career shot.
// Career Stats: 3-1-1-2-2

Mike Siltala, Washington Capitals

NHL Debut: December 14, 1981 / Washington Capitals 3 at Montreal Canadiens 6
Goal: Siltala (MacKinnon, Gustafsson) 10:21 1st

Called up from the Kingston Canadians earlier in the day, the 18-year-old Siltala made sure he got to Montreal in time—and then he went to work. He scored the team's first goal by deflecting a Paul MacKinnon shot, and that tied the score, 1–1. The Habs, however, bounced back to win the game. Siltala didn't get into a second game until three months later, and he played only seven career games.
// Career Stats: 7-1-0-1-2

Pierre Giroux, Los Angeles Kings

NHL Debut: October 14, 1982 / Los Angeles Kings 4 at Quebec Nordiques 4
Goal: Giroux (Korab, M Murphy) 7:56 3rd

When Dan Bonar dislocated his left elbow the previous night in a game in Winnipeg, the centreman flew back to Los Angeles and the Kings recalled Pierre Giroux from New Haven. Giroux was considered that team's best centre and was to fill in on the fourth line alongside J.P. Kelly and Mike Murphy.

Giroux had only recently signed with the Kings as a free agent, but he was assigned to the farm team in the AHL. He scored early in the third on his first career shot, giving the Kings a 4–3 lead, but in the end they had to settle for a 4–4 road tie.
// Career Stats: 6-1-0-1-17

Pierre Rioux, Calgary Flames

NHL Debut: December 7, 1982 / Los Angeles Kings 4 at Calgary Flames 4
Goal: Rioux (Nilsson, Hislop) 2:30 1st

First shift, first shot, first goal. The Flames had seven regulars unable to play, so Pierre Rioux got a promotion from the farm team in Colorado and promptly staked his team to a 1–0 lead. In fact, Calgary built a 3–0 lead only to let it slip through their proverbial fingers and settle for a 4–4 tie.

Rioux was sent down before the Flames' next game, though he did get recalled in January (two games) and again in March (11 games), dressing for an additional 13 games but going without a goal.
// **Career Stats: 14-1-2-3-4**

Geordie Robertson, Buffalo Sabres

NHL Debut: February 12, 1983 / Buffalo Sabres 2 at Calgary Flames 4
Goal: Robertson (Housley, Cyr) 5:35 2nd

Called up from Rochester for five games, Robertson scored early in the second period of his debut game to give the visiting Sabres a 2–1 lead. It was the only goal of the period, but the Flames rallied with three goals in the third to win.
// **Career Stats: 5-1-2-3-7**

Bob LaForest, Los Angeles Kings

NHL Debut: October 5, 1983 /
Minnesota North Stars 3 at Los Angeles Kings 3 (5:00 OT)
Goal: LaForest (Dionne, Hardy) 2:05 1st (pp)

Both lucky and good, Bob LaForest wasn't able to parlay his good timing and good fortune into anything much beyond his NHL debut. A late draft choice by the Kings the previous summer, LaForest turned heads during training camp with his strong play and offensive skills. Add to that the fact that Dave Taylor had had wrist surgery in the summer and wasn't expected to play for another month, and voila! LaForest was in the lineup for the Kings' first game of the season.

"When a guy goes in the fifth round [of the draft], you don't expect him to be with the team, but he's there," coach Don Perry said honestly. "He caught a break because there was a spot open." That spot wasn't any generic spot. It was a spot on the top line with Marcel Dionne and Charlie Simmer. Dionne-Simmer-Taylor formed the Triple Crown Line, one of the NHL's greatest scoring threesomes of their generation.

Even better, Dionne was at his dominant best, scoring two goals and assisting on LaForest's marker. Dionne's two goals put him past Maurice Richard on the all-time list, now with 546. LaForest scored the game's first goal on the power play. Dionne's shot was stopped by Gilles Meloche, but LaForest lifted the rebound in. Incredibly, Dionne had 11 of the team's 26 shots, and LaForest had a front row seat watching one of the greatest players of all time.
// **Career Stats: 5-1-0-1-2**

Jim Archibald, Minnesota North Stars

NHL Debut: March 20, 1985 / Minnesota North Stars 2 at Winnipeg Jets 5
Goal: Archibald (Broten, Wilson) 1:32 3rd

Dino Ciccarelli was a no go, not feeling well, so Archibald came in and played on Minnesota's top line with Neal Broten and Dirk Graham. The Stars fell behind, 3–0, but Archibald's goal gave the Stars a bit of life early in the third. It was a big-league goal, that's for sure. He took a pass from Broten and skated down the right side, blasting a high slapshot over the glove of Brian Hayward from the top of the faceoff circle.

Graham scored just nine seconds later to make it 3–2, but that's as close as it got. The Jets pulled away for the win. Still, coach Glen Sonmor was delighted by Archibald's debut. "It appears we've got ourselves a very good prospect," he beamed after the game. "Whether he will help us immediately is still a question. We've got guys like [Willi] Plett and [Tony] McKegney coming back from injuries, but you never know."

Archibald played only 16 NHL games and never scored again. True—you never know.
// **Career Stats: 16-1-2-3-45**

Ted Speers, Detroit Red Wings

NHL Debut: March 3, 1986 / Minnesota North Stars 8 at Detroit Red Wings 5
Goal: Speers (Ogrodnick, Larson) 0:55 1st

The 25-year-old Ted Speers and 20-year-old Bob Probert were recalled from Adirondack on March 3, 1986. Probert had played on two occasions earlier in the season, and Speers had been recalled once previously but didn't play. This night was different. Playing on a line with Ron Duguay and John Ogrodnick, Speers scored in the first minute of the game, one of the fastest first goals ever.
// **Career Stats: 4-1-1-2-0**

Todd McLellan, New York Islanders

NHL Debut: December 28, 1987 / New York Islanders 4 at New Jersey Devils 6
Goal: McLellan (Henry, Dalgarno) 2:54 2nd

McLellan's goal early in the second period gave the Islanders a 3–1 lead and seemed to take the crowd out of the game, but the Devils didn't give up and scored

three in the second and three more in the third for the win. Despite his short career on ice, he has had a paradoxically long career behind the bench as NHL coach.
// Career Stats: 5-1-1-2-0

Rod Dallman, New York Islanders

NHL Debut: February 21, 1988 / New York Islanders 7 at Hartford Whalers 2
Goal: Dallman (Makela, Trottier) 14:40 2nd

It was 2 p.m. and Marty Dallman wasn't expecting the call, but Rick Kromm had an abdominal strain and Greg Gilbert a sore knee, so coach Terry Simpson, who knew Dallman from their time together in Prince Albert of the WHL, called on Dallman as a last-minute replacement.

It got better. "I was so pumped up, coming here, getting the chance to play. And then when Terry told me I'd be playing with Bryan Trottier and Mikko Makela, then I felt no pressure right away."

At five-foot-eleven and 185 pounds, Dallman brought skill to the team but also a little sandpaper. He demonstrated both in his debut, scoring a nice goal off a Makela pass that gave the Isles a comfy 6–1 lead, and later getting into a pushing-and-shoving match with Kevin Dineen that earned him a double-minor penalty.
// Career Stats: 6-1-0-1-26/1-0-1-1-0

Justin Hodgman beat Roberto Luongo for his only NHL goal and earned the Coyotes' player of the game belt for the feat (see story page 135).

John English, Los Angeles Kings

NHL Debut: March 30, 1988 / Calgary Flames 7 at Los Angeles Kings 9
Goal: English (Kontos, Robitaille) 1:34 3rd (pp)

The Kings were missing seven regulars for this game, so John English, up from the AHL's New Haven Nighthawks, got a chance to shine. And he did. He assisted on a Jimmy Carson marker late in the first period to bring the Kings to within a goal of the Flames, 3–2.

Soon after, he took a minor penalty, and after a wild scoring spree by both teams he scored his goal early in the third to give L.A. a 6–5 lead. His long shot from the right point on the power play beat Doug Dadswell. Incredibly, English had four career points in the NHL, and three came on this night, his first.
// Career Stats: 3-1-3-4-4/1-0-0-0-0

Dean Morton, Detroit Red Wings

NHL Debut: October 5, 1989 / Detroit Red Wings 7 at Calgary Flames 10
Goal: Morton (Habscheid, Yzerman) 12:52 1st

Steve Yzerman was starting a new season as captain of Detroit, with a whopping new contract paying him $6 million over five seasons. The legendary Borje Salming signed with the Wings in the off-season, and Detroit acquired another future Hall of Famer, Bernie Federko, in a trade with St. Louis. The talented Petr Klima had a court case and took up boldface news space because of alcohol problems.

And then there was newcomer Dean Morton, a defenceman who caused barely a ripple of attention when he made the team out of camp. Morton was a low draft choice in 1986, but he was on the opening night roster for a road game against the Calgary Flames, Stanley Cup champions.

The Flames were up 3–0 by the 12-minute mark, but shortly thereafter Morton scored, with Yzerman's help, to get the Wings in the game. Morton later incurred a penalty, though, and the Flames kept scoring, racking up a huge win and forcing Jacques Demers to make changes for their game the next night in Vancouver.

Morton was out—and he never got back in.
// Career Stats: 1-1-0-1-2

Andrew McKim, Boston Bruins

NHL Debut: December 26, 1992 / Boston Bruins 9 at Hartford Whalers 4
Goal: McKim (unassisted) 13:58 3rd

Polar opposite to Randy MacGregor, Andrew McKim's only career goal was a beaut. But first, the backdrop. McKim was tiny, five-foot-seven and 165 pounds, generously, and after four years in the Q there was no NHL interest. He played in the minors and drew enough looks from the Bruins that they invited him to training camp in September 1992. He was cut quickly, though, and assigned to the AHL team in Providence with the promise that he'd get a chance at some point. He was quite sick early in the season and needed time to get his legs, but on December 23, he was told to pack his bags.

McKim spent Christmas Day in a hotel and skated with the team before the game. Coach Brian Sutter even put McKim out for the opening faceoff. He scored a goal in the third period to give the Bruins a commanding 7–3 lead, and it was one to remember.

He got control of the puck near his own blue line and darted up the right side. He then split the defencemen—Steve Konroyd and Murray Craven—and when he saw goalie Frank Pietrangelo dip slightly, McKim roofed a quick shot to the top corner. Truly, a highlight-reel goal, a goalscorer's goal.

"He goes down, you have to go upstairs," he said with delight afterwards. Of all the players in the category of one career goal scored in the first game, no one played more games than McKim. He went dry in six more games with the Bruins this season, went goalless for them a year later in 29 games, and played two games for Detroit in 1994–95, without scoring. But the one he caught was a gem.
// **Career Stats: 38-1-4-5-6**

Jeff McLean, San Jose Sharks

NHL Debut: October 31, 1993 / San Jose Sharks 2 at Mighty Ducks of Anaheim 1 (OT)
Goal: McLean (Makarov, Larionov) 7:34 3rd

It's maybe not fair to call it the MLM Line, but McLean scored the tying goal playing with two-thirds of the greatest international line of all time. The Soviets' vaunted

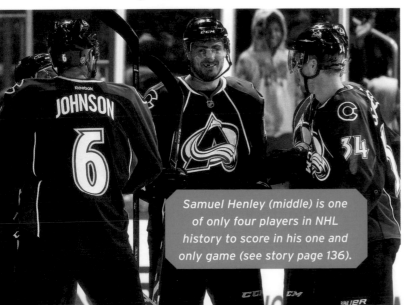

Samuel Henley (middle) is one of only four players in NHL history to score in his one and only game (see story page 136).

KLM line featured Vladimir Krutov, Igor Larionov, and Sergei Makarov, but the NHL's Sharks version swapped Krutov for McLean—at least for one game.

McLean never scored again but his one goal was important in the game and also significant historically.
// **Career Stats: 6-1-0-1-0**

Pat Neaton, Pittsburgh Penguins

NHL Debut: November 16, 1993 / Philadelphia Flyers 5 at Pittsburgh Penguins 11
Goal: Neaton (Stevens, Murphy) 17:27 3rd (pp)

The Penguins made one change to their lineup for this home game against state rivals, Philadelphia. They recalled Pat Neaton from the Cleveland Lumberjacks and sent Ladislav Karabin down.

For Neaton, the night was unforgettable. For fans watching, however, it was Jaromir Jagr they would remember. Number 68 had a goal and five assists, while Neaton scored the final goal late in the third when the game was way out of reach.

The other unique factoid about this game is that it was officiated by "scabs," replacement officials hired by the league because the usual zebras were on strike, looking for better pay.
// **Career Stats: 9-1-1-2-12**

Paul Brousseau, Colorado Avalanche

NHL Debut: January 10, 1996 /
Florida Panthers 4 at Colorado Avalanche 4 (5:00 OT)
Goal: Brousseau (Wolanin, Kamensky) 13:10 3rd

Despite playing 26 career games in the NHL, Brousseau scored in the third period of his first game and never again. It was a big goal all the same, though. Florida jumped into an early 3–0 lead, but the Avs clawed their way back. Brousseau scored the game-tying goal at 13:10 of the final period, and that's how the game ended, 4–4.
// **Career Stats: 26-1-3-4-29**

Petr Hubacek, Philadelphia Flyers

NHL Debut: October 5, 2000—Vancouver Canucks 3 at Philadelphia Flyers 6
Goal: Hubacek (Tocchet, Stevens) 3:18 2nd

It was a tale of two cities, but instead of cities it was players. Specifically, 19-year-old Justin Williams and 21-year-old Petr Hubacek, both were making their NHL debuts. Eric Lindros, debilitated by concussions, was not in the lineup for the Flyers for the first time in nine years.

All the same, the start of a new NHL season for the Flyers was full of hope and promise and mystery as coach Craig Ramsay had several new faces in the lineup, including young Canadian Williams and Czech Hubacek. "If they show me they can play, they'll get a chance," Ramsay said of his two prized young players before the team's season opener at home against Vancouver.

That night, they played as advertised. Williams, playing on a line with John LeClair and Keith Primeau, scored the game's first goal at 3:14, his career first, and he later added two assists. Hubacek scored early in the second to tie the game, and the fairy-tale game ended a 6–3 victory for the Flyers.

Mikko Lehtonen scored just seven seconds after stepping onto the ice in his first game. He never scored again (see story page 133).

Just 28 days later, Hubacek played what turned out to be his last NHL game, and this goal remained his only one. Williams? He's still playing in the NHL more than 1,200 games and 300 goals later. You just never know.
// **Career Stats: 6-1-0-1-2**

Miroslav Zalesak, San Jose Sharks

NHL Debut: March 11, 2003 / St. Louis Blues 4 at San Jose Sharks 2
Goal: Zalesak (Cheechoo) 8:55 2nd

St. Louis jumped into an early 3–0 lead in San Jose, but the Sharks got their first of the night on a sensational play by Marco Sturm. He one-handed the puck past Blues goalie Chad Johnson, beating the goalie to the puck and swatting it in. Moments later, Jonathan Cheechoo had the puck in centre ice along the right boards and spotted Zalesak free and clear on the left. He got Zalesak the puck, and the rookie wired a great shot to the top corner to score his first goal and make it a 3–2 game. It was Zalesak's first career shot in 14:25 of ice time, but it also proved to be his one and only NHL goal.
// **Career Stats: 12-1-2-3-0**

Damian Surma, Carolina Hurricanes

NHL Debut: March 18, 2003 / Ottawa Senators 6 at Carolina Hurricanes 5
Goal: Surma (O'Neill, St. Jacques) 2:50 3rd

Very few players can lay claim to scoring such a gorgeous baseball-like goal as their first, but Surma displayed great hand-eye coordination on a two-on-one rush with Jeff O'Neill.

Ottawa was leading 4–2 early in the third period when O'Neill made a great tip of the puck inside his own blue line to get by a pinching Wade Redden and create the odd-man rush with Surma.

O'Neill streaked down the right side and let fly a shot. Patrick Lalime made the save but the puck bounced in the air and Surma, skating towards the goal, batted it in as he leaped over the sprawling goalie.
// **Career Stats: 2-1-1-2-0**

Peter Sarno, Edmonton Oilers

NHL Debut: November 4, 2003 / Edmonton Oilers 4 at Montreal Canadiens 2
Goal: Sarno (Isbister, Salmelainen) 7:15 2nd

Jarret Stoll's pain was Peter Sarno's gain. Stoll's case of tonsillitis kept him in bed and forced the Oilers to recall Sarno from the Toronto Roadrunners. This is a trivia question in itself given that the Roadrunners played in T.O. for only one season. Be that as it may, Sarno arrived in Montreal and practised on a line with Tony

Salmelainen and Brad Isbister. The next day's *Edmonton Journal* wasn't shy about Sarno's debut, running the headline "Sarno notches first goal in first game."

An ecstatic Sarno was in step time with the banner, saying, "I've waited my whole life for this opportunity. It feels like a dream." His goal made it 4–0 for the visitors, cementing an impressive road win. Sarno lifted the puck over Mathieu Garon for the score.

"The puck was lying there, and when I saw the net, my hands were shaking," he described. It was his first shot on goal and came in 8:12 of ice time.
// Career Stats: 7-1-0-1-2

Josh Olson, Florida Panthers

NHL Debut: March 11, 2004 / Florida Panthers 3 at Montreal Canadiens 2 (OT)
Goal: Olson (Audette, Huselius) 1:40 3rd

Donald Audette had the puck behind the Montreal goal and thought he had a moment. He came out front quickly, trying to sweep the puck in, but goalie Mathieu Garon made the save. Olson, though, was right there and snapped in the rebound. That made it 2–1 for the visiting Panthers early in the third. Montreal later tied the game, but the Panthers won in OT on an Olli Jokinen goal.

Olson played four more games in the next nine days, but he never registered another point and never played in the NHL thereafter. On this night, he had his goal in 8:15 of ice time.
// Career Stats: 5-1-0-1-0

Brad Fast, Carolina Hurricanes

NHL Debut: April 4, 2004 / Carolina Hurricanes 6 at Florida Panthers 6 (5:00 OT)
Goal: Fast (Brind'Amour, Cole) 17:34 3rd
See page 23
// Career Stats: 1-1-0-1-0

Petr Kanko, Los Angeles Kings

NHL Debut: December 16, 2005 /
Los Angeles Kings 4 at Mighty Ducks of Anaheim 3 (5:00 OT/SO)
Goal: Kanko (Giuliano) 5:26 3rd

Called up from the Kings AHL affiliate in Manchester, Kanko connected when it mattered the most. Los Angeles let slip an early 2–0 lead, and after two periods found themselves trailing, 3–2. Kanko, though, delivered the tying goal early in the third period. His time with the team lasted but 10 games, and the rest of his career played out in the minors and overseas.
// Career Stats: 10-1-0-1-0

Jonathan Ferland, Montreal Canadiens

NHL Debut: January 3, 2006 / Pittsburgh Penguins 6 at Montreal Canadiens 4
Goal: Ferland (Higgins, Begin) 6:43 2nd

It's both special and a drag when your career highlight is merely a footnote in a game, but them's the facts. On the morning of January 3, 2006, Montreal coach Claude Julien sent Alexander Perezhogin to the AHL team in Hamilton and recalled Jonathan Ferland, Jean-Philippe Cote, and Andrei Kostitsyn.

The trouble was that all of the news emanating from Montreal that day was about the visiting Pittsburgh Penguins and rookie Sidney Crosby's first trip to the Bell Centre. The only thing worse? Crosby did, indeed, steal the show, scoring twice and creating a buzz all night long, on ice and in the stands.

So although Ferland scored his goal early in the second to give the Habs their only lead of the night, history barely remembers that brief moment in time because of No. 87's dominating performance. In all, Ferland had four shots in 9:12 of ice time, and he scored the only NHL goal of his career.
// Career Stats: 7-1-0-1-2

Mikko Lehtonen, Nashville Predators

NHL Debut: October 7, 2006 / Nashville Predators 5 at Minnesota Wild 6
Goal: Lehtonen (Dumont, Suter) 1:41 1st

Every player has a story to tell, and in the case of defenceman Mikko Lehtonen it's an uncommon one. Never a top prospect, he was drafted a distant 271st overall by Nashville in 2001. For perspective, note that there were a total of 289 players chosen, so Lehtonen was way *way* down the list.

He was also very happy playing in the Finnish league and never considered the NHL seriously for several years, but in 2006 he thought he'd give it a try. Coach Barry Trotz put him in the lineup for the team's second game of the season, figuring Lehtonen's speed on the blue line would help negate Minnesota's speed up front.

Well, lo and behold, Lehtonen scored just 101 seconds into his first game and eight seconds into his first shift. He never scored again, though, ended up in the minors for most of the year, and then returned to Finland where he continued a successful career with Karpat before retiring in 2014. He made The Show; he just didn't stay long.
// Career Stats: 15-1-2-3-8

Bjorn Melin, Anaheim Ducks

NHL Debut: January 7, 2007 / Detroit Red Wings 2 at Anaheim Ducks 4
Goal: Melin (Selanne) 10:36 2nd

A goal is a goal. That's what it says on the scoresheet. But some are gems and some are dogs, and Melin's fell into the latter category. But that's okay, because it took him eight years to get into his first NHL game.

Melin was drafted late in the 1999 Entry Draft by the New York Islanders, but he never played for them. Instead, they traded him to Anaheim early in 2002, but still Melin continued to play in Sweden and pine for the NHL. "It was always a dream for me to come here," he started. "I always wanted to play in this league, but I

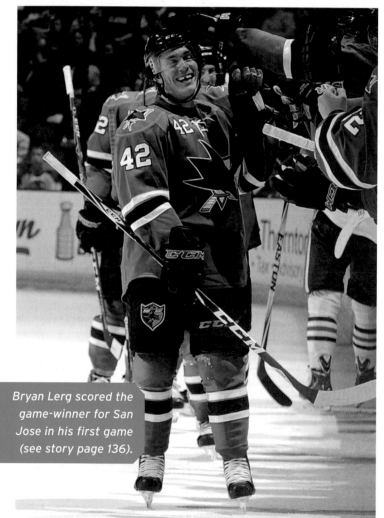

Bryan Lerg scored the game-winner for San Jose in his first game (see story page 136).

probably wasn't good enough. I had to work on everything, had to be more physical and get more mature."

The Ducks finally signed him in 2006 and after training camp that fall assigned him to Portland, where he showed great improvement. He was called up on Friday and was in the lineup two nights later against Detroit where he played on the first line with Teemu Selanne and Andy McDonald.

And then the big moment happened. Selanne stole the puck near centre, came over the line and dropped a pass to Melin. Melin fired a pass over to McDonald, but the puck hit Detroit defenceman Brett Lebda's stick and went in past Dominik Hasek, who was playing the pass. It was Melin's first career "shot" and goal, and in only three games it turned out to be his only one as well.
// Career Stats: 3-1-0-1-0

Petteri Wirtanen, Anaheim Ducks

NHL Debut: October 17, 2007 / Nashville Predators 1 at Anaheim Ducks 3
Goal: Wirtanen (Parros, Huskins) 4:47 3rd

Although Wirtanen had a mere 2:52 of ice time, he managed not only to score on his first shot but also to score the game-winning goal for the Ducks. He had been the team's last cut at training camp but got a chance to strut his stuff this night because Todd Marchant had an ankle injury.

Early in the third period, George Parros made a nice pass to Wirtanen who moved the puck past Nashville defenceman Greg de Vries and then deked goalie Chris Mason to score the 2–1 goal. "It's a moment that I can't imagine," Wirtanen said. "The chance came, and I just put it in. It felt awesome."
// Career Stats: 3-1-0-1-2

Petr Vrana, New Jersey Devils

NHL Debut: October 18, 2008 / New Jersey Devils 4 at Washington Capitals 3
(5:00 OT/SO)
Goal: Vrana (Elias, Oduya) 12:48 1st

Vrana's goal midway through the first tied the game. It was his first career shot in 7:02 of ice time. The game ended up in a shootout, but he never took a shot. He played 16 games during an injury-plagued year, the only ones of his NHL career.
// Career Stats: 16-1-0-1-2

Ray Sawada, Dallas Stars

NHL Debut: February 19, 2009 / Edmonton Oilers 2 at Dallas Stars 4
Goal: Sawada (Ribeiro, Daley) 16:36 1st

Called up from the Manitoba Moose of the AHL, Sawada played five games in a two-week stretch in 2008–09, and then only six more games in the subsequent two seasons. On his debut night, his goal late in the first period gave the Stars a 2–0 lead. He scored on his first shot, beating Dwayne Roloson with a low wrister between the pads.
// **Career Stats: 11-1-0-1-0**

Lee Sweatt, Vancouver Canucks

NHL Debut: January 26, 2011 / Nashville Predators 1 at Vancouver Canucks 2
Goal: Sweatt (D Sedin) 12:31 3rd

Called up from the Manitoba Moose after a spate of injuries reduced the Canucks' list of healthy players, Sweatt made his debut the night of Wayne Gretzky's 50th birthday. The defenceman not only scored—he scored the game winner. Teams had failed to put a puck in the net in either of the first two periods, but the visiting Preds opened the scoring early in the third. Alexandre Burrows tied the game midway through, and two minutes later Sweatt beat Pekka Rinne for the final goal of the night on his first career shot.
// **Career Stats: 3-1-1-2-2**

Kevin Henderson, Nashville Predators

NHL Debut: April 19, 2013 / Nashville Predators 4 at Chicago Blackhawks 5 (OT)
Goal: Henderson (Mueller, Butler) 10:42 1st

Losers of seven straight games heading to Chicago, the Predators were also decimated by injury. Out were Colin Wilson (shoulder), Paul Gaustad (shoulder), Gabriel Bourque (knee), Mike Fisher (hand), Brandon Yip (lower body), and Patric Hornqvist (upper body). As a result, Henderson was recalled from Milwaukee of the AHL and got into his first career NHL game.

Lo and behold, he jammed a puck past Corey Crawford in the Chicago goal midway through the opening period, giving the Predators a 2–1 lead. It was his first career shot, but by the end of the night the Hawks had pulled out a victory thanks to a Jonathan Toews goal in overtime.

Henderson played 12:57 and had a memory to last a lifetime. "I was fortunate to get the goal there and help the team out, but it was just an amazing experience for me. I'll remember that moment for a long time," he said afterwards.
// **Career Stats: 4-1-0-1-0**

Mark Cundari, Calgary Flames

NHL Debut: April 21, 2013 / Calgary Flames 4 at Minnesota Wild 1
Goal: Cundari (Brodie, Cammalleri) 13:37 1st (pp)

The Flames acquired Cundari just three weeks earlier in a package that sent Jay Bouwmeester to St. Louis. Coming to the Flames with Cundari were goalie Reto Berra and a first-round draft choice in 2013 (Emile Poirier, 22nd overall). Two days shy of his 23rd birthday, Cundari was small (five-foot-nine, 195 pounds), but he was used to playing a physical game against bigger players.

The defenceman played with T.J. Brodie and had 24:54 of ice time. He scored his first career goal on the power play, wiring a shot from the top of the left faceoff circle over the shoulder of Nicklas Backstrom in the Minnesota goal. Teammate Mike Cammalleri fished the puck out of the net, later calling the impressive shot a "big-time goal."

Cundari's goal made it 1–0, and he assisted on another Flames score on a third-period power play to make it 3–1. All in all, a sensational debut, but his first, last, and only goal came in this game.
// **Career Stats: 8-1-2-3-2**

John Albert, Winnipeg Jets

NHL Debut: December 2, 2013 / Winnipeg Jets 5 at New York Rangers 2
Goal: Albert (Byfuglien) 10:00 2nd

Say no more. Albert's opening salvo in the NHL was a highlight-reel goal. The venue was Madison Square Garden and exactly at the midway point of the game he scored on his first ever shot.

The play started inside the Jets blue line when a dangerous Rangers rush was expertly broken up by Dustin Byfuglien. He carried the puck outside the line and hit Albert with a breakaway pass. Albert out-skated two Rangers and drilled a bullet shot short side on Cam Talbot to give his team a 2–1 lead. A thing of beauty.
// **Career Stats: 9-1-0-1-0**

Justin Hodgman, Arizona Coyotes

NHL Debut: October 25, 2014 / Florida Panthers 1 at Arizona Coyotes 2 (OT)
Goal: Hodgman (Korpikoski, Yandle) 9:51 3rd (pp)

On July 1, 2014, Hodgman signed a one-year, two-way contract with the Coyotes and made the team out of training camp. But he was a healthy scratch for the first two games of the season and was sent to the farm team in Portland. After three games, though, he was recalled and got his NHL start at home on October 25.

Even better, his power-play goal midway through the third period tied the game with Florida, and the 'Yotes went on to win in OT. Hodgman was at the back side of goalie Roberto Luongo and took a nice pass from Keith Yandle, burying it without thinking. He had taken a slashing penalty in the first period, which turned out to be harmless. Over the rest of the season, he appeared but sporadically, never scoring again.
// **Career Stats: 5-1-0-1-2**

Bryan Lerg, San Jose Sharks

NHL Debut: April 9, 2015 / San Jose Sharks 3 at Edmonton Oilers 1
Goal: Lerg (Couture, Fedun) 17:08 3rd

Goalie Laurent Brossoit and Curtis Hamilton, both of Edmonton, also made their NHL debuts on the final day of the 2014–15 season. Brossoit shone brightest in that he stopped 49 of 51 shots and was sensational in the Oilers' goal. Hamilton remains a one-game wonder to this day, and Lerg played only a few games, his first being his most memorable. He scored the game-winning goal late in the third period, breaking a 1–1 tie and sending the Sharks to victory.
// **Career Stats: 8-1-0-1-0**

Hudson Fasching, Buffalo Sabres*

NHL Debut: March 26, 2016 / Winnipeg Jets 2 at Buffalo Sabres 3
Goal: Fasching (Pysyk, Nelson) 8:37 1st

Still an active player, the last chapter may not yet be written in the chronicles of Fasching's NHL career, but the opening lines focus on the end of the 2015–16 season. Fasching had finished his third year with the University of Minnesota when the Sabres signed him to an entry-level contract, effectively ending his NCAA career and starting his pro career.

Fasching's goal was fantastic. He forced his way down the left wing, simply out-muscling Jacob Trouba along the boards. Finding himself in the corner of the Jets end, he continued to barge right in on goal and stuffed a shot past Michael Hutchinson.

"It's really exciting. It's kind of a dream come true," Fasching said. "I was talking to my buddies and my parents and I was like, 'If I score in my first game I don't know what I'm going to do.' I'm going to be blacked out on adrenaline and so excited. That was almost the case. I was so excited out there. It was a really happy moment for me."
// **Career Stats: 22-1-2-3-8** *active

Samuel Henley, Colorado Avalanche

NHL Debut: December 1, 2016 / Columbus Blue Jackets 3 at Colorado Avalanche 2
Goal: Henley (Barrie) 14:25 2nd

"I was extremely nervous playing my first game," Henley admitted after his debut. He had but 5:18 of ice time, but his goal late in the second period tied the score, 2–2.

It came on a quick play. As the puck was rolling near the Columbus blue line, Henley, back to the goal, corralled the disc and in one motion turned and fired.

The puck drifted by several players, fooling goalie Sergei Bobrovsky in the process. "Tyson Barrie made a really nice play to me," he described. "I shot, and I actually wasn't sure first of all if it was really in the net."
// **Career Stats: 1-1-0-1-2**

Wade Megan, St. Louis Blues*

NHL Debut: December 22, 2016 / St. Louis Blues 2 at Tampa Bay Lightning 5
Goal: Megan (Reaves, Edmundson) 14:43 1st

"I tried to think of it as just another game for me and tried to prepare mentally the same I do every night," Megan said after his terrific debut.

Whatever he did worked because midway through the first period, Megan scored his first career goal. It came off the rush, and it came on a play he started. Coming down the left side on a three-on-two, Megan dropped the puck to Ryan Reaves. Reaves's quick blast was stopped by Andrei Vasilevskiy, but the puck came right back to Megan, who snapped the rebound in.

"I definitely got pretty wide-eyed there," Megan said of the play, "but I had to re-focus and bear down and put it in. Great shot by Reaves." The goal gave the visiting Blues a 2–0 lead, but the Lightning stormed back with five unanswered goals over the final 40 minutes to win.
// **Career Stats: 15-1-1-2-2** *active

Nathan Walker, Washington Capitals*

NHL Debut: October 7, 2017—Montreal Canadiens 1 at Washington Capitals 6
Goal: Walker (Smith-Pelly, Beagle) 18:05 2nd

Nathan Walker is not just another name in the annals of NHL play. Born in Cardiff, Wales, he grew up in Sydney, Australia, and on this night became the first player from that country to make it to the NHL. He had been drafted 89th overall by the Capitals in 2014 and spent the next three years with Hershey in the AHL.

Walker made the team out of training camp and was in the lineup for the Caps' first game of the 2017–18 season. Although he scored in his first game, it wasn't a gem. Off a faceoff in the Montreal end, Devante Smith-Pelly got the puck back to Jay Beagle at the point. His quick shot hit Walker in front and eluded Al Montoya, giving the Aussie his first, and still only, goal.

In fact, the goal was originally credited to Smith-Pelly and only changed after video review. "I don't have any words, to be honest," a humbled Walker said. "It's so incredible. Just to be out on the ice with those guys . . . it was really fun."
// **Career Stats: 12-1-1-2-8** *active

Crazy Post-Debut Slump

Andrew McKim

BOSTON BRUINS // DECEMBER 26, 1992

Of the 7,863 players in NHL history, exactly 520 have one career goal to their credit. Of that number, 66 scored their only goal in their first game. Some played only a few more games, while others played many more games, never scoring after their debut.

The granddaddy of players who scored in their debut and never again is none other than Andrew McKim. He scored in the third period of his first game with Boston, but over the course of three partial years in the league but a total of 38 regular-season games (no playoff appearances), he never scored again.

What's even more striking about McKim's slump is that he was a scorer wherever he went. In his final two years of junior, first with Verdun and then Hull, McKim scored 50 and then 66 goals. With St. John's in 1991–92, he scored 43 goals. He was only five-foot-seven and 165 pounds, so the perpetual knock on him was that he was too small and not strong enough, but at every level he graduated to, he proved the naysayers wrong.

He had been playing with the Providence Bruins during the 1992–93 season, but just before Christmas he was alerted that he'd play on Boxing Day, in Hartford. "It's been pretty tough to sleep the last few nights," he admitted after his debut with the Bruins. "But it's great. I worked hard for a long while, and I'm here after a lot of people said I'd never make it."

The Bruins hammered the Whalers by a 9–4 score, and McKim scored the seventh Boston goal.

In all, he played seven games that year with the Bruins, never scoring again. The next year he was called up for 29 games, not scoring once. The year after, now with Detroit, he got a two-game look, and after not scoring, he never played in the NHL again.

At the end of that 1994–95 season, he played for Canada at the World Championship, and again he was sensational, scoring six goals and 13 points in eight games and leading the team to a bronze medal.

In the NHL, though, he could muster only that one amazing goal—but that's still better than nothing.

Other long one-goal careers:

Paul Brousseau	26 regular-season games
Greg Parks	23 regular-season games + 2 playoff games
Hudson Fasching	22 regular-season games
Jim Archibald	16 regular-season games
Bobby Crawford	16 regular-season games
Ben Hanowski	16 regular-season games
Petr Vrana	16 regular-season games

Andrew McKim started big and ended with a lengthy scoring slump.

Debuts Across the Pond

// The only player who can say he scored his first career NHL goal overseas is Bobby Ryan of Anaheim. He beat Jonathan Bernier in the third period during the Ducks' 4–1 loss to Los Angeles.

// Only two goalies have made their debuts in Europe—the aforementioned Bernier and, a day later at the other end of the ice, Swiss-born Jonas Hiller for the Ducks.

// Only two other players recorded their first points overseas, Greg Classen and Maxime Macenauer.

Bobby Ryan (white) scored his first career goal at the O2 Arena in London, England.

NHL Debuts in Europe					
Player/ Goalie (team)	Date (City)	G/ Mins	A/ GA	P	PIM/ Decision
Mattias Ohlund (VAN)	October 3, 1997 (Tokyo)	0	0	0	4
Dave Scatchard (VAN)	October 3, 1997 (Tokyo)	0	0	0	0
Greg Classen (NAS)	October 6, 2000 (Tokyo)	0	1	1	0
Scott Hartnell (NAS)	October 6, 2000 (Tokyo)	0	0	0	0
Roman Simicek (PIT)	October 6, 2000 (Tokyo)	0	0	0	4
Milan Kraft (PIT)	October 7, 2000 (Tokyo)	0	0	0	2
Josef Melichar (PIT)	October 7, 2000 (Tokyo)	0	0	0	0
Jonathan Bernier (LA)	September 29, 2007 (London)	59:59	1		W
Brady Murray (LA)	September 29, 2007 (London)	0	0	0	0
Bobby Ryan (ANA)	September 29, 2007 (London)	1	0	1	0
Jonas Hiller (ANA)	September 30, 2007 (London)	60:00	1		W
Paul Bissonnette (PIT)	October 4, 2008 (Stockholm)	0	0	0	0
Vladimir Mihalik (TB)	October 4, 2008 (Prague)	0	0	0	0
Janne Niskala (TB)	October 4, 2008 (Prague)	0	0	0	0
Steven Stamkos (TB)	October 4, 2008 (Prague)	0	0	0	0
Dmitri Kulikov (FLO)	October 2, 2009 (Helsinki)	0	0	0	0
Jordan Caron (BOS)	October 10, 2010 (Prague)	0	0	0	0
Maxime Macenauer (ANA)	October 7, 2011 (Helsinki)	0	1	1	0
Devante Smith-Pelly (ANA)	October 7, 2011 (Helsinki)	0	0	0	0

The NHL has periodically sent teams to Europe to play exhibition games and, starting in 1997, regular-season games. As a result, there is a small group of players who made their NHL debuts not in an NHL rink but in a rink in Europe.

Some unique notes from the 19 players to date who made their NHL debuts overseas:

// No European player has ever made his debut in his home country. The closest is defenceman Vladimir Mihalik of Tampa Bay, who played in Prague. Although he was born in the old Czechoslovakia, he is Slovakian, so there was a little extra special meaning playing in Prague.

Nothing to See Here, Folks

Christian Soucy

CHICAGO BLACKHAWKS // MARCH 31, 1994

Chicago coach Darryl Sutter used Christian Soucy to make a point, and a good thing he did because it was the only NHL action Soucy ever experienced.

The 23-year-old Soucy was undrafted, signed by the Hawks as a free agent, and called up from Indianapolis to act as Jeff Hackett's backup on March 31, 1994, a home game against Washington.

The Caps scored three times in the first period, throwing the coach into paroxysms of anger. He pulled Hackett after the last of those three, at 16:39, and Soucy entered the game.

Well, wouldn't you know it, the Hawks played better and didn't allow a shot the rest of the period. Sutter put Hackett back in to start the second, but the Caps went on to win, 6–3.

After playing just 3:21 at the end of that first period, Soucy went back to the minors, where he played for the better part of a decade, but he never got into another NHL game.

His stats line is all zeroes—no wins or losses, no goals allowed, no shots faced. He was there, but he wasn't.

One-Game-Wonder Goalies–Briefest Appearances	Mins	GA	Decision
Jorge Alves, Carolina Hurricanes, December 31, 2016	0:08	0	nd
Jordan Sigalet, Boston Bruins, January 7, 2006	0:43	0	nd
Martin Houle, Philadelphia Flyers, December 13, 2006	2:12	1	nd
Shawn Hunwick, Columbus Blue Jackets, April 7, 2012	2:33	0	nd
Mathieu Chouinard, Los Angeles Kings, February 29, 2004	2:43	0	nd
Rob McVicar, Vancouver Canucks, December 1, 2005	2:44	0	nd
Robbie Irons, St. Louis Blues, November 13, 1968	2:59	0	nd
Christian Soucy, Chicago Blackhawks, March 31, 1994	3:21	0	nd
Sean Gauthier, San Jose Sharks, March 6, 1999	3:29	0	nd
Brian Foster, Florida Panthers, February 4, 2012	4:52	0	nd
Jerome Mrazek, Philadelphia Flyers, February 7, 1976	6:17	1	nd
Riku Helenius, Tampa Bay Lightning, January 30, 2009	6:52	0	nd
Tom McGratton, Detroit Red Wings, November 9, 1947	7:40	1	nd
Joe Junkin, Boston Bruins, December 14, 1968	8:56	0	nd
Matt Keetley, Calgary Flames, November 5, 2007	9:22	0	nd
Corrie D'Alessio, Hartford Whalers, December 11, 1992	11:00	0	nd
Greg Redquest, Pittsburgh Penguins, March 19, 1978	12:47	3	nd
Jordan Binnington, St. Louis Blues, January 14, 2016	12:47	1	nd
Scott Foster, Chicago Blackhawks, March 29, 2018	14:01	0	nd
Tyler Weiman, Colorado Avalanche, October 4, 2007	15:46	0	nd
Jeremy Duchesne, Philadelphia Flyers, April 1, 2010	16:44	1	nd
Ken Brown, Chicago Black Hawks, March 31, 1971	17:49	1	nd
Olivier Michaud, Montreal Canadiens, October 30, 2001	18:05	0	nd

NOTES

// There have been 94 one-game-wonder goalies, of which 32 played the full game and 61 came in to replace the starting goalie. Only once, in the case of Jim Stewart, did a one-game-wonder goalie start the game and was pulled.

One-Game Wonders

There have been but 10 players who made their NHL debuts in the playoffs and then, as time would tell, turned out to be one-game wonders. And of those 10, nary a one was a goaltender and none recorded a point. They came and went quickly.

Not surprisingly, all 10 got into their playoff game because of either injury or the coach's desire to mix things up. Four of this number turned out to have participated in a Stanley Cup–winning run, but only one, Doug McKay, played in the finals and got his name on the hallowed trophy.

Gord Haidy is part of a small group of one-game wonders whose only game came in the playoffs.

// Buck Davies, New York Rangers
April 4, 1948

Davies was one of four players called up by the Rangers from New Haven for Game 6 of the semi-finals against Detroit (Nick Mickoski, Jack Lancien, and Dunc Fisher were the others), but the Red Wings didn't give him or anyone else on the Blueshirts a chance to shine. Detroit scored the only three goals of the first, came back with a scoreless second, and coasted to a 4–2 win to eliminate the Rangers and advance to the Stanley Cup Finals

// Gord Haidy, Detroit Red Wings
April 4, 1950

The 1940s belonged to the Toronto Maple Leafs, but the first half of the 1950s were the greatest years in the long history of the Detroit Red Wings. And, after losing to the Leafs in the playoffs in 1947, 1948, and 1949, the Wings exacted a measure of revenge in 1950—but it wasn't easy. The Leafs split the first two games of their semi-finals series in Detroit, and won Game 3 on home ice. If they won Game 4, their 3–1 series lead would be tough to overcome.

Making matters worse, the Wings had lost Gordie Howe to a serious injury in one of the most controversial plays in hockey history. In Game 1, Howe skated hard to check Ted Kennedy and fell head first into the boards. He suffered a fractured skull and nearly died.

Some reports indicated that Howe lost his balance in trying to hit Kennedy as hard as he could; other reports suggest Kennedy saw Howe at the last moment and tripped him. A photo in the *Detroit Free Press* days after showed Howe in hospital, bandages covering his head and right eye, his bed filled with fan letters encouraging his recovery. The headline said, "Howe Doesn't Blame Kennedy."

In Game 3, Jimmy Peters twisted his knee and returned to Detroit for treatment. As a result, coach Tommy Ivan summoned Gord Haidy from the farm team in Indianapolis. Haidy played on the third line and got a regular shift. The game went to overtime and Leo Reise scored the 2–1 winner for the Red Wings, tying the series.

For Haidy, though, the news was doubly bad. First, it seemed Peters would be healthy enough for Game 5, but also the Omaha Knights were eliminated from the USHL playoffs. GM Jack Adams scouted the farm team's final game and brought three new players to Detroit—defenceman Marcel Pronovost and brothers Johnny and Larry Wilson.

Haidy's playoffs were over, and as time would tell so was his NHL career. He skated for many more years in senior leagues, never to return to The Show. The Wings beat the Leafs and then the Rangers to win the Cup, but Haidy didn't play in the finals and didn't play enough to get his name on the Cup.

// Doug McKay, Detroit Red Wings
April 15, 1950

How's this for trivia? Doug McKay is part of a rare group of playoff one-game wonders, but he's the only one of this contingent whose only game was in the Stanley Cup Finals. And, to add a little mystery, he played in neither his home rink (the Detroit Olympia) nor the opponent's rink (New York's Madison Square Garden).

How is this possible?

In a unique playoffs, the New York Rangers played a seven-game finals with Detroit and never played a home game. Madison Square Garden had been booked by a circus, so Game 1 was played in Detroit, Games 2 and 3 at Maple Leaf Gardens in Toronto, and Games 4 through 7 back at the Olympia.

The Red Wings opened with a solid 4–1 win and followed with a lacklustre 3–1 loss. That loss prompted massive panic attacks by Jack Adams and coach Tommy Ivan. Holed up in a Hamilton hotel with owner Jim Norris, the triumvirate strategized a major shakeup for Game 3.

Marcel Pronovost, who had played so well, was benched, as were Steve Black, Pete Babando, and Larry Wilson. In their places would go Gord Haidy, who had made his NHL and playoff debut the previous series (see page 140), Jimmy Peters (recovered from an eye injury), and the aforementioned McKay, making his NHL debut.

That was the plan on game day, but by the time players went out onto the ice, Pronovost was in and Haidy out. McKay played a regular shift and the Red Wings cruised to a 4–0 win. McKay, however, never played in the NHL again, but the Wings won the Cup in seven games and McKay got his name on the hallowed trophy. In fact, Pete Babando scored in overtime of Game 7, the first time this had happened in NHL history.

// Don Cherry, Boston Bruins
March 31, 1955

The news was bad all around for Boston as it hoped to fight and claw its way back into the semi-finals series against Montreal in 1955. They were heading to the Forum, trailing 3–1 in games, so Game 5 was a win-or-go-home moment for the team.

Worse, their number-one goalie, Sugar Jim Henry, had had his cheek shattered by a Baldy McKay shot in Game 4, meaning the Bruins had to rely on 22-year-old John Henderson to save them.

As well, their top defenceman, Fern Flaman, suffered torn knee ligaments in that game, so coach Milt Schmidt called up another defenceman, Don Cherry. Tom Fitzgerald wrote the following introduction of the newcomer in the *Boston Globe*: "To fill the gap in the roster Schmidt will dress Don Cherry, rugged-looking 21-year-old Hershey farmhand."

Offered Bruins general manager Lynn Patrick: "He's a kid who can hit hard and who likes to hit."

Schmidt partnered Cherry, wearing number 24, with veteran Bill Quackenbush, but the youngster didn't distinguish himself and the Bruins lost easily, 5–1. Before the game, Boston scout Baldy Cotton was singing Cherry's praises and suggested the team was counting on him to step up and be a regular the following season.

By the time the next training camp came around, however, Cherry was back in the minors where he famously remained for the next 15 seasons. Reports are sparse, but it would seem he took a regular shift in his lone NHL contest. Warren Godfrey, who had a bad left wrist, was also a late scratch, leaving the Bruins with just five blueliners.

Don Cherry played only once in the NHL, but, of course, fans know him for his later colourful appearances on Coach's Corner.

Regardless, Cherry played enough to get into the record books as an NHLer who made his debut in the playoffs, and, most rarely, an NHL playoff one-game wonder.

Much later, he became the Grapes we all know from *Coach's Corner*.

// Jack Stanfield, Chicago Black Hawks
   April 14, 1966

Stanfield got into Game 4 of the 1966 Stanley Cup semi-finals between Chicago and Detroit, and he can thank Gordie Howe for that. Or perhaps Stan Mikita. Or, worst of all, Chico Maki. Or, ultimately, Doug Mohns.

In Game 3, Maki made a simple pass to Chicago teammate Mikita. Mikita was then checked by Howe, but he got the better of the great Red Wings star, which only got Howe angrier. Howe lunged at Mikita, who got out of the way. Howe instead fell onto Maki, and Maki suffered a knee injury and had to be carted off on a stretcher.

This injury, however, was not enough to get Stanfield into the lineup, nor was the injury to defenceman Moose Vasko. No, these players were replaced by Ken Hodge and John Miszuk.

But, when Doug Mohns was injured during the warmup and couldn't play, coach Billy Reay put both Stanfield and Dennis Hull into the game to fill in for the ever-reliable Mohns. The loss of three top players, though, was too great, and Detroit skated to an easy 5–1 win, tying the playoff series at two games each.

Stanfield didn't play a lot, but he can remember his first game because his brother, Fred, also played. Two years younger, Fred had a long NHL career. Jack, however, didn't dress again in this series. Detroit won Game 5, 5–3, and Game 6, 3–2, to win the Cup. Jack played for several years in the minors, but he never got another NHL chance.

Jack Stanfield (left) hams it up with teammate Gerry Melnyk.

// Chris Hayes, Boston Bruins
   April 23, 1972

Derek Sanderson had colitis, so Chris Hayes had a date with greatness that he will never forget.

The 1972 playoffs started with Boston taking out the Leafs in five games and St. Louis edging Minnesota in seven. That set up a Boston-St. Louis semi-finals that was a repeat of the 1970 finals, made famous by Bobby Orr's flying celebration after scoring the Cup-winning goal.

Two years later, not much had changed. The Bruins were still the dominant force, and the Blues couldn't hope to keep up with them. Indeed, Boston won the first two games by 6–1 and 10–2 clobberings, and Game 3 promised more of the same.

That's when Hayes stepped in. Sanderson couldn't play in Game 3, so Hayes, who had played with Oklahoma City in the CHL all season, was called in to take his place.

Wearing No. 29, Hayes found himself in the same dressing room as Orr, Phil Esposito, and Gerry Cheevers. The Bruins hammered the Blues again that night, 7–2, and although Hayes's stats sheet shows all zeroes, there is one asterisk.

At 7:25 of the first period, the Bruins were assessed a too-many-men penalty, and coach Tom Johnson tapped Hayes on the shoulder to serve the bench minor.

The Bruins went on to sweep the series and win the Stanley Cup, and Hayes's contribution to the victory was so negligible as to be forgotten. But, a longtime friend of his later informed the Bruins that Hayes had never received his Stanley Cup ring, so current club president Cam Neely went to work. In 2018, 46 years later, Hayes got his finger furniture.

One game, one Cup memory, one ring.

// Michel Deziel, Buffalo Sabres
   May 1, 1975

A promising prospect, Deziel was selected 47th overall by Buffalo in the 1974 Amateur Draft. He spent that 1974–75 season in the AHL, with Hershey, but during the playoffs the Sabres called him up.

In the post-season, the Sabres easily beat Chicago in five games in the quarter-finals, setting up a semi-finals date with Montreal. Back in the day that series was called Series I while the other semis between Philadelphia and the Islanders was Series J.

Michel Deziel's NHL career was only one game long, but it came in the 1975 playoffs.

Buffalo won the first two games on home ice and ventured to the Forum for Games 3 and 4. Deziel played in Game 3, but the Habs hammered Buffalo to the tune of 7–0. Not only did Deziel never play again in the series, he never played again in the NHL.

// Dave Salvian, New York Islanders
April 7, 1977

The preliminary round best-of-three between the Islanders and Black Hawks had a twist. The Islanders won the first game, 5–2, and the teams were expected to go to Chicago for Game 2. However, a previously booked Led Zeppelin concert rendered the stadium unavailable for hockey, so the Nassau Coliseum hosted Chicago's home game.

Called up from Fort Worth of the CHL, Salvian was with the Islanders but not expected to play. Then, just before the start, J-P Parise declared himself unfit because of a knee injury, and just like that, 21-year-old Salvian was in the lineup.

"I didn't expect to play," Salvian acknowledged. "It was some thrill."

The Islanders won, 2–1, and Salvian assisted on the team's first goal from Jude Drouin late in the opening period, tying the game, 1–1.

But it was Chicago goalie Tony Esposito who was the star of the game, keeping the score tight despite facing 38 shots. Indeed, he stopped all 16 in the third period and earned an ovation from the Nassau Coliseum fans as well as many Islanders players.

"Incredible," Salvian said of Esposito's performance. "I have to go back tomorrow to begin our playoffs against Kansas City, but I don't expect to find any goaltending like that."

Although coach Al Arbour was also generous in praise ("He handled himself well"), Salvian was sent back to the farm the next day—and he never made it back to The Show.

// Brock Tredway, Los Angeles Kings
April 19, 1982

The Smythe Division finals of the 1982 playoffs featured Los Angeles and Vancouver. The Canucks were ahead two games to one as teams prepared for Game 4 at the Fabulous Forum in Los Angeles on April 19, 1982.

These were the days when the two home games in a city were played on consecutive nights, so injuries and replacements were more frequent. Game 3 saw Jim Fox of the Kings suffer a charley-horse injury. With another game the next night,

he couldn't play, so Tredway, who had played with the team's AHL affiliate in New Haven all year, got the call.

His presence was to no avail. The Canucks won, 5–4, and they eliminated the Kings in Game 6 back in Vancouver. Tredway didn't play in that game, skated for three more seasons with the Nighthawks, and retired in 1986.

// Igor Nikulin, Mighty Ducks of Anaheim
April 27, 1997

The Phoenix Coyotes were in the driver's seat of this Western Conference quarter-finals matchup. They won Game 5 to take a 3-2 series lead and were coming home with a chance to eliminate Anaheim, but the Ducks were having none of it. Coach Ron Wilson made two changes, one to the blue line, one up front. He scratched defenceman Dan Trebil and dressed Darren van Impe, and he also removed forward Sean Pronger in favour of Nikulin.

The Coyotes had to fight back late in the game to tie the score, 2–2, and force overtime, but Paul Kariya's second goal of the game, off a lovely pass from Teemu Selanne, gave the Ducks the win. Anaheim also won Game 7, eliminating the 'Yotes and ending their season in the desert.

Nikulin had played in the IHL and AHL this regular season and was with the Ducks as insurance during the playoffs. He didn't see a great deal of ice time this game, and didn't play at all in the next series, a four-game sweep by Detroit. After realizing he wasn't going to get another chance at the NHL, Nikulin returned home to play in Russia for several years.

Playoff One-Game Wonders				
Player	Team	Date of Only Game	Result–Series	Series Summary
Buck Davies	NYR	April 4, 1948	L–SF	Game 6 of 6 (lost)
Gord Haidy	DET	April 4, 1950	W–SF	Game 4 of 7 (won)
Doug McKay	DET	April 15, 1950	W–SF	Game 3 of 7 (won)
Don Cherry	BOS	March 31, 1955	L–SF	Game 5 of 5 (lost)
Jack Stanfield	CHI	April 14, 1966	L–SF	Game 4 of 6 (lost)
Chris Hayes	BOS	April 23, 1972	W–SF	Game 3 of 4 (won)
Michel Deziel	BUF	May 1, 1975	L–SF	Game 3 of 6 (win)
Dave Salvian	NYI	April 7, 1977	W–Pre	Game 2 of 2 (won)
Brock Tredway	LA	April 19, 1982	L–DF	Game 4 of 5 (lost)
Igor Nikulin	MDA	April 27, 1997	W–CQF	Game 6 of 7 (won)

21st Century Firsts

Kyle Freadrich

TAMPA BAY LIGHTNING // JANUARY 1, 2000

Kyle Freadrich can lay claim to being the first player to make his debut in the 21st century—although not by much. January 1, 2000, fell on a Saturday, and the first games on the NHL slate were a San Jose at Nashville matchup at 2:30 p.m. ET and a Florida at Tampa Bay game with a start 30 minutes later.

Freadrich was called up from the Detroit Vipers to play for the Lightning. The behemoth stood six-foot-seven and tipped the proverbial Toledos at 250 pounds, and he was

Kyle Freadrich has the distinction of being the first newcomer to the league in the 21st century.

recalled because the last time the two teams met, just a few days earlier, things got out of hand. Tampa coach Steve Ludzik wanted to be sure they had a big guy in the lineup to prevent a repeat beating.

The numbers told the tale. Freadrich had played 27 games with the Vipers, incurring 127 penalty minutes and recording not a single point. He goaded Florida tough guy Peter Worrell into taking a roughing penalty in the first period and then himself took a roughing penalty in the third.

In all, Freadrich played just 2:54 in the game, won by the Panthers, 7–5, and extending the Lightning's winless streak to eight games.

Meanwhile, in Nashville, goalie Evgeni Nabokov took over for Steve Shields in the Sharks net early in the third period after the Predators scored to make it a 3–1 game. This was Nabokov's first game, but his appearance didn't happen until about 4:30 p.m. ET, a good hour after Freadrich's debut.

Nabokov played the final 15:06 of his game, stopping the only four shots he faced, and a brief Sharks rally ended in a 3–2 loss. Shields was saddled with the loss, but Freadrich narrowly beat Nabokov to claim the distinction of being the first new player of the new century.

Lots of Rubber

Legace and Brossoit Sparkle

Of the 775 goalies who have played in the NHL, two have the distinction of having made the most saves in their first game. Although a shutout is a rare achievement, of course, a first-game goalie who has to face 50 shots or more is exceptional.

Manny Legace, Los Angeles Kings / October 21, 1998

It started with an injury to number-one goalie Stephane Fiset a few days earlier. The backup, Jamie Storr, then became the go-to puckstopper. But he, too, was injured later in the same game, so the Los Angeles Kings recalled Stephane Fiset from the Long Beach Ice Dogs of the IHL to start the road game on October 21, 1998, against Florida, the team's fifth game of the new season. As well, 18-year-old Alexei Volkov was recalled from Halifax of the QMJHL to serve as Legace's backup.

> As it turned out, Legace stole the show. The Panthers dominated the game and outshot the Kings by a 50-19 margin, yet 60 minutes of regulation and another five of overtime produced a 1-1 tie.

"I've got to give their goaltender a lot of credit," noted Florida coach Terry Murray. "He's on an emergency recall situation. Fifty shots. I'll give him a lot of marks."

"I would rather face a lot more shots than just stand there," Legace offered. "Personally, my mind would start to wander if I got only nine shots in the first two periods," he added, in reference to the Kings' shot tally through 40 minutes. Indeed, shots after two periods were 29-9 in favour of Florida, but the score was 1–1.

> The 49 saves marks the most in NHL history for a goalie's debut, matched only by Laurent Brossoit nearly 17 years later.

Laurent Brossoit, Edmonton Oilers / April 9, 2015

Although Brossoit allowed two goals to Legace's one and lost the game in regulation, he holds the record for most shots faced by a goalie in his debut—51.

In Brossoit's case, it was a matter of one man's birth being another man's NHL debut. That is, Edmonton's Richard Bachman, himself a recent call-up, was sent back to the Oklahoma City Barons so that he could be with his wife, who was about to give birth. That allowed for Brossoit to be recalled from the same Barons, for which he had made 25 consecutive starts, to face the San Jose Sharks in an NHL game.

Said interim head coach Todd Nelson: "He's had a lot of growth. Just like any young goalie, there was some inconsistency, but he put together a really good stretch [with Oklahoma City]. He's been controlling play. He's been very efficient in net."

It was the final home game of the season for the Oilers, another terrible year that saw them finish out of the playoffs again. Brossoit was amazing. He stopped the first 41 shots he faced into the third period, but the Oilers' tenuous 1–0 lead vanished when Patrick Marleau finally beat the rookie.

Seven minutes later, Bryan Lerg, in his debut, scored. The Sharks added an empty-netter and won, 3–1, despite the heroics of Brossoit.

"It's something you look forward to, something I wanted to happen all year, and to be honest, I couldn't be happier," the 22-year-old said after. "But it's just one game. It's not going to make or break my career. I'm not going to put too much emphasis on it."

Edmonton goalie Laurent Brossoit faced a record 51 shots in his NHL debut.

Sid vs. Ovi—Day One

**Sidney Crosby (Pittsburgh Penguins)
and Alexander Ovechkin
(Washington Capitals)
Debut in Parallel Universes
October 5, 2005**

October 5, 2005, saw a record 45 players make their first NHL appearance, a number bolstered by the lost season of 2004–05 when not one game was played, not one player debuted, and the Stanley Cup was not awarded. As well, helping to bump the numbers, all 30 teams were in action to signal the return of the NHL.

> The list of great players to debut on October 5 was impressive, including Corey Perry, Ryan Getzlaf, Duncan Keith, Zach Parise, and Dion Phaneuf. But really, only two names mattered—Sidney Crosby and Alexander Ovechkin.

It was a match made in heaven, a rivalry so natural it needed no hype to be special. It was a matchup that began in 1954, when the Soviet Union played in its first ever World Championship and defeated Canada. It grew to unheard-of heights in September 1972 when the Summit Series was played, and it continued through 1987 when the Canada Cup finals produced what many say were the three greatest games ever played.

And yet when the Soviet Union gave way to Russia in the early 1990s and Russian players joined the NHL in record numbers, there was no one-on-one rivalry like Crosby and Ovechkin. Gretzky and Bure? Hardly. Lemieux and Mogilny? Nope.

But Ovechkin was drafted first overall by Washington in 2004 and Crosby a year later by Pittsburgh. Ovechkin's NHL debut was delayed a year by the lockout, and so on October 5, 2005, the two top prospects started their careers. Canada versus Russia, the individual player version.

There was a difference, though. Crosby was the face of the post-lockout NHL. He was that special player who followed in the Canadian footsteps of Orr, Gretzky, and Lemieux. Ovechkin had talent, of course, but Russians were always considered enigmatic, and his grasp of English then wasn't great, so fans could only watch and wait and see if he turned out to be as good as he might be. Crosby was destined to be as good as expected, if not better.

The Penguins started their 2005–06 season in New Jersey, and on Crosby's first shift he had a great scoring chance, but his backhand—the shot for which he has become famous—was stopped by Martin Brodeur, the Hall of Famer who holds virtually every important goaltender record.

In the end, the Devils cruised to a 5–1 win, but late in the third period Crosby picked up an assist on the team's only goal of the night, a shot by Mark Recchi from in close. In all, Crosby was a -2 on the night, played nearly 16 minutes,

Sidney Crosby's debut changed the fortunes of the Pittsburgh Penguins franchise.

and had three shots. It was a solid beginning, but nothing other-worldly.

"I think I played well, but it's my first game, and I'm still getting my feet wet," the 18-year-old Crosby said after.

Meanwhile, in Washington, Ovechkin scored twice to lead the Capitals to a 3–2 come-from-behind win over Columbus. The Blue Jackets led 1–0 midway through the second period when Ovechkin scored what can only be described as a typical goal, wiring a one-timer from the high slot off a pass from Dainius Zubrus in the corner and beating Pascal Leclaire before the goalie knew what had happened.

Four and a half minutes later, Ovi scored number two. On a power play, the Caps moved the puck around well, and Leclaire made a nice save going down. The puck came to Jeff Halpern, and he made a great back-door pass to the young Russian, who found the wide-open net to score again.

The rivalry has taken many forms over the last decade and a half, Crosby winning all international games in which the two have played, and both players have accomplished pretty much what everyone might have expected.

They started their careers on the same day, but likely won't finish on the same day. They have been the defining players of their generation, and they have dealt with pressure and expectations that few have experienced.

Alexander Ovechkin scored two goals in his first game—and never looked back.

Brotherly Tandems

Of all of the hundreds of brothers to have played in the NHL, six are very special because the brothers made their debuts together, on the same night and with the same team. It doesn't get more memorable than that.

// Bill and Bun Cook, New York Rangers
November 16, 1926

See page 14

// Des and Earl Roche, Montreal Maroons
November 11, 1930

Opening night of the 1930–31 NHL season saw a weak Montreal Maroons team visit Ottawa. In Montreal's lineup were brothers Des and Earl Roche, replacing the injured Babe Siebert and Archie Wilcox.

Earl played on a line with Nels Stewart and Hooley Smith, but that threesome did little to create many dangerous chances. Des didn't play very much, and the home-town Senators skated to a convincing 2–0 win. The brothers played several games together this year and again in later years with Ottawa and St. Louis.

// Conrad and Jean Bourcier, Montreal Canadiens
December 19, 1935

Something had to be done. The Canadiens had not won in nine games (managing three ties), so coach Sylvio Mantha decided to scratch Wildor Larochelle and Paul Runge and call up newcomers Conrad and Jean Bourcier from the Verdun Maple Leafs for a game against Chicago. Mantha put Conrad at centre, Jean on the left wing, and rookie Joffre Desilets on the right side to form a Kid Line of sorts.

Jean and Desilets teamed with Pit Lepine for the game's first goal, midway through the opening period, when Lepine's long shot trickled over the goal line past Mike Karakas. In the second, they counted again, Lepine getting his second and Bourcier drawing an assist.

The Hawks scored twice in the third to tie the game, though, and 10 minutes of overtime solved nothing. Another tie, another game without a win for the Habs. But the Bourcier brothers, who often played on a line together, had an excellent night in their co-debuts.

// Johnny and Larry Wilson, Detroit Red Wings
February 15, 1950

In 1949–50, Detroit and Chicago were heading in opposite directions. The Red Wings had a core of exceptional talent that was on the verge of winning the Stanley Cup four times in six years, and the Black Hawks were a last-place team that was to remain in the basement for quite some time.

As the season was drawing to a close, the Red Wings were comfortably in first place in the standings and the Hawks clearly in last. In their previous meeting, Detroit had won, 9–2. As a result, general manager Jack Adams decided not to dress Ted Lindsay, the league's top point-getter, and he relegated captain Sid Abel to a sub. That meant two-thirds of the famed Production Line (Gordie Howe being the third) would not play much of a role in the encounter in Chicago on February 15, 1950.

Adams called up two farmhands from Omaha for the game, and what made that decision particularly special was that they were brothers—Johnny and Larry Wilson.

It was a memorable night for the duo—for the obvious reasons—but also one they'd like to forget. The Hawks won the game, 3–0, and neither Wilson made a big impression. Larry, a centreman, and Johnny, a winger, were both demoted after the game and didn't see the NHL again for two years.

// Anton and Peter Stastny, Quebec Nordiques
October 9, 1980

It wasn't just a game, and it wasn't just about brothers. On this night, history, politics, and skates mixed together. The Stastnys didn't just make their NHL debuts together this night; they beat a political system, and they risked their lives doing so. Anton and Peter defected from Czechoslovakia to play for Quebec in the NHL, leaving behind a brother, Marian, and the rest of their family to an uncertain future.

The opener to the 1980–81 season took place in Calgary, and that was also special. The Atlanta Flames had left town and moved north to Alberta, so the game of October 9, 1980, was also the franchise's first.

It wasn't pretty. The Flames had a 4–1 lead but let it slip away as the Nordiques rallied for a 5–5 tie. Anton and Peter played on a line with Jacques Richard, but the trio was held in check most of the night. Richard scored late in the second on a pass from Peter to complete the comeback and make it 4–4.

Calgary coach Al MacNeil and Quebec coach Maurice Filion got into a strategic war. MacNeil wanted to match lines, so he put the trio of Don Lever–Bill Clement–Brad Smith out against the Stastnys and Richard. In turn, Filion started playing his top line every other shift, meaning his best players were out the most and MacNeil had to sit his best trio in the name of his checking line. In the end, though, it worked out for MacNeil. "That was a line that really concerned us, and I thought we handled them pretty well," MacNeil said.

// Daniel and Henrik Sedin, Vancouver Canucks
October 5, 2000

There have been only five sets of twins who have played in the NHL, each different in their own way. Rich and Ron Sutter were the first to play together; Patrik and Peter Sundstrom were the first Europeans; Chris and Peter Ferraro almost never didn't play together; Henrik and Joel Lundqvist represented a goalie (Henrik) and a forward; and Daniel and Henrik Sedin were the cornerstones of a new era in Vancouver.

"Of course it was tough," said Daniel, after a 6–3 opening night loss to Philadelphia in which he and brother Henrik were held off the scoresheet. "These are the best players in the world, and we have to get used to it. You have to do everything quite a bit faster."

"Twins tip-toe to loss" blared the unkind headline in the *Vancouver Province*. Daniel wore number 22 and Henrik number 33, symbolic of their order of selection in the 1999 Entry Draft (Daniel was selected second overall and Henrik third).

"I was nervous, then I felt pretty good," said Henrik. "Maybe in 20 or 30 games we won't think so much about it and just go out and play."

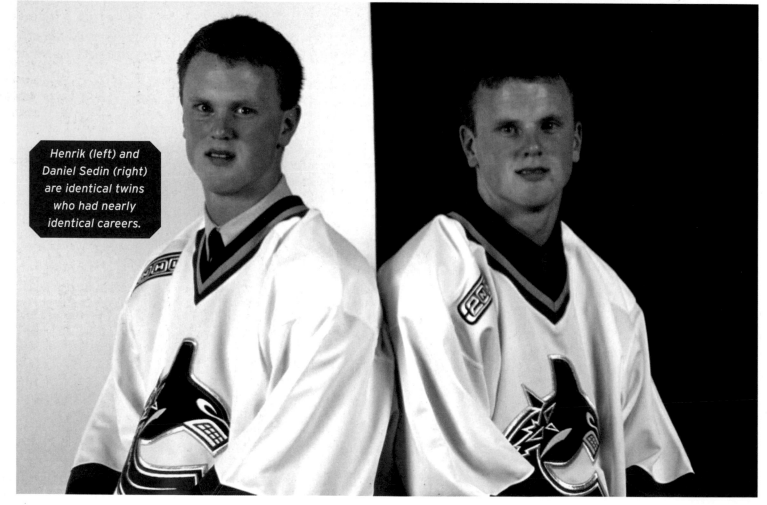

Henrik (left) and Daniel Sedin (right) are identical twins who had nearly identical careers.

Brothers Bill Cook (left) and Bun Cook (right) made their NHL debuts together and were terrific on a line with Frank Boucher (middle).

Goalie Assists

Of the 1,463 players who recorded at least one point in their NHL debuts, only nine are goalies.

// Rick Heinz, St. Louis Blues
January 10, 1981

Rick Heinz not only wasn't even supposed to play against the L.A. Kings on this night, he didn't want to play. He was called up from Salt Lake City because Blues backup goalie Ed Stanowski had suffered a shoulder injury the day before this game, but Heinz understood that Mike Liut would start the game.

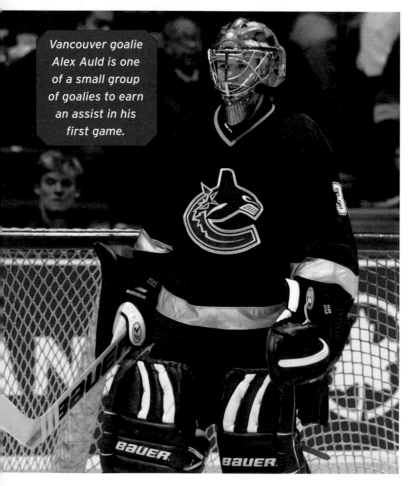

Vancouver goalie Alex Auld is one of a small group of goalies to earn an assist in his first game.

The trouble was that early in the game Liut took a shot from Mike Murphy right in the crown jewels. After a lengthy delay, he managed to finish the period but allowed four goals and clearly wasn't himself. As a result, Heinz was forced into action.

"When Mike got hurt, I said to myself, 'C'mon, you gotta get up,'" Heinz admitted after the game. "I played last night in Oklahoma City and faced a lot of rubber—46 shots. I was pretty tired and really didn't want to play."

But play he did—and well. Although the Blues trailed 4–2 after 20 minutes, they rallied to make it a 6–6 game by the end of the night. Along the way, Heinz stopped 12 of 14 shots, including a clear-cut chance by Marcel Dionne, one of the greatest scorers of all time. "The way it worked out, I'm glad I got a chance to play. You can't believe what a thrill it is, but it was pretty scary, especially when Dionne had that breakaway."

The back-and-forth game didn't get its last goal until 15:23 of the third, and it came when St. Louis forward Jorgen Pettersson scored off an L.A. player. Heinz touched the puck on the play, earning the first ever goalie assist in an NHL debut, making his memorable night even better.

// Bob Froese, Philadelphia Flyers
January 8, 1983

On January 6, the Flyers hosted a touring Soviet team that hammered the Flyers, 5–1. During the game, goalie Pelle Lindbergh also suffered a wrist injury. That forced the team to recall 24-year-old Froese from the Maine Mariners, where he had been playing well.

The Flyers were in Hartford two nights later, and the newcomer got the start over Lindbergh's backup, Rick St. Croix, for two reasons. One, St. Croix had played only once in two months, so he was rusty. Two, because he had lost the starter's job to Lindbergh, St. Croix was upset and had asked for a trade.

Led by Darryl Sittler's hat trick, the Flyers beat the Whalers, 7–4, their seventh straight road victory and their eighth in a row overall. Froese got his assist midway through the first period on a Bill Barber goal, moving the puck up to defenceman Brad McCrimmon who set up Barber.

Froese stopped 20 of 24 shots, got the win, and earned an assist. Not a bad NHL debut.

One day Jason Bacashihua was playing with the Peoria Rivermen (above) and the next he was in the NHL with St. Louis.

// Ron Tugnutt, Quebec Nordiques
December 29, 1987

"He played a heck of a game," said Buffalo head coach Ted Sator of Quebec Nordiques goalie, Ron Tugnutt, who stopped 29 of 30 shots in a 5–1 win in his first game. And the icing on the cake was that the goalie also assisted on Peter Stastny's second-period goal, the 300th of his illustrious career.

// Mike Greenlay, Edmonton Oilers
February 25, 1990

Grant Fuhr? Injured. Bill Ranford? Injured. Pokey Reddick? Injured, too. With nowhere else to turn, the Edmonton Oilers recalled 21-year-old Mike Greenlay from the Cape Breton Oilers for their Sunday evening game in Calgary.

As it turned out, Reddick and his two bruised shoulders deemed themselves healthy enough to start, and Greenlay almost didn't dress. His equipment got lost

en route from the east coast and didn't arrive until an hour before game time. Ranford had already started to dress as backup and was relieved when Greenlay's armour arrived.

Just as well. The Flames pumped six goals past the wounded 'tender, and coach John Muckler put the healthy but untested Greenlay in to start the third period. Greenlay, however, didn't fare any better, allowing four goals on just 17 shots, but he did earn an impressive assist on Craig MacTavish's league-best sixth short-handed goal early in the final period.

"Overall, I guess I was okay," Greenlay said. "I knew when I came in, I wasn't going to be the difference whether we won or lost. But I had a reputation from the minors to uphold."

// David Goverde, Los Angeles Kings
December 26, 1991

Called up from New Haven for Los Angeles' first game after the holiday break, Goverde couldn't have been happier. "I've got to rate this with the best Christmas presents I've ever had," he said after leading the struggling Kings to an impressive 5–3 win over San Jose. And to make the victory all the sweeter, he earned an assist on Wayne Gretzky's empty-net goal with 64 seconds remaining in the game.

The 21-year-old Goverde stopped 28 of 31 shots on the night. "It doesn't happen too often that I'm nervous the whole game," he said. "Usually it goes away, but tonight it didn't."

Goverde got the start again three days later in Calgary, gave up six goals, and didn't play again all season. In fact, he has but five career games to his credit, but he also has that one assist on a goal by No. 99. Even more impressive, of all goalie assists in NHL debuts, his is the only one that's the lone assist.

// Joaquin Gage, Edmonton Oilers
May 1, 1995

With two games left in a regular season delayed by a lockout, the Oilers needed to win both contests and get help along the way in order to qualify for the playoffs. Yet, with everything on the line, their top goalie, Bill Ranford, was out with back spasms that wouldn't go away.

Gage got the call-up from Cape Breton for this game against the visiting Maple Leafs, but Ranford's backup, Fred Brathwaite, got the start. He gave up four goals in the first period, though, putting the Oilers in a 4–1 hole after 20 minutes. With the season on the line, Gage came out to start the second, and the Oilers promptly rallied to tie the game, 4–4. Shayne Corson's goal early in the second got the rally going, and it was on that play that Gage earned an assist.

The Leafs went up 5–4, but Edmonton tied it seconds later. But Mats Sundin spoiled the party, scoring a power-play goal on a wicked shot late in the third that the Oilers couldn't match. A 6–5 loss meant the season was over.

"I wanted more than anything in the world to win this game," a dejected Gage said after. "I'd stopped [Sundin] on three really good chances. On this one, I yelled to Luke [Richardson] I couldn't see the puck. I moved to the short side, and Luke got out of the way. If I'd stayed there, the puck probably would have hit me."

Rick DiPietro made history in 2000 as the first goalie ever selected first overall at the NHL Entry Draft.

// Rick DiPietro, New York Islanders
January 27, 2001

The first ever goalie to be selected first overall at the NHL Entry Draft, Rick DiPietro was supposed to be the next great thing in the blue ice when the Islanders chose him in the summer of 2000. He spent the first half of the succeeding 2000–01 season with Chicago in the IHL, then played for the U.S. at the 2001 World Junior Championship in Russia. He was called up to play against the Buffalo Sabres on January 27, 2001, because John Vanbiesbrouck's back spasms wouldn't go away.

The 19-year-old DiPietro played well, but the Isles trailed 1–0 after two periods. Early in the third, though, he helped the team tie the game. DiPietro controlled the puck near his goal and fired a long pass up to Claude Lapointe. Lapointe fed Dave Scatchard, who scored. DiPietro had his first career point.

"One of his strongest points is his ability to handle the puck," Scatchard noted. "The older he gets, the better he's going to get at it, and he's pretty great right now."

Unfortunately, the Sabres scored a minute later, and then with four minutes left in the game, DiPietro, suffering from dehydration, had to call it a night.

// Alex Auld, Vancouver Canucks
January 23, 2002

Auld had a tempting taste of NHL life earlier in the month when he was recalled from the Manitoba Moose of the AHL, but he didn't get to play. A bit later, when Dan Cloutier hurt his left ankle, Auld's chances improved because that injury seemed more serious.

Indeed, Auld started on January 23, in Dallas, and was excellent, turning aside 20 of 22 shots. He even assisted on Markus Naslund's empty netter to seal the 4–2 victory.

// Jason Bacashihua, St. Louis Blues
December 16, 2005

Expecting to sit on the bench as backup to Curtis Sanford in Chicago, Bacashihua had to do a mental flip-flop when the starter was injured in the second period and couldn't continue. The Hawks were leading, 2–0, and just six minutes later Bacashihua earned an assist on a goal by Dean McAmmond that brought the Blues to within a goal.

Soon after, the Hawks made it 3–1, though. They added an empty netter in the third, and then scored again at 19:58. In all, Bacashihua stopped 14 of 16 shots but did not take the loss.

Blinded by the Light

Mikko Lehtonen

NASHVILLE PREDATORS // OCTOBER 7, 2006

An "old" rookie, Mikko Lehtonen didn't play his first NHL game until he was 28.

The Nashville Predators lost their 2006–07 season opener to Chicago by an 8–5 score to Chicago, prompting coach Barry Trotz to make some changes for their second game, in Minnesota, a couple of nights later.

Out was defenceman Greg Zanon, and in his place was Mikko Lehtonen, a 28-year-old who had played pro in Finland for the previous seven seasons. "Minnesota is a fast team, and he's got some good speed," Trotz explained of the change. "We've got to find out a little bit about him, and that's a change we felt we could make."

Wearing No. 42, Lehtonen opened the scoring, putting the puck past Nicklas Backstrom at 1:41 of the opening period on a long shot. More incredible, it was just eight seconds into his first career shift, and it came on his first ever shot.

The defenceman played 9:14 over 13 shifts and had one other shot. The Preds lost, 6–5, but his incredibly quick first goal was something to remember. Amazingly, Lehtonen didn't score again. Some 14 games later, he was sent to the AHL and was later traded, and at the end of the season he returned to Finland. He attained his NHL dream, but to the tune of exactly one goal.

The Great Dane

Frans Nielsen

NEW YORK ISLANDERS // JANUARY 6, 2007

By birth certificate, Poul Popiel was the first Dane to make it to the NHL. But his family moved to Canada when he was small, and he didn't start playing hockey until he arrived in his new homeland and gained a Canadian passport.

Frans Nielsen was different, though. Born in Herning, he started skating in Denmark, developed there before moving to Sweden to start his professional career, and has played for Denmark internationally on many occasions.

Indeed, he is the first truly Danish player to make it to the NHL. Drafted 87th by the New York Islanders in 2002, shortly after his first year with Malmo in Sweden, Nielsen did not come to North America until he was 22. In the interim, he played in Sweden and represented Denmark at several World Championships during an historic period for the small hockey nation.

The Danes hadn't played at the top level of the Worlds since 1949, when they experienced the worst loss in the tournament's A Pool history,

47–0, to Canada. They struggled in lower divisions for decades, but after 54 years, thanks to Nielsen and others, they earned promotion to the top level for 2003.

Nielsen came to the Islanders' training camp in the fall of 2006 and was assigned to Bridgeport of the AHL, but during a losing streak early in the new year, he got the call to go to Carolina for a road game. The 'Canes handed the Islanders their sixth loss in a row, 4–2, and Nielsen played just 7:38 of game time.

Nevertheless, he has developed into a superb two-way centreman, now on the cusp of playing his 1,000th career game, and he has inspired several other Danes to reach for the sky.

Since 2007, another 10 Danes have made it, and the country has maintained its place in the top level of the World Championship every year since 2003.

Frans Nielsen made Danish history—and many have followed since.

Wonder Brothers

Jordan and Jonathan Sigalet

Another unique chapter in the story of the NHL is the Sigalet brothers, Jordan and Jonathan, from British Columbia. They are the only brothers who are both one-game wonders. Their reasons and experiences, though, were different.

Jordan was a goalie. Five years older than Jonathan, he was drafted a lowly 209th overall by Boston in 2001, before starting his NCAA career at Bowling State. In his final year, he was diagnosed with multiple sclerosis but continued to play, proving an inspiration to people with MS everywhere.

After he graduated in 2005, the Bruins assigned him to their farm team in Providence, but on January 7, 2006, he was recalled to act as backup for Andrew Raycroft, who was starting in place of the injured Hannu Toivonen.

The game went along, nothing special. The Bruins were cruising, leading 5–3, when Pat Leahy scored into an empty net with 42.5 seconds remaining to make it 6–3. But as the team celebrated the goal, Raycroft skated to the Bruins bench and left the ice. He had tweaked his knee a bit earlier and didn't want to risk worsening a potential injury. Sigalet came on and played the final seconds, not facing a shot.

"My leg just kind of got stuck in the post, and I rolled on it a little bit," Raycroft explained. "It's not my knee. It's just a bit of a tweak, just below it. It's not a big deal. I just didn't want to make it much worse."

Sigalet was sent back down after the game and a year later collapsed during an AHL game. He retired soon after.

His brother, Jonathan, also went to Bowling Green and was drafted by the same Bruins, 100th overall in 2005. The brothers were also teammates in Providence, and almost a year to the date that Jordan got into his game, Jonathan was recalled.

On January 9, 2007, Jonathan was told to fly to Ottawa for the game that night against the Senators. A defenceman, he was needed because Zdeno Chara was injured and Brad Stuart was with his wife, who was in labour with their first baby.

Sigalet was paired with Matt Lashoff as the third defensive unit. He played 14:41 over the course of the game and incurred two minor penalties in the second period, neither of which resulted in a goal. Still, Ottawa won handily, 5–2.

"We wanted to have a look at Jonathan . . . and felt this was our chance to do it," said Bruins GM Peter Chiarelli.

It was a brief look. Sigalet was sent down before the team's next game, and although he has continued to play since, he has never had another NHL appearance.

As a result, Jordan and Jonathan Sigalet are the only one-game wonder brothers in NHL history.

A Japanese First

Yutaka Fukufuji

LOS ANGELES KINGS // JANUARY 13, 2007

Yutaka Fukufuji grew up in Kushiro, a town in the Hokkaido region of Japan where most of the nation's hockey activity is centred. He made his way to the Cincinnati Cyclones of the ECHL, signing as a free agent in 2002 at the age of 20.

Fukufuji returned home after a year, but he had made enough of an impression that the L.A. Kings used a late draft choice to select him 238th overall in 2004 and assigned him to the Bakersfield Condors in the ECHL.

In 2006–07, Lady Luck was on his side. The pecking order for L.A. Kings goalies had Mathieu Garon as the starter and Dan Cloutier as the backup, but Cloutier underwent surgery on a torn labrum in his hip. The Kings had Jason LaBarbera in the minors, but he'd have to clear waivers to

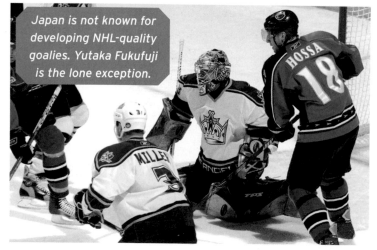

Japan is not known for developing NHL-quality goalies. Yutaka Fukufuji is the lone exception.

be recalled, and the Kings were sure he'd be claimed. As a result, Barry Brust, LaBarbera's backup in Manchester (AHL), moved up in the team's rankings and was given a chance to dress as Garon's backup. But on December 16, Cloutier couldn't play, so Brust got the start and Fukufuji was recalled on an emergency basis (but never played).

A month later, Garon suffered a finger injury and Brust got the start for a road game in St. Louis, and Fukufuji again dressed as the backup. But after the Kings were trailing, 5–4, through 40 minutes, coach Marc Crawford decided to put Fukufuji between the pipes for the final period.

Dennis Wideman scored at 7:32 for St. Louis, giving the Blues a 6–4 lead, but Fukufuji had a bit of bad luck when his own teammate, Rob Blake, scored on the power play with five minutes remaining.

Why was this bad luck? Because the Kings never got the tying goal, meaning Wideman's goal was the winner and Fukufuji, who faced only five shots, took the loss by allowing just the one goal.

"I was so nervous, but I was very excited, too," the goalie said after the game, his historic appearance now in the record books.

Debuts Far from Home

The date was September 29, 2007. The teams were the Stanley Cup champion Los Angeles Kings and division rivals Anaheim Ducks.

The location: O2 Arena in London, England. For the first time in NHL history, regular-season games were being played outside North America.

As well, for the first and still only time, some four NHLers made their career debuts outside North America. The four in question were Anaheim's Bobby Ryan and Brady Murray and 19-year-old goaltender Jonathan Bernier of L.A. Jonas Hiller made his debut one night later in the second of the two games in London.

Brady Murray (left) made his debut in London, England, with Los Angeles.

Making it doubly special, this marked the earliest NHL debuts in league history. No players before or since have played their first games in September.

These were the first games of the 2007–08 season, and the Kings won the opener, 4–1. Ryan, also 19, got the only goal for the Ducks, adding to the historic night, and Bernier stopped 26 of 27 shots to earn the European win. The 23-year-old Murray was held pointless.

Bernier earned the start after a strong training camp, but he played only three more games over the next couple of weeks (all losses) and was returned to junior. Still, he became the first goalie to make his NHL debut outside North America, and win.

Ryan also played only four games before being sent to the minors, while Murray was a more interesting case. The son of coach Andy Murray, he played two years of college before moving to Switzerland to continue his career. The Kings signed him, but four games later sent him to the minors. Murray returned to Switzerland the following year, where he stayed for the remainder of his career.

The next night, the teams reversed the score, 4–1, for the Ducks, and Swiss goalie Hiller stopped 22 of 23 shots to earn his first win in his first game, also at the O2 Arena.

Fighting to Make the Show

David Koci

CHICAGO BLACKHAWKS // MARCH 10, 2007

One of the very few European NHLers who was truly nothing more than a fighter, David Koci was determined to make the NHL, and when he did he left nothing to chance.

Drafted 146th overall by Pittsburgh in 2000, Koci, who was born in Prague, Czechoslovakia, moved to Canada and played a year of junior in the WHL with Prince George. A year later he was in the ECHL and then AHL, where he settled in for the better part of six years. During that time he amassed more than 1,100 penalty minutes and scored a measly five goals.

In the summer of 2006, Koci signed with Chicago, and late in the 2006–07 season he got that call he had waited so long for. The game was in Phoenix, and both the Hawks and Coyotes were out of the playoffs. It was an otherwise meaningless contest.

Given his reputation, however, he knew he wasn't being asked to score goals during his audition, and he responded accordingly.

Koci and Josh Gratton got into a fight less than three minutes into the game. When he got out of the box, Koci got into a shoving match with Daniel Carcillo, and each received minors (and Carcillo got an extra two minutes for elbowing).

Koci and Gratton fought again at 15:04 of the period, adding five minutes each to their stats for the evening.

Early in the third, Koci made it a hat trick of fights. He incurred a charging major and then fought Nick Boynton. That third fight of the game triggered an automatic game misconduct.

The grim scoresheet showed that Koci had "played" a total of 2:31 during which time he amassed 42 penalty minutes, a record for first games that will take some doing to better.

Other brawling debuts

On four other occasions a player has incurred at least 25 penalty minutes in his debut.

// Tie Domi, Toronto Maple Leafs, March 2, 1990 / 37 minutes

John Kordic had sore tonsils, so Domi was called up from Newmarket of the AHL to fill the fighter's gloves, as it were. The Wings also called up tough guy Chris McRae, so the stage was set for a pair of "tough" Toronto-Detroit weekend games early in March.

"I was drafted here to fulfill a role, and I realize that it's the only way I'm ever going to make it," Domi said, unapologetically. "I'll do whatever I have to do to stay here."

And he did.

In less than two minutes of actual playing time, Domi earned a roughing penalty midway through the opening period, a misconduct just a few seconds after that penalty expired, a fighting major in the second, and a misconduct in the overtime. Detroit won, 4–3, but Domi had started his career the only way he knew how—with his fists.

// Florent Robidoux, Chicago Black Hawks, October 9, 1980 / 27 minutes

A truculent winger, Robidoux fought Jim Schoenfeld of Buffalo twice, the first time earning a minor and misconduct and the second time a major and misconduct. Chicago won the game, 4–3, but the real story was Denis Savard, making his NHL debut in style by assisting on three of the Hawks' goals.

// Paul Stewart, Quebec Nordiques, November 22, 1979 / 27 minutes

Before he was a love-him-or-hate-him referee, Paul Stewart was a "resident tough guy" plying his trade for, firstly, the Quebec Nordiques. And he made his splashy debut in the cozy confines of the Boston Garden, becoming the first player ever to incur three fighting majors in his debut (the aforementioned Koci remains the only other member of this exclusive and dubious club).

Two days earlier, in Quebec, the Nordiques' Robbie Ftorek cut Boston's Bobby Schmautz accidentally. The Bruins didn't buy the "accidentally" part and vowed revenge, so Quebec coach Jacques Demers brought up not one, not two, but three fighters for the rematch in Boston.

Stewart made history of sorts when, over the course of the game, he fought three players—first Terry O'Reilly, then Stan Jonathan, and, finally, Al Secord. The last carried with it an automatic game misconduct, and an earlier delay-of-game penalty gave Stewart 27 PIM for his first game. Ironically, the delay of game was the result of an O'Reilly-Stewart set-to that the linesmen cut short.

// Jason Simon, New York Islanders January 7, 1994 / 25 minutes

They say fights don't mean much, but there was a time when sometimes they did. Consider the New York Islanders home game against Calgary on January 7, 1994. The visiting Flames were playing really well, leading 1–0 late in the first period, when newcomer Simon started a fight against the Flames' Paul Kruze. The set-to energized the Nassau Coliseum crowd, and the energy, in turn, filtered down to the players.

The Islanders scored two goals before the end of the period, taking a surprising 2–1 lead to the dressing room. In the second, Simon and Sandy McCarthy earned misconducts in the early going, and the Islanders again scored. The two

combatants were at it again early in the third, and the Isles scored two more, skating to an easy 6–2 win.

David Koci amassed 42 penalty minutes in his first game.

Who Gets the Puck?

It is not common for a team to have more than one player make his NHL debut in the same game, but it is also not altogether rare. But what is rare is that three players, all playing in their first NHL game for one team, combine on the same goal.

Indeed, it has been accomplished only three times in 102 years of NHL play.

October 31, 1942
New York Rangers 2 at Toronto Maple Leafs 7

Rangers / Bend (Bell, Gooden), 19:21 1st

It was the start of the 1942–43 season. The war was on, and player departures for God and country had depleted talent from the NHL. The Rangers were at Maple Leaf Gardens for the season opener, but they had many new faces in the lineup, starting with goalie Steve Buzinski (who later earned the nickname, probably as a joke, probably long after he retired, "the puck goes inski").

In addition, the Blueshirts had Scotty Cameron, Joe Bell, Lin Bend, Gord Davidson, Bill Gooden, and Bob Kirkpatrick in the lineup, one and all playing in their first NHL game. Including Buzinski, that's seven players—nearly half the team.

The Leafs had newcomers Bobby Copp, Jack Hamilton, Shep Mayer, and Bud Poile making their debuts.

The Leafs scored early and often, but three newbie Rangers combined on a goal late in the first to bring the visitors to within two. Bend got the goal on assists from Bell and Gooden, the first time in league history that three debutants had combined on a goal.

October 10, 1979
Winnipeg Jets 2 at Pittsburgh Penguins 4

Jets / Lukowich (Marsh, Melrose), 13:24 3rd

The start of a new hockey season is always an exciting time, but in Pittsburgh, on the night of October 10, 1979, most sports fans had their minds—and TVs—on Game 1 of the Pittsburgh-Baltimore World Series.

As a result, only 8,752 souls came out to the Civic Arena to watch the Pens take on the Jets in the season opener. Those who came, though, were treated to a home win and a little bit of history. This marked the Jets' first NHL game. They had won the Avco Cup in the WHA the previous spring and joined the NHL over the summer along with the Edmonton Oilers, Hartford Whalers, and Quebec Nordiques.

The Pens were ahead 3–0 midway through the third when Morris Lukowich scored, assists going to Peter Marsh, whose shot Lukowich redirected, and Barry Melrose. All three were playing their first NHL game, and it was the first such goal in almost 37 years.

October 4, 2007
St. Louis Blues 2 at Phoenix Coyotes 3

Coyotes / Winnik (Hanzal, Weller), 7:30 3rd

Wayne Gretzky was the coach of the Coyotes. The team played its home games at a place called Jobing.com Arena, and three first-year players combined on a goal that proved to be the game winner.

Gretzky's Coyotes were starting the season with youth. Peter Mueller was 19; Martin Hanzal, 20; Keith Yandle, 21; Daniel Winnik, 22. The team was ahead 2–0 early in the third when Winnik scored to make it 3–0. Assists were credited to Hanzal and Craig Weller, all first-game players.

Winnik got the puck because it was his goal—scored on his first career shot—and his parents were in the stands. "It feels great," he enthused after. "Before the game I kind of convinced myself it was just another pre-season game, and not to put on any added pressure. It felt great to hear the crowd roaring, and thanks to my linemates, it was something special."

Winnik's goal gave the Coyotes what appeared to be a comfortable 3-0 lead midway through the final period in the team's season opener, but two late goals from the Blues ensured the goal was, in fact, the game winner.

Daniel Winnik (right) is checked by Eric Brewer of St. Louis during Winnik's memorable first game.

Playoff Debut Goalscorers

It's a rare and exclusive group. A small section of the 7,863 NHLers are those players who made their NHL debuts in the playoffs. To date only 144 (1.8 percent) have done so.

And of that 144, a mere seven scored a goal in their NHL-playoff debut.

// Eddie Emberg, Montreal Canadiens
March 29, 1945

By the time Game 5 of the Stanley Cup semi-finals rolled around in late March 1945, the Maple Leafs were in command and the Canadiens reeling. Toronto had won three of the first four and threatened to end the series in Montreal on March 29. All of Toronto's wins were by a single goal, while Montreal took Game 3 by a 4–1 score.

Making matters infinitely worse for the Habs were injuries. Buddy O'Connor and Fern Gauthier were gone for the year; Elmer Lach, Frank Eddolls, and Ken Mosdell had been injured. Coach Dick Irvin had to call up amateurs Nils Tremblay and Ulric Tondreau of the Quebec Aces and Rosario Joannette from Valleyfield.

But there was a wild card. Eddie Emberg had played so well for the Quebec Aces in his last game, watched by Montreal executives Senator Donat Raymond and Tommy Gorman, that they sought to acquire his services. They had recalled Tondreau only if the Habs couldn't use Emberg.

In the end, Emberg and Tremblay played, and they were effective in a landslide 10–3 win. Wrote Dink Carroll in the next day's *Montreal Gazette*: "The crippled Canadiens underwent a blood transfusion for this game with the injection of two new forwards, Nils Tremblay and Eddie Emberg, into the lineup. The former Quebec Aces, teaming on a line with Dutch Hiller, played smart, effective hockey both ways and accounted for a goal on a pretty piece of stickhandling by Eddie Emberg in the first period. In the opening stages, before the big line opened fire, it was the Canadiens' best line."

Lauri Korpikoski scored a great goal in his playoff debut to help the Rangers eliminate Pittsburgh.

// Les Costello, Toronto Maple Leafs
April 3, 1948

You would think a team ahead 3–1 in a playoff series heading home for Game 5 would be content, but such was not the case in early April 1948 in Toronto. General manager Conn Smythe and coach Hap Day were none too pleased with how the Leafs played in Boston in Game 4, a 3–2 loss that gave the Bruins a bit of life.

As a result, Smythe hinted after the game that Les Costello might play in place of Don Metz in Game 5. Metz was unimpressive the previous match after missing Games 2 and 3, and Smythe felt the team needed a spark.

The move worked as Costello became only the second NHLer ever to score in a playoff game that was his NHL debut.

Costello won a battle for the puck in the corner and passed to Max Bentley in front. Bentley's shot was stopped by Frank Brimsek, but Costello hustled to the front of the net and pounced on the rebound, giving the Leafs a 2–1 lead at 16:13 of the first period. The play capped off a great rush by defenceman Gus Mortson, who had missed the previous game with a knee injury and made a valiant return.

The Leafs won the game, 3–2, and advanced to the Cup Finals where they swept the Red Wings to claim their second straight Cup and third in four years. Impressively, Costello played in every game for the victors.

// Doug Volmar, Detroit Red Wings
April 11, 1970

The quarter-finals of the 1970 Stanley Cup playoffs between Chicago and Detroit started predictably. The Hawks, at home, won the first two games, and as the series headed to Detroit, the Wings hoped to do the same—win a pair in front of the home fans.

Indeed, as Jack Berry wrote in the *Detroit Free Press* prior to Game 3: "A sweep of the Saturday-Sunday games at Olympia is almost imperative."

Chicago's wins were by identical 4–2 scores, so the Wings were in the thick of things. But head coach Sid Abel decided to make one important lineup change. He put in Doug Volmar on right wing to replace defenceman Poul Popiel. Volmar had a great slap shot, and given that one of the reasons for losses in the first two games was Chicago's potent power play and Detroit's ineffective one, Abel saw value to putting Volmar and his heavy shot on the point during the man advantage.

As well, Volmar, who had played the year with the farm team in Fort Worth (CHL), was a standout at Michigan State University in the mid-1960s, where he had success against Chicago goalie Tony Esposito, who played for Michigan Tech during the same three-year period (1964–67).

Volmar acquitted himself well, but the Wings didn't follow suit. The newcomer unleashed a high, rising slapshot in the second period that caught Esposito on the shoulder and forced him to the bench for a quick talk with the trainer, but two goals in the second gave the visiting Hawks a 3–1 lead.

Volmar scored midway through the third period on a hard, low shot from the slot, making it a 3–2 game. Almost as quickly as the puck went in, Volmar skated to the goal to pluck it out of the twine for a most cherished souvenir.

Chicago, however, had the last laugh, adding an empty netter to win, 4–2. Volmar was in the lineup the next afternoon, and the Hawks won again, by the same 4–2 score, eliminating the Red Wings.

// Rod Brind'Amour, St. Louis Blues
April 11, 1989

The division semi-finals of the Clarence Campbell Conference had St. Louis playing Minnesota. The Blues won the first three games before losing Game 4 in Minnesota, but they headed home with a chance to eliminate the North Stars and move on.

Rod Brind'Amour had no reason to expect he'd see any action. Drafted 9th overall by the Blues in 1988, he had had an outstanding first year at Michigan State University, so much so that when his NCAA season ended the Blues signed him to a contract (April 3).

That was at the start of this series, but coach Brian Sutter had the 18-year-old watch the first four games from the press box. That all changed only a short time before the opening faceoff for Game 5.

"Just before the game, Sudsy [Sutter] told me that I was going to play," Brind'Amour related later in the evening of April 11, 1989, after he had become only the fourth NHLer to score in his playoff-game debut.

This was the only lineup change Sutter made between Games 4 and 5, but the coach wasn't particularly philosophical in explaining it. "I just thought it would be a good opportunity to play him," Sutter said. "He just wanted to contribute, and I thought he played really well."

Brind'Amour didn't step on the ice until 16:54 of the opening period, skating on a line with Gino Cavallini and Herb Raglan. He scored on his fourth shift, at 9:48 of the second period, to give the Blues a solid 3–1 lead.

"It wasn't much of a goal," he said. "Tom [Tilley] and Doug [Evans] did most of the work. It's kind of funny. Tom ripped a shot from the point, and I wound up tapping it in. I'll take it."

The Blues won, 6–1, to advance, but lost the next round to Chicago in five games. Brind'Amour played in four of those games, scoring one more goal.

// Adam Mair, Toronto Maple Leafs
May 11, 1999

It was the best of times, the worst of times . . . memorable times all around.

Adam Mair was a little bit of everything. Big and strong, he played a tough game. Skilled, he had good touch around the net. The Leafs drafted him 84th overall at the 1997 Entry Draft after his second impressive season with the Owen Sound Platers of the OHL.

During his fourth season, the end of his junior career, he also played for Canada at the World Junior Championship, helping the team win silver in Winnipeg. Once his season was done, the Leafs sent Mair to St. John's to play in the AHL playoffs, and after that they brought him up to the big club.

Toronto beat Philadelphia in a demanding six-game series of the conference quarter-finals and faced Pittsburgh next. The teams split the first two games in Pittsburgh, meaning the Leafs had home-ice advantage moving to Game 3 at home.

Coach Pat Quinn put Mair in the lineup as a late decision because Steve Sullivan's back problems had returned and he couldn't play. The 20-year-old Mair responded in spades, scoring at 12:58 of the second to give the Leafs a 3–2 lead. It wasn't the prettiest goal—he merely banged in a rebound after barging his way to the front of the net.

The Leafs' Adam Mair banged in a shot from close range for his first career goal.

Mair also took a high-sticking penalty during a scoreless opening period, but more significantly he was on the ice midway through the third when the Penguins scored the game winner.

In all, Mair played only 4:43, nine shifts, mostly on a physical line with Kris King and Tie Domi.

// Lauri Korpikoski, New York Rangers
May 4, 2008

There was little wrong with the Pittsburgh Penguins as they made their way through the 2008 playoffs. They swept Buffalo to start their march to the finals and won the first three games against the Rangers to take a commanding lead in the next series. The Rangers managed a 3–0 win in Game 4, but the Penguins were going home to try to eliminate the Blueshirts.

The Rangers, meanwhile, had eliminated New Jersey in five games before earning a date with Pittsburgh. After falling behind so badly, though, there seemed little hope. So when Blair Betts couldn't play in Game 5 because of an injury, coach Tom Renney decided to insert the 21-year-old Korpikoski, who had yet to skate on a sheet of NHL ice.

The Rangers fell behind in the pivotal game, 2–0, after two periods, but Korpikoski scored early in the third to start a comeback. He got the puck in his own end and rushed up on a two-on-one. Not wanting to make a mistake on a pass, he fired a shot that beat Marc-Andre Fleury cleanly. Nigel Dawes made it 2–2 just 83 seconds later, but Marian Hossa scored in overtime for the Penguins to eliminate New York.

// Cale Makar, Colorado Avalanche
April 15, 2019

See page 197

Playoff Debut Scorers				
Player	Team	Date	Result	Series Summary
Eddie Emberg	MTL	March 29, 1945	W	Game 5 of 6 (lost)
Les Costello	TOR	April 3, 1948	W	Game 5 of 5 (won)
Doug Volmar	DET	April 11, 1970	L	Game 3 of 4 (lost)
Rod Brind'Amour	STL	April 11, 1989	W	Game 5 of 5 (won)
Adam Mair	TOR	May 11, 1999	L	Game 3 of 6 (won)
Lauri Korpikoski	NYR	May 4, 2008	L	Game 5 of 5 (lost)
Cale Makar	AVS	April 15, 2019	W	Game 3 of 5 (won)

One Night Hype

Derek Stepan

NEW YORK RANGERS // OCTOBER 9, 2010

Drafted 51st overall by the New York Rangers in 2008, Stepan started his college career at the University of Wisconsin after leaving Shattuck St. Mary's prep high school in Minnesota. The highlight of the next two years was surely the 2010 World Junior Championship. Captaining the U.S. team, Stepan led the tournament in scoring and took the Americans to a gold medal, defeating Canada in overtime.

That fall, he was in the starting lineup for the Rangers' season opener against the Buffalo Sabres, and he had one of the greatest debuts in league history. Stepan scored three goals on three shots.

Goal number one gave the Rangers a 1–0 lead and was a deflection off a Dan Girardi point shot that fooled Ryan Miller.

Goal number two was similar. In this case, it was a Marc Staal point shot that got to Miller. The goalie made the save but couldn't control the puck. Stepan pounced on the rebound to give the Rangers a 3–1 lead late in the second period.

Three and a half minutes later, Stepan completed his hat-trick debut, and this was a first-rate goal. Linemate Sean Avery got the puck behind the net off a pass from Girardi and snapped the puck to an unguarded Stepan in the slot.

Stepan fired a quick shot past a helpless Miller. Bang, bang, in. Three goals in less than two periods of his career.

Stepan played all 82 games for the Rangers in 2010–11, scoring 21 goals, but none were as memorable as the three he netted on opening night.

Three goals on three shots. Pretty nice start for Derek Stepan.

Spectacular Shorties

There is no more difficult a goal to score than a short-handed goal, but to score a "shortie" in your first NHL game is even more special. Indeed, only seven players have ever done as much.

// Dit Clapper, Boston Bruins
November 15, 1927

Not only did Dit Clapper score short-handed, he scored while the Bruins were two men short! And his goal gave the team a 1–1 tie with Chicago.

The 20-year-old Clapper was known to fans of the Bruins because he had played the previous season with the Boston Tigers of the CAHL, but in his NHL debut, the young star was memorable.

John Hallahan described Clapper's sensational tally in the *Boston Globe*: "The Bruins had two men shy when Clapper, carrying the puck at a slow pace, outwitted [Teddy] Graham and Corbett Denneny, and got free with the disk. From close up, he beat Gardiner with the tying goal."

// Wally Boyer, Toronto Maple Leafs
December 11, 1965

The Boston Bruins were a terrible team in the immediate years before the arrival of Bobby Orr, and on this night an 8–3 thrashing by Toronto at Maple Leaf Gardens was another indicator of their woes. It marked Boston's sixth straight loss, and insult was added to injury by a great play from first-gamer Wally Boyer.

That Boyer was in the lineup was the result of extraordinary fortitude and perseverance. He graduated from the Toronto Marlies back in 1958, after which he kicked around in four leagues trying to earn a spot in the lineup. But nine years later, coach Punch Imlach called him up to the Leafs, and Boyer didn't waste this career opportunity.

The Leafs had led 4–1 only to see Boston claw back to within a goal, and the Bruins seemed to have a great chance to tie the game when they went to the power play late in the second period. Al Arbour sprung Boyer free, however, and he made a great move on two Bruins defenders before beating Gerry Cheevers with a wrister to make it 5–3. It was the first shot of his NHL career.

Boyer played nearly 11 minutes in this game, most of it as a penalty killer, and he set up Orland Kurtenbach for another shortie in the third period, giving him two points in his inaugural game while playing four men to five.

// Morris Stefaniw, Atlanta Flames
October 7, 1972

This wasn't just a short-handed goal, this was a goal for the record books and a goal that came out of odd circumstances. For starters, the Atlanta Flames were in New York to play the Islanders. It was not only the opening game of the 1972–73 season, it was the first game in franchise history for the Flames.

The Islanders came out flying, of course—home fans, first game—but their momentum was derailed when referee Ark Skov was injured and the game delayed for several minutes. That unexpected timeout settled down the Flames, but their own Randy Manery incurred the first penalty of the game at 11:13.

Jake Dowell scored short-handed in his first game, a rare accomplishment.

Playing short-handed, Stefaniw tipped a shot from penalty-killing partner Lew Morrison that eluded Gerry Desjardins to give the Flames a 1–0 lead. It was Stefaniw's first goal on his first shot in his first game, and it was also the Flames' first goal in franchise history. They went on to win, 3–2.

// Teppo Numminen, Winnipeg Jets
October 6, 1988

At home to open the 1988–89 season, the Vancouver Canucks were playing well in front of 22-year-old goalie Kirk McLean. Late in the third period, it seemed all but certain they'd beat the visiting Winnipeg Jets; they were ahead 2–1 and on the power play as the game approached the final minute.

But Jets defenceman Teppo Numminen got the puck at the Canucks blue line and fired a quick shot on goal. It was a knuckleball, and at the last minute dipped out of McLean's reach, off the post, and in. The game ended 2–2, and Numminen had scored his first goal on his first shot, short-handed no less.

// Jake Dowell, Chicago Blackhawks
November 22, 2007

Dowell and Kris Versteeg were called up from Rockford the day before Chicago was set to play in Calgary. "I want to bring anything I can to the table," Dowell enthused upon arriving at the Pengrowth Saddledome. "I want to bring energy, play well defensively, and try to be really good on the penalty kill."

The two players were needed because both Rene Bourque and Jason Williams were injured and unavailable. Playing on a checking line with Dustin Byfuglien and David Koci, Dowell acquitted himself well.

Early in the second period of a scoreless game, Koci took a penalty, but it was Dowell who scored. He collected a loose puck just inside the Calgary end and beat Miikka Kiprusoff with a great shot to make it 1–0.

"To play my first NHL game and to get my first NHL goal, I know it's a cliche but every kid dreams about doing that. To be able to say I got that is a great feeling."

The Flames tied the game late in the period and then Dowell inadvertently figured on the Hawks' game-winning goal early in the third. He incurred a tripping penalty late in the second period, and while he was still in the box, Patrick Sharp scored short-handed. Chicago won the game, 2–1, and Dowell's memorable debut was in the books.

// Jordan Eberle, Edmonton Oilers
October 7, 2010

The gold standard for NHL debut goals is surely Mario Lemieux's. First shift, strips Ray Bourque of the puck, and makes a magnificent move to score. Jordan Eberle's first career goal is every bit as magical. The only difference is that it came early in the third period in an Edmonton-Calgary game in which he took a regular shift.

It wasn't a gem, but Alan Quine's first goal came during a Buffalo power play.

The goal was incredible. The Oilers were short-handed. The puck was deep in the Edmonton end, and the Flames had a great chance to score but didn't. Oilers blue-liner Jim Vandermeer got the puck and gently banked it off the boards out to centre where Eberle chased it down. This created a two-on-one with Shawn Horcoff, with Ian White the only Flames defenceman back.

Eberle took a quick look at Horcoff, but it was clear he was going to take the puck to the net. White sensed this and dove to try to block the shot. At just the right moment, Eberle made a toe drag with the puck, avoiding both White and his sweeping stick.

In the same moment that he was on the other side of the fallen White, Eberle glided through the high slot. Miikka Kiprusoff went down, expecting a shot, but Eberle hung onto the puck fractionally longer and slid the puck into the net. It was a sensational play, giving the Oilers a 2–0 lead in a game they won, 4–0.

// Alan Quine, New York Islanders
April 9, 2016

Called up from Bridgeport of the AHL earlier in the day, Quine made his debut with the Islanders a special one, although in the end the team lost, 4–3, to Buffalo, in overtime.

Quine's shortie came early in the third and tied the game, 2–2. The Islanders won a faceoff deep in their own end, and defenceman Zach Boychuk rifled the puck down the ice. Sabres goalie Linus Ullmark mishandled the puck, and Bracken Kearns got to it first. He passed it in front, and it went off the body of Quine and in. Not a beauty by any means, but a short-handed goal all the same and his first career marker to boot.

Unluckiest Loss Ever

Mike Murphy

CAROLINA HURRICANES // DECEMBER 6, 2011

Every NHL game must have, statistically speaking, a winning goalie and a losing goalie. Makes sense.

The winning goalie is the one who is in goal when his team scores the winning goal, so in a 5–2 win, if he's in net for the third goal, he's awarded the win. Makes sense.

The losing goalie is the one who is in goal when the opposing team scores the winning goal, so in a 6–3 loss, if he's in net for the fourth goal, he's given the loss. Makes sense.

Mike Murphy was perfect in his debut, but he managed to be the losing goalie of record all the same.

But the Carolina-Calgary game of December 6, 2011, made no sense whatsoever, especially to Hurricanes goalie Mike Murphy.

Calgary went up 3-0 early in the second. It was 5–2 early in the third, but the Flames made it 6–3 soon after. 'Canes coach Kirk Muller pulled starting goalie Cam Ward to give Murphy some ice time, his first career minutes, no less.

Murphy played 8:37, the rest of the game, facing only two shots and stopping them both. His team, though, scored soon after he came on, making it 6–4, so Muller pulled Murphy late in the game to try to tie the score. The Flames scored into the empty net, though, with 69 seconds remaining, making it a 7–4 game. And that was that, right?

Nope. The 'Canes managed to score two late goals to make it 7–6, the last coming with only five seconds remaining. The 7–6 final score meant that whoever was in goal for that seventh goal was the losing goalie, but it was scored into the empty net.

Regardless, NHL rules are NHL rules, so Murphy, who didn't allow a goal, was assessed the loss. A cruel loss, to be sure, but so noteworthy and unique perhaps it was worth it.

Small Start to a Record

Matt Hackett

MINNESOTA WILD // DECEMBER 6, 2011

Goalie Matt Hackett was called up from the Houston Aeros of the AHL on December 6, 2011, to dress as backup to starter Josh Harding. The Minnesota Wild were in San Jose for a game against the Sharks, and Harding started for the Wild, as expected.

Joe Pavelski scored exactly one minute into the game for the Sharks, ruining Harding's shutout hopes, and just 11 seconds later, Wild teammate Nick Schultz collided with Harding, knocking the goalie cold. When he came to, he left the game, of course, and the 21-year-old Hackett was pressed into service.

Playing his first career game, Hackett was sensational, stopping all 34 shots he faced in 58:49 of ice time. Two nights later, he earned the start, his first, against Los Angeles. Again, he was fantastic, allowing his first goal only early in the third period. The Wild won, 4-3.

This all added up to two crazy facts. Hackett won the first two games of his career, allowing only two goals, but he didn't even have a shutout to show for his great start.

What he did have, though, was an NHL record 102:48 shutout streak to start his career.

No goalie played longer shutout hockey to start a career than Minnesota's Matt Hackett.

Tick, Tick, Done

Kellan Lain

VANCOUVER CANUCKS // JANUARY 18, 2014

It was old time hockey for a couple of seconds, and that's not a good thing. After, there were accusations all around, but in the end, the start to this Calgary at Vancouver game was not the way hockey was meant to be played in the 21st century.

Trying to "set the tone," visiting Calgary coach Bob Hartley put his fourth line out to start the game. Now, "fourth line" can sometimes mean "checkers," but sometimes, as in this case, it is a euphemism for "fighters."

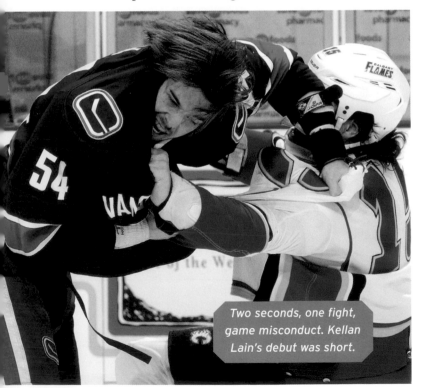

Two seconds, one fight, game misconduct. Kellan Lain's debut was short.

Vancouver coach John Tortorella felt he had no recourse but to start his fourth line/fighters, including Kellan Lain, a huge six-foot-six prospect who had been playing for the Utica Comets, Vancouver's AHL affiliate, before being called up.

Predictably, as soon as the puck was dropped to start the game a line brawl ensued. When the dust had settled, 10 players received assorted penalties, including fighting majors and game misconducts to eight, including Lain.

The Flames lost Chris Butler, Blair Jones, Kevin Westgarth (who also got an instigating minor), and Ladislav Smid, and the Canucks lost Lain (who fought Westgarth), Dale Weise, Kevin Bieksa, and Jason Garrison. Brian McGratton (Calgary) and Tom Sestito (Vancouver) also received majors and misconducts.

For Lain, it was a terrible way to "begin" his NHL career. Even Tortorella admitted as much. "That's my biggest mistake, to put Lainer in the lineup, and I'll kick myself forever not having someone else there."

The Canucks won, 3–2, and there were 204 penalty minutes in the game. Lain had 15 of that total, even though his debut game lasted but two seconds.

79 Seconds Is All

Brian White

COLORADO AVALANCHE // NOVEMBER 21, 1998

Drafted a distant 268th overall by Tampa Bay in 1994, Brian White was the Pluto of players, so far from the Gretzkys and Lemieuxs of the NHL world that he could barely see their light.

Be that as it may, history shows he played two games in the NHL during the 1998–99 season—the sum total of his career—with the Colorado Avalanche.

White made his debut on November 21, 1998, against Montreal. It made sense; the Avs had six regular defencemen out of the lineup with an assortment of injuries. White was playing with Hershey in the AHL and having a decent season, but Avs coach Bob Hartley leaned heavily on his number one and two defencemen, Aaron Miller and Greg de Vries, both playing more than half a game each.

Fifth defencemen Jeff Buchanan played just 1:18, and White, almost confounding time itself, was on the ice for just two seconds.

The Avs won, 3–2, in Montreal, and four days later White appeared again for the team in Edmonton. This time he played 1:17. He never saw NHL action again.

Total stats: two games, 1:19 of ice time.

Brian White (No. 59) appeared on the ice for but two seconds in his first game.

Come the Shootout

There are different levels of participation in an NHL debut game, to be sure. Getting one shift, then a few, is the least a player gets. Playing regularly is another compliment from the coach, and playing on the power play or penalty kill—those critical moments in a game that often decide the outcome—is yet another.

Playing in overtime is an even higher level, and taking part in a shootout the ultimate. A goalie has little choice, of course. If it's his debut game and he played well enough to get the team to the shootout, the coach is hardly going to pull him.

But for a player in his first game to be selected by the coach to take a shootout shot is surely special, and scoring a goal is the penultimate achievement in a first game. But scoring the shootout winner? Almost unheard of. Almost.

The shootout began at the start of the 2005–06 season, after the lockout, as the NHL tried to woo fans back to empty arenas with extra excitement. Since then, hundreds of games have gone to overtime and more than 2,000 players have made their first appearance in a game.

Yet in all that time only three first-game goalies have participated in a shootout—and all won the game. As well, only 12 skaters have taken shootout shots in their debuts. Six scored with their chance, and four of those were game winners—Tim Stapleton, Linus Omark, Evgeni Svechnikov, Ryan Poehling.

Anaheim goalie Viktor Fasth found himself in a shootout in his first game. He won.

Goalies

Josh Harding, Minnesota Wild / April 4, 2006
Tied 4–4 after regulation and overtime, the Wild and St. Louis Blues went to extra shots. Keith Tkachuk beat Harding with the first shot, but Mikko Koivu and Brian Rolston scored for Minnesota to give Harding a win in his first game.

Viktor Fasth, Anaheim Ducks / January 26, 2013
The Ducks and Predators went to overtime tied 2–2, but Corey Perry scored for Anaheim and Fasth stopped all three Nashville skaters to earn the victory.

Martin Jones, Los Angeles Kings / December 3, 2013
The king of all goalies in the shootout so far, Jones stopped 26 of 28 shots in 65 minutes of playing time in a 2–2 game to take his Kings to a shootout against state rivals Anaheim. And even then Jones had to work overtime as the shot-taking process extended to nine rounds. Amazingly, Jones stopped all nine shots he faced, staring down the likes of Corey Perry, Ryan Getzlaf, Saku Koivu, and Teemu Selanne. An historic and impressive first-game win.

Skaters

Jakub Klepis, Washington Capitals / November 4, 2005

A call-up from Hershey, Klepis scored a goal in the second period of his debut. But the game, against the now-defunct Atlanta Thrashers, went to a shootout, and Klepis took the second Washington shot, which was stopped by Mike Dunham. Happily, Alexander Ovechkin had scored on the team's first shot, and the Caps won the game, 4–3.

Claude Giroux, Philadelphia Flyers / February 19, 2008

The Flyers had lost seven in a row by the time they got to Ottawa for this mid-February game. In dire need of a change, they called up 20-year-old junior Claude Giroux, who was playing nearby for Gatineau in the QMJHL. He saw only 9:20 of ice time in the game, one that went to a shootout after the Flyers and Sens played to a 2–2 tie. Giroux was selected to take the first shot after Ottawa's Daniel Alfredsson missed, but Giroux was stopped by Ray Emery. Ottawa went on to win the game.

Tim Stapleton, Toronto Maple Leafs / February 26, 2009

The Leafs did things the hard way against Tampa Bay this night, squandering a 4–2 lead in the third period and needing to go to a shootout. Stapleton, a 26-year-old who went undrafted and started his career in Finland, got the call to take the final shot.

Edmonton's Linus Omark scored the greatest debut shootout goal ever.

Each team had already scored a goal, so the situation was simple. A goal, and the Leafs win. A miss, and the shootout continues. The right-shooting Stapleton collected the puck at centre and immediately moved to his left. As he came in on goal, he simply rifled a hard shot over Joey MacDonald's glove to give the Leafs the win. Nothing fancy. Juts a quick, accurate shot.

Linus Omark, Edmonton Oilers / December 10, 2010

Not only did Omark score a shootout goal in his first game, he scored one of the most famous shootout goals of all time. The Oilers and Tampa Bay went to the shots contest after playing to a 3–3 tie through 65 minutes. Omark earned an assist on a power-play goal by Tom Gilbert in the second, but that was nothing compared to his shootout goal.

Teammate Taylor Hall called the move "ballsy." Lightning forward Ryan Malone called it "a *bleeping* joke." "You could say he's very confident," said Oilers goalie Nikolai Khabibulin with a laugh.

Here's what happened. Jordan Eberle scored for Edmonton on the first shot, and Khabibulin stopped the first two Tampa Bay shooters. Omark was up next. If he missed, Tampa would still have one more shot; if he scored, game over. He started back in his own end and built up breakaway speed by the time he hit centre ice. He got the puck on his stick and immediately did a 360-degree spin between centre ice and the blue line. Still at top speed, he then wound up for a slapshot from close range, hesitated, and then snapped a shot along the ice between the pads of Dan Ellis, sending the crowd into a frenzy. Pretty cool Game One!

Mats Zuccarello, New York Rangers / December 23, 2010

The eighth Norwegian-born player to make it to the NHL, Zuccarello is also the country's best to date. He made his NHL debut against Tampa Bay, playing 17:52 and looking every bit the part of a solid player. The teams played to a 3–3 tie through 65 minutes, and in the shootout Zuccarello was the third Rangers player to take a shot.

Tampa led 2–1, so if he missed, it was game over. The diminutive Zuccarello, however, skated in on Dan Ellis, then slowed right down and made a quick deke to score. Celebrations had to wait, though, because the shootout kept going and going. It wasn't until the 22nd shot that the Lightning's Ryan Malone scored the winner.

Reid Boucher, New Jersey Devils / December 4, 2013

Drafted 99th overall by New Jersey in 2011, Boucher was called up from Albany to play a home game against Montreal. The Habs took a 1–0 lead into the third period, but teams combined for five goals in that final 20 minutes to force overtime.

Boucher contributed, setting up Michael Ryder for the go-ahead goal midway through that wild third period. Then, when nothing was settled in the OT, teams went to a shootout, and the first shooter was Boucher.

He skated in on goal with speed, made a little head fake, and beat Peter Budaj to the stick side. Unfortunately, the Habs scored on two of their shots to win the game, 4–3, but Boucher did his part in his first NHL game.

John Persson, New York Islanders / March 27, 2014

The 21-year-old Swede was called up for 10 games late in the 2013–14 season, and although he got good ice time in his debut, 12:49, he didn't register a point during the game. In the shootout, he was stopped by Tampa Bay's Ben Bishop. What's special about this game, though, is that Persson's was the 18th shot of a shootout that went to 26 total before the home side Lightning won. It was one of the longest shootouts in NHL history.

Andrei Burakovsky, Washington Capitals / October 9, 2014

Only 19 when he made his NHL debut, the Austrian made an immediate impact, scoring just 6:43 into the game to give the Caps a 1–0 lead over Montreal. The game ended, 1–1, and went to an extended shootout. Burakovsky was the ninth shooter, but he was stopped by Dustin Tokarski. Brendan Gallagher then scored for Montreal to give the Habs the victory.

Tyson Jost, Colorado Avalanche / March 31, 2017

Just a couple of weeks after turning 19, Jost joined the Avs for six games at the end of his first season at the University of North Dakota. He didn't get a point in regulation, but he did get a chance to take a shot in the shootout. He was stopped by St. Louis goalie Jake Allen, but the Avs won, 2–1.

"It's something I'm going to remember for a long, long time," Jost said after. "Having my family come down and being in the crowd is pretty special. They've done a lot for me throughout my life."

Evgeni Svechnikov, Detroit Red Wings / April 3, 2017

Drew Miller woke up with the flu on Monday morning, so the Red Wings recalled 20-year-old Evgeni Svechnikov from the AHL farm team in nearby Grand Rapids, and he made his NHL debut at home that night against Ottawa. It turned out to be quite a debut.

Svechnikov played 13:10 during a game that ended in a 4–4 tie after 60 minutes of regulation and five minutes of OT, and in the shootout he wasn't among coach Jeff Blashill's first choices. But as the shots went to a fourth and fifth round, the coach had to look farther down the bench, and when it got to round seven he tabbed Svechnikov. The left-shooting rookie went in on goalie Cam Anderson on the off wing, faked a shot to the far side, and then whipped a low backhand to the back side that fooled Anderson.

Ottawa coach Guy Boucher then selected Colin White to take a must-score shot, and White, also playing in his first career game, couldn't match Svechnikov's effort. The Russian had just scored the winning goal.

"Coach pointed at me and said 'Go,' and the guys told me to do my thing," Svechnikov said. "I did that move in Grand Rapids a couple times and scored, so I knew that's what I wanted to do. This is just an unbelievable moment. I'm 20 years old, and I'm starting a game at Joe Louis Arena. It felt like there were bubbles in my body."

Colin White, Ottawa Senators / April 3, 2017

"They put their kid on, so we put our kid on," said Ottawa coach Guy Boucher, explaining why White, in his first game, was chosen. "Their kid" refers to Detroit's Evgeni Svechnikov, who scored. White missed. Game over. (See Svechnikov's story above.)

Ryan Poehling, Montreal Canadiens / April 6, 2019

See page 196

Evgeni Svechnikov celebrates his shootout winner.

Fastest Man on Blades

Connor McDavid

EDMONTON OILERS // OCTOBER 8, 2015

Although some members of the media tried to generate interest in the 2015 NHL Entry Draft by wondering if Connor McDavid or Jack Eichel would be the first overall selection, it was a non-starter. The only question was whether the Buffalo Sabres, last in the league in 2014–15, would win the draft lottery or not.

They did not. Nor did the second-last team, the Arizona Coyotes. As fate and lottery-luck would have it, the third-worst Edmonton Oilers won rights to the top pick, something they also won in 2010 (Taylor Hall), 2011 (Ryan Nugent-Hopkins), and 2012 (Nail Yakupov).

Of course, the Oilers selected McDavid, and he was in the starting lineup for the first game of the 2015–16 season, a road date in St. Louis. Playing on a line with Hall and Anton Slepyshev, McDavid was held without a point in his debut, a 3–1 loss to the Blues.

"I did some good stuff, did some bad stuff, along with the team. I think as the game went on, I felt better about it."

Back in Edmonton, bars were packed, fans wore No. 97 sweaters everywhere, and the sense of a new era was in the air. The Oilers hadn't been in the playoffs since 2006, but that long and painful drought was surely about to end.

McDavid wasn't just a great star—he was special, magical. By far the fastest skater the league had ever seen, he could make moves and stickhandle at top speed, something astonishing to behold.

This opening night was nothing to brag about, and yet it hailed the start of a time that had people thinking about Sidney Crosby in the past tense, as no longer the face of the NHL, as the second-best player to this speedy wunderkind in Edmonton.

Connor McDavid took speed to a new level when he came to the NHL.

Auston, Ontario

Auston Matthews

TORONTO MAPLE LEAFS // OCTOBER 12, 2016

Without question, the biggest sigh of relief in Toronto Maple Leafs history occurred on April 30, 2016. That was the day the NHL's draft lottery determined the order of selections for that year's Entry Draft.

That was the day the Toronto Maple Leafs had a 20 percent chance of winning, and that was the day NHL commissioner Gary Bettman showed the Winnipeg Jets logo for the second position, meaning the Leafs, the league's worst team in 2015–16, had the first overall choice.

That was the moment Toronto president Brendan Shanahan sighed. His master plan—the Shanaplan, as Lou Lamoriello later dubbed it—could now take effect.

The Toronto Maple Leafs drafted Auston Matthews first overall three and a half weeks later, marking the first time the team had the top choice since 1985, when they selected Wendel Clark.

Matthews was supposed to be the team's saviour, the "generational player" who could finally deliver a Stanley Cup to a hockey-mad city that had not won the hallowed

trophy since Canada's centennial celebrations in 1967.

Not surprisingly, Matthews showed up to training camp in great shape and ready to prove his worth, and coach Mike Babcock had an easy time naming the young star from Arizona to his starting lineup.

In his first career game, October 12, 2016, in Ottawa, Matthews didn't disappoint.

He scored on his first shot, from in close off a pass from Zach Hyman, at 8:21 of the first period.

He scored on his second shot, six minutes later, rifling a low drive past Senators goalie Craig Anderson.

He scored on his third shot, early in the second period to give the Leafs a 3–2 lead on another low shot, this time converting a feed from defenceman Morgan Rielly.

And he scored on his fourth career shot with three seconds left in the second.

Matthews scored four goals on four shots. This is the last of that number as he beat Ottawa goalie Craig Anderson.

Incredibly, the Leafs lost the game, 5–4, in overtime, but the night belonged to Matthews. The NHL proved to be party poopers and declared this night was not a record night. It said that Harry Hyland and Joe Malone had scored five goals in their debuts in 1917–18, the NHL's first season of play, and Reg Noble also scored four to start that season.

Of the 641 players (of more than 7,863 in league history) to score in their first game, 52 have scored two goals, and five have scored three goals. And then there are Matthews, Noble, Hyland, and Malone.

In his first three years in the league, Matthews has played 212 games and recorded 111 goals and 205 points. Some 56 of those games (more than a quarter) have been multiple-point outings. He has three four-point games, including his debut; 13 three-points games; and 40 two-pointers.

His most impressive stretch was the first seven games of the 2018–19 season, when he had 10 goals and 16 points. Oddly, he has never had another hat trick since his first game and has three times had three assists in a game.

First Overall Draft Debuts

Since 1979, when the NHL Entry Draft started (previously it was known as the Amateur Draft and featured only players under 20), most first overall draft choices have started in the team's first game after draft day, meaning they made the NHL at 18. The overwhelming majority of players did not have great debuts, the notable exception, of course, being Auston Matthews, who scored four goals.

Year	Player				Team	NHL Debut Date
	G	**A**	**P**	**PIM**		**First Game After Draft**
1979	Rob Ramage				COR	October 11, 1979
	0	0	0	0		season opener
1980	Doug Wickenheiser				MTL	October 15, 1980
	0	0	0	0		healthy scratch first two games
1981	Dale Hawerchuk				WJE	October 6, 1981
	0	0	0	2		season opener
1982	Gord Kluzak				BOS	October 7, 1982
	0	0	0	0		season opener
1983	Brian Lawton				MNS	October 5, 1983
	0	0	0	0		season opener
1984	Mario Lemieux				PIT	October 11, 1984
	1	1	2	0		season opener
1985	Wendel Clark				TOR	October 10, 1985
	0	0	0	0		season opener
1986	Joe Murphy				DET	October 11, 1986
	0	0	0	2		recalled from minors after one game
1987	Pierre Turgeon				BUF	October 8, 1987
	0	0	0	2		season opener
1988	Mike Modano				MNS	April 6, 1989
	0	0	0	0		played season in Prince Albert (WHL)
1989	Mats Sundin				QUE	October 4, 1990
	1	0	1	2		played '89-'90 in Sweden
1990	Owen Nolan				QUE	October 4, 1990
	0	0	0	4		season opener
1991	Eric Lindros				PHI	October 6, 1992
	1	0	1	0		holdout/played '90-'91 with Canada's national team
1992	Roman Hamrlik				TB	October 7, 1992
	0	0	0	0		season opener
1993	Alexander Daigle				OTT	October 6, 1993
	0	2	2	0		season opener
1994	Ed Jovanovski				FLO	November 2, 1995
	0	0	0	0		played '94-'95 in Windsor (OHL)
1995	Brian Berard				NYI	October 4, 1996
	0	0	0	0		played '95-'96 in Detroit (OHL)
1996	Chris Phillips				OTT	October 1, 1997
	0	0	0	0		played '96-'97 in Lethbridge (WHL)
1997	Joe Thornton				BOS	October 8, 1997
	0	0	0	0		injured-missed start of season
1998	Vincent Lecavalier				TB	October 9, 1998
	0	0	0	0		season opener
1999	Patrik Stefan				ATT	October 2, 1999
	0	1	1	0		season opener
2000	Rick DiPietro				NYI	January 27, 2001
	Mins	GA	Decision			
	55:54	2	L*			recalled from minors
2001	Ilya Kovalchuk				ATT	October 4, 2001
	0	0	0	2		season opener
2002	Rick Nash				CBJ	October 10, 2002
	1	0	1	0		season opener
2003	Marc-Andre Fleury				PIT	October 10, 2003
	Mins	GA	Decision			
	59:30	2	L			season opener
2004	Alexander Ovechkin				WAS	October 5, 2005
	2	0	2	2		debut delayed a year by lockout
2005	Sidney Crosby				PIT	October 5, 2005
	0	1	1	0		season opener
2006	Erik Johnson				STL	October 4, 2007
	0	1	1	0		season opener

Year	Player	Team					Date
2007	Patrick Kane	CHI					October 4, 2007
			0	0	0	0	season opener
2008	Steven Stamkos	TB					October 4, 2008
			0	0	0	0	season opener
2009	John Tavares	NYI					October 3, 2009
			1	1	2	0	season opener
2010	Taylor Hall	EDM					October 7, 2010
			0	0	0	2	season opener
2011	Ryan Nugent-Hopkins	EDM					October 9, 2011
			1	0	1	2	season opener
2012	Nail Yakupov	EDM					January 20, 2013
			0	0	0	0	debut delayed by lockout/season opener
2013	Nathan MacKinnon	AVS					October 2, 2013
			0	2	2	2	season opener
2014	Aaron Ekblad	FLO					October 9, 2014
			0	1	1	0	season opener
2015	Connor McDavid	EDM					October 8, 2015
			0	0	0	0	season opener
2016	Auston Matthews	TOR					October 12, 2016
			4	0	4	0	season opener
2017	Nico Hischier	NJ					October 7, 2017
			0	0	0	0	season opener
2018	Rasmus Dahlin	BUF					October 4, 2018
			0	0	0	0	season opener

*also recorded an assist

NOTES

// Only twice has a goalie been selected number one, and both lost their debuts.

// Of the 40 names on this list, 22 have retired and five have been inducted into the Hockey Hall of Fame—Hawerchuk, Lemieux, Modano, Sundin, and Lindros.

// Mike Modano is the only first overall selection to make his NHL debut in the playoffs.

// The last first overall draft choice who did not play right away with the team was goalie Rick DiPietro with the New York Islanders in 2000. He started the year with the Chicago Wolves of the AHL before being recalled mid-season.

Buffalo's Rasmus Dahlin is part of a trend that has seen the first overall draft choice jump straight into the NHL.

Most Goals in a Game

There have been exactly 61 multi-goal games by players in their NHL debuts. Interestingly, of the 10 to score at least three goals, Real Cloutier is the only one to score all his goals in one period (3rd). And, of the 51 to score two goals in their debut, 23 scored both in one period. Of all players to score at least two goals in a period, only seven did so in the first period—Harry Cameron, Jake Guentzel, Bill Hay, Al Hill, Harry Hyland, Joe Malone, Auston Matthews. The fastest two goals were scored by George Hay, who had two career goals after only 4:20 playing time.

5 goals	2	Harry Hyland, Joe Malone
4 goals	2	Auston Matthews, Reg Noble
3 goals	6	Fabian Brunnstrom, Real Cloutier, Cy Denneny, Ryan Poehling, Alex Smart, Derek Stepan
2 goals	51	Greg C. Adams, George Allen, **Dave Archibald**, **Ralph Barahona**, Todd Bergen, Gus Bodnar, Nikolai Borschevsky, **Rob Brown**, **Harry Cameron**, **George Carey**, **Chris Cichocki**, Brad DeFauw, Corb Denneny, John Ferguson, Thomas Gradin, **Jake Guentzel**, **George Hay**, Alex Hicks, Al Hill, Scott Howson, **Wingy Johnston**, Aurele Joliat, Bob Joyce, **Anze Kopitar**, George Lyle, **Mark Marquess**, **Joe A. Matte**, **Dan McCarthy**, **Rick Middleton**, Bill Miller, Don Murdoch, Dmitri Nabokov, **Ralph Nattrass**, Ivan Novoseltsev, Peanuts O'Flaherty, **Alexander Ovechkin**, Doug Palazzari, **Mark Parrish**, Gerry Pinder, Dave Poulin, Dave Ritchie, Pavel Rosa, **Mike Rupp**, **Devon Setoguchi**, **Babe Siebert**, **Duane Sutter**, Vladimir Tarasenko, Fred Thurier, **Jiri Tlusty**, Eddie Wares, Vitali Yachmenev

bold=both goals in one period

Los Angeles forward Anze Kopitar (left) celebrates his second goal in his debut.

Leap Year Debuts

February 29 comes but once every four years, and it's not a particularly conducive time of year to new players anyway, so the number of NHL debuts on that day are very few and far between.

However, one year and one team stand above all others—Toronto, in 2016. On that date, some *four* Leafs made their NHL debuts—Zach Hyman, Kasperi Kapanen, William Nylander, and Nikita Soshnikov. The Leafs lost at home to Tampa Bay that night, 2–1, and none of the four figured in the lone Leafs goal.

Soshnikov was the only one of the quartet who never made an impact with the team. The others, of course, are a huge part of the Cup hopefuls.

Additionally, there are nine other skaters who made their debuts on February 29:

Player, Team, Year	G	A	P	PIM
Ron Schock, Boston Bruins, 1964	1	0	1	0
Darren Lowe, Pittsburgh Penguins, 1984	0	1	1	0
Pat Flatley, New York Islanders, 1984	1	1	2	0
Pat LaFontaine, New York Islanders, 1984	0	0	0	0
Brian Leetch, New York Rangers, 1988	0	1	1	0
Ken McRae, Quebec Nordiques, 1988	0	0	0	0
Quintin Laing, Chicago Blackhawks, 2004	0	0	0	0
Brandon Bollig, Chicago Blackhawks, 2012	0	0	0	5
Garnet Hathaway, Calgary Flames, 2016	0	0	0	0

Mathieu Chouinard

Lone Goalie in Unique Game

The only goalie to make his debut on this date was Mathieu Chouinard of the L.A. Kings, in 2004. He replaced Cristobal Huet briefly during a 6–3 loss to state rivals Anaheim Ducks, stopping the only two shots he faced during just 2:43 of ice time. This game was, in fact, one of the strangest ever.

The game was tied 3–3 after 40 minutes, but the Ducks scored three in the first half of the third to go up 6–3. Kings coach Andy Murray then pulled Huet in favour of Chouinard, but less than three minutes later the team got a power play. Murray pulled Chouinard and kept him on the bench most of the rest of the game. That is, Los Angeles played with an empty net for an extraordinary seven minutes without surrendering another goal.

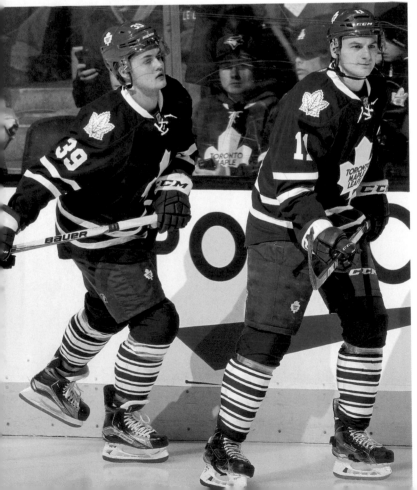

Maple Leafs forwards William Nylander (left) and Zack Hyman were two of four Leafs to make their debuts on February 29, 2016.

Managing the Crease

Jorge Alves

CAROLINA HURRICANES // DECEMBER 31, 2016

On the afternoon of Saturday, December 31, 2016, Jorge Alves signed a one-day contract with the Carolina Hurricanes. The team's equipment manager became an NHL backup goalie because Eddie Lack was feeling ill and the team didn't have time to get a substitute from their system.

Lack had been a 'tender in high school and then joined the Marines in 1997, where he trained for four years. After leaving, he played minor pro for a few years before joining the Hurricanes staff in 2003. He became the full-time equipment manager in 2012 but often filled in as a goalie during practice.

That night, the 'Canes were in Tampa Bay to play the Lightning, and, of course, Cam Ward started for Carolina. Wearing No. 40, Alves led the players onto the ice for the warmup, doing a "rookie lap" on his own before the rest of the team joined him.

During the intermissions, Alves would sharpen players' skates and carry out his duties as equipment manager, all the while wearing his goalie equipment. Late in the third period, Tampa Bay was winning the game, 3–1, and there was only 7.6 seconds remaining in the game with a faceoff in the Lightning end after an icing call.

Carolina coach Bill Peters then called to the end of the bench and told Alves to go in. The game ended quietly, and Alves didn't face a shot, but he did get into the record books as having played eight seconds.

"When I did realize it was going to happen it was kind of disbelief," he enthused after. "For years it's always been kind of a joke around the locker room that I might go in. That was an amazing experience."

The 37-year-old now holds the record for briefest NHL career by a goalie, and his short debut has been "shortened" only by Kellan Lain and Brian White (two seconds each).

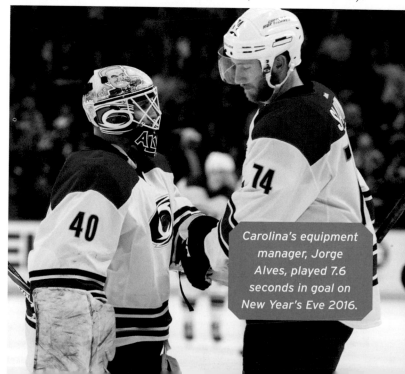

Carolina's equipment manager, Jorge Alves, played 7.6 seconds in goal on New Year's Eve 2016.

Goalie Penalties

Some 21 goalies have incurred a penalty in their NHL debut, most commonly for delay of game (10). Some of the penalties meant little; some were costly.

// Claude Pronovost, Boston Bruins
January 14, 1956

Oh, the good old days. This is the kind of story that made the Original Six so amazing. It all started with Boston goalie Terry Sawchuk. He fractured a finger on his right hand in practice on January 13, so the team called up John Henderson from Hershey for its game the next night against the Canadiens. It was a daunting assignment in that the Bruins had lost a club-record 11 straight games and were playing in the difficult Forum in Montreal.

But as game time approached the next night, Henderson's equipment still hadn't arrived, so the Bruins had to use Montreal's goalie, Claude Pronovost! The 20-year-old was the backup for the Montreal Royals in the Quebec league behind Gerry

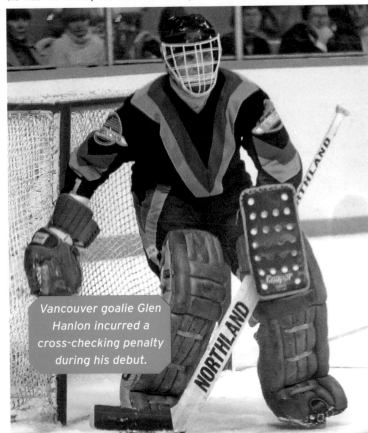

Vancouver goalie Glen Hanlon incurred a cross-checking penalty during his debut.

McNeil and had never played in the NHL, and at the other end of the ice was the great Jacques Plante.

Nevertheless, Pronovost was nothing short of sensational playing against his own team. He stopped all 31 shots in a 2–0 win, became one of a rare group of goalies to earn a shutout in his NHL debut, and was given rousing cheers all night by the fans at the Forum. He didn't play in the NHL again for three years (with the Habs).

Midway through the third period he received a penalty for delay of game (holding the puck) because of an extended period of Montreal pressure, but he made up for it, of course, by not allowing a goal on this power play or at any other time. History shows he was the first goalie to incur a penalty in his NHL debut.

// Gary Bromley, Buffalo Sabres
October 10, 1973

Bromley's road appearance for the Sabres in Toronto was greatly overshadowed by the NHL debut of Borje Salming. Bromley didn't have as special a night, allowing six goals in the first two periods before being replaced by Roger Crozier for the third. He incurred a tripping penalty late in the second, but no goal came from the Leafs' power play.

// Glen Hanlon, Vancouver Canucks
March 31, 1978

Curt Ridley tore knee ligaments in the Canucks' previous game, thus forcing Vancouver to recall 20-year-old Hanlon from Tulsa of the Central Hockey League where he was having a sensational rookie season.

After a rough first period, Hanlon settled down, but his teammates couldn't get the job done, and they lost to Philadelphia, 3–2. Hanlon gave up his first goal in the second minute of play on a breakaway by Mel Bridgman. The goalie later took a cross-checking penalty, which the team killed off, and gave up two more before his first 20 minutes was in the books.

// Mario Lessard, Los Angeles Kings
October 26, 1978

Another of the rare group to record a shutout in his NHL debut, Lessard also incurred a delay-of-game penalty for holding the puck early in the second period. No matter. He stopped all 18 shots and got plenty of goal support as his L.A. Kings beat the visiting Sabres, 6–0. In the process, he became an instant hero, and by the end of the game fans were chanting, "Mario! Mario!" in praise of his sensational shutout debut.

// Reggie Lemelin, Atlanta Flames
December 2, 1978

Part of a rare group of goalies, Lemelin allowed a goal on his first ever shot, which didn't come until eight minutes into the game. The Flames lost to Minnesota, 4–3. Lemelin also took a cross-checking penalty at 13:33 of the first period, along with J-P Parise of the North Stars. Lemelin was spotting for Dan Bouchard in goal after Bouchard had played in 24 of the previous 25 games and needed a rest.

// Don Cutts, Edmonton Oilers
January 29, 1980

Oilers goalie Cutts didn't waste any time getting into the game. Less than a minute into his NHL debut he took a high-sticking penalty after mixing it up with Perry Turnbull of St. Louis, who also took two for the same offence.

Cutts lost, 3–2, but played really well. Two of the goals were scored on breakaways, and the goalie's play impressed coach Glen Sather. "Cutts played very well and couldn't be faulted on any of the goals. I think I'll play him tomorrow night in Los Angeles."

Sather was true to his word, but in that game Cutts pulled himself after 21:18 of play because, of all things, his contact lenses weren't working and he couldn't see properly.

// Marc D'Amour, Calgary Flames
October 11, 1985

See page 108

// Darrell May, St. Louis Blues
October 29, 1985

Rick Wamsley was injured, so the Blues recalled May from Peoria of the IHL for a night. By all accounts in the St. Louis dressing room after the game, second-year referee Dan Marouelli had had a bad night, and the Blues lost to Washington, 6–3. Symptomatic of his officiating, they felt, was a slashing call assessed to May.

"Our goaltender was just going after the puck. He calls that a slash," lamented coach Jacques Demers. That penalty came midway through the first period and changed the game. Mark Hunter scored on the power play to tie the score, 1–1, and the Capitals reeled off five in a row to go ahead, 5–1.

"I made a few nervous mistakes," May said. Demers was more lenient. "There were a few giveaways we made that caught him by surprise. It's his first game in the NHL. He tried his best; that's the main thing."

Darrell May had a rough first night, allowing six goals and taking a penalty for good measure.

// Rick Tabaracci, Pittsburgh Penguins
October 21, 1988

"I can't wait!" was how Tabaracci reacted the day he was told by coach Gene Ubriaco he'd be playing on this Friday night in New Jersey, his first career game. He had started the season third on the depth chart for the Penguins, but Wendell Young struggled mightily after being named number one, and Steve Guenette had been pulled in each of his last two games.

Ubriaco and GM Tony Esposito had liked Tabaracci's feistiness and competitive spirit and kept the 19-year-old on the roster rather than send him back to his junior team in Cornwall. This debut night, however, was far from sweet. Tabaracci surrendered four goals on 21 shots over 33 minutes and was replaced by Young midway through the second period.

With the game tied, 2–2, Tabaracci took an interference penalty, but Mario Lemieux scored a short-handed goal to give the Penguins a 3–2 lead. Soon after, the Devils scored two quick goals, spelling the end for Tabaracci and his first game.

// Andrei Trefilov, Calgary Flames
November 4, 1992

A thinking man's coach, Calgary bench boss Dave King decided he wanted to look at goalie Andrei Trefilov, who had had a great start in the minors with Salt Lake of the IHL. But not to ruffle feathers, namely the pride of starter Mike Vernon or back-ups Trevor Kidd, Jeff Reese, and top prospect Jason Muzzatti, King stressed it was a look-see and no more.

"It's not a long-term thing. It's just a chance to look at a young prospect. It's fine to be a good minor league and international goalie, but you've got to know what he can do in the NHL." And what better time, King thought, than now, after the team got off to a great 9–4 start for the 1992–93 season.

It was a rough outing for the Soviet goalie, though, but a late goal by Joel Otto, followed by a scoreless overtime, gave the visiting Flames a 5–5 tie with the Canucks. Along the way, Trefilov and Vancouver's Cliff Ronning received offsetting slashing minors midway through the third period, but the next day, true to his word, King sent Trefilov back to the minors.

// Garth Snow, Quebec Nordiques
December 3, 1993

The appearance of Garth Snow in the Nordiques goal this night was the result of a major decision by the goalie. Playing with the U.S. Olympic team preparing for Lille-hammer just two months later, Snow was wooed away from that team to sign with the NHL Nords. And his first start was seamless. The only nugget of anxiety came after Snow took a delay-of-game penalty midway through the third. The Islanders scored to cut the Quebec lead to 3–2, but Snow was solid the rest of the way and won his debut by that score.

// Patrick Labrecque, Montreal Canadiens
October 7, 1995

This was a night Labrecque absolutely, positively did not think he'd be playing. Yes, he was dressed as the backup, but Patrick Roy was the starting goalie and Montreal was hosting Philadelphia in the team's season opener. And, in an inspiring pre-game ceremony, the Habs officially retired Jacques Plante's No. 1. The stage was set for a great game for Roy.

But on this rare occasion, "Saint Patrick" played like the devil, allowing five goals on 15 shots over just 22:12 of playing time. Cue the hook, and Labrecque had to come in, playing 37:48 and allowing two goals on only 12 shots. He also incurred an interference penalty late in the second period, but the game was long lost by this point (7–1 was the final score), and the Flyers didn't add to their tally during the power play.

// Derek Wilkinson, Tampa Bay Lightning
November 8, 1995

"I can't approach the game any differently," Derek Wilkinson said after being recalled from the IHL to play in his first game, thanks to an injury to number-one man Daren Puppa. "The players may be a little better, but the puck is the same size, and the net is the same size."

It was the right attitude, but the outcome was disappointing. The Lightning cruised to an early 3–0 lead and then all but collapsed, losing 5–4 to the visiting New York Rangers. "I have no qualms with the goaltending," coach Terry Crisp said after. "The kid played well. It was breakdowns that cost us."

The Rangers got back into the game late in the first period thanks in part to Wilkinson, who took a slashing penalty. Soon after, teammate Eric Charron also took a penalty, and on the ensuing five-on-three New York scored, clawing their way back into the match. They also scored the only three goals of the final period.

// Steve Shields, Buffalo Sabres
December 23, 1995

Number four worked out well for Steve Shields, who got into his first NHL game for the Buffalo Sabres in Ottawa, a dismal team. The Sabres' top goalie, Dominik Hasek, was out with a strained stomach muscle. His backup, Andrei Trefilov, got the start, but Robb Stauber, the team's top minor-league prospect, had a torn rotator cuff. So Shields, fourth on the team's depth chart, got the call to be Trefilov's backup.

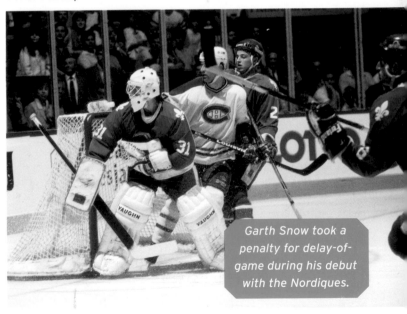

Garth Snow took a penalty for delay-of-game during his debut with the Nordiques.

Then, less than five minutes into the game, Trefilov suffered a knee injury and had to leave. Shields came in and won the game, 4–2, handing the Senators their 21st loss in the last 23 games. And he had to face only 15 shots to get the W. Easy.

Worse for Ottawa, their two goals were the result of nervous Shields errors, but the team wasn't able to test the newcomer more often. Shields got his name on the scoresheet by taking a delay-of-game penalty with only nine seconds left in the final period, but, of course, nothing came of it.

Marty Turco set a record of sorts by being the only goalie to incur two minors during his debut.

// Marty Turco, Dallas Stars
October 10, 2000

Double trouble.

Turco has the distinction of being the only goalie to incur two minor penalties during his NHL debut, both for delay of game. What's more, they came within 85 seconds of each other, putting the Stars down two men. He did his bit, though, by not allowing a power-play goal to Carolina. The 'Canes won anyway, 5–2.

// Patrick DesRochers, Phoenix Coyotes
November 23, 2001

DesRochers was drafted 14th overall by Phoenix in 1998, but it took him a while to get into a game. In 1999–2000, he was recalled twice from Springfield of the AHL, but he didn't play. In 2000–01, he was called up four times, but saw no ice time. Finally, early in the 2001–02 season, he got his chance. The Coyotes were in Minnesota when starting goalie Robert Esche had a tough two periods, and with the Wild leading 5–1, coach Bobby Francis decided to give DesRochers some time. The 22-year-old faced only six shots, stopping them all, so his delay-of-game penalty didn't do further damage. Final score, though, was 5–2.

// Neil Little, Philadelphia Flyers
March 28, 2002

Few players in the history of the NHL had to persevere to the degree Little did to get into his first NHL game. Never a top prospect, he was drafted 226th overall by Philadelphia in 1991 after finishing his first year of NCAA play with RPI.

Little graduated in 1994 and then played with the Hershey Bears in the AHL. He remained in the Flyers system for a decade in all, finally getting the call nearly 11 years after draft day (thanks to an injury to starting goalie Roman Cechmanek).

Unfortunately for Little, his teammates didn't give him much support against Carolina this night, and things went from bad to worse late in the second period. Billy Tibbetts, a thug for the Flyers, pulled down the 'Canes Craig Adams in the crease, knocking Little over. With the goalie down, Jaroslav Svoboda scored.

Incensed, Little got up and started punching Adams, precipitating a brawl. In the end, five players received a total of 72 penalty minutes, including Little, who got a 10-minute misconduct. Carolina won the game, 4–1, but Little had an NHL debut to remember.

// Jan Lasak, Nashville Predators
April 9, 2002

Mike Dunham and Tomas Vokoun were injured, so Nashville had to call up both Chris Mason and Jan Lasak for a late season game in St. Louis. In the end, coach Barry Trotz decided to start Lasak, who stopped 39 of 42 shots but lost, 3–2.

Lasak stopped Keith Tkachuk on a penalty shot midway through the opening period, but the goalie was part of the outcome in the third. First, Nathan Perrott took a five-minute major for spearing, and just 17 seconds later Lasak inadvertently shot the puck over the glass, incurring a penalty and putting the team down two men. With the five-on-three, Ray Ferraro scored the winning goal.

// Adam Munro, Chicago Blackhawks
March 1, 2004

It was an impressive debut for goalie Munro as he stopped 33 of 35 shots and helped the Hawks tie Nashville through 60 minutes of regulation and five more of overtime. And then, after the game was over, a skirmish broke out and Predators goalie Tomas Vokoun went ballistic. He incurred a rare triple minor penalty while teammate Scott Walker earned a roughing minor. For Chicago, Munro was assessed a minor for leaving the crease to join the fracas, and Mark Bell and Tuomo Ruutu also drew minors.

// Ondrej Pavelec, Atlanta Thrashers
October 20, 2007

Kari Lehtonen's (groin) pain was Ondrej Pavelec's gain, so when the former couldn't dress as backup to Johan Hedberg, the latter was called up from the AHL's Chicago Wolves for a game in Tampa Bay. Then, when Hedberg gave up five goals in two periods, Pavelec got the nod to play the final 20 minutes, which he did, giving up one goal on six shots. Late in that period, he incurred a delay-of-game penalty, but it wasn't costly. Still, the Lightning whipped the Thrashers, 6–2.

Casey DeSmith of Pittsburgh allowed a goal on the first shot he faced. He took a penalty later in the game.

// Casey DeSmith, Pittsburgh Penguins
October 29, 2017

DeSmith's NHL career was exactly 11 seconds old when he surrendered his first goal on the first shot he faced. The context: DeSmith was backup to Matt Murray in the Pittsburgh net, but the hometown Jets were on fire this night, scoring four goals and chasing Murray at the 18:07 mark. Two of those goals came from Blake Wheeler, and Wheeler completed his hat trick at 18:18.

"I was kind of like, 'Oh, this is happening. This is going to be the ol' debut here,'" DeSmith related of his surprise entry into his inaugural game. "Then I got in there and they scored that shift, first shot, so not ideal."

Early in the second, he accidentally flipped the puck over the glass to put his team down a man, but the Jets didn't score. No matter. Winnipeg skated to an easy 7–1 win, DeSmith giving up three goals on just 15 shots.

Philadelphia's Neil Little was assessed a misconduct after a brawl precipitated by a controversial goal.

Debut Highlights, 2018–19

Goalies

Of the 10 goalies who made their debuts this past season, five came in during the game in relief. Of the five who started (and finished—none was pulled), only one managed to win—Philadelphia's Carter Hart. Hart stopped 20 of 22 shots as the Flyers beat Detroit, 3–2.

No goalie appeared in a shootout, and only Sam Montembeault (Florida) went as far as overtime, losing to Carolina, 4–3.

As well, no goalie incurred a penalty or drew an assist.

Skaters

Of course, head and shoulders above all debuts in 2018–19 was Ryan Poehling, who scored a hat trick and the shootout winner for Montreal on the final day of the regular season.

The only other multi-point games came from Vancouver sensation Elias Pettersson, who had a goal and an assist for the Canucks on October 3, 2018, the team's first game of the year; and Maxime Lajoie (Ottawa), who also had one plus one on October 4, 2018, the first game for the Sens.

Jacob MacDonald of Florida (right) celebrates his debut goal with teammate Vince Trocheck.

Only 11 players scored a goal in their debut: Drake Batherson (Ottawa), Michael Bunting (Arizona), Dennis Cholowski (Detroit), Max Comtois (Anaheim), Carl Grundstrom (Los Angeles), Jacob MacDonald (Florida), Zach Senyshyn (Boston), Lajoie, Pettersson, Poehling, and Cale Makar (for Colorado in the playoffs).

Comtois's goal stands out. It came just 49 seconds into the game and ensured his name was added to the list of players who scored on their first shot and shift in the first minute of play in their debut.

MacDonald, a defenceman, didn't score on his first shift, but he did score on his first shot in front of his family, less than six minutes into the game.

In all, 14 players were credited with an assist during their first game: Mason Appleton (Winnipeg), Ben Gleason (Dallas), Taro Hirose (Detroit), Quinn Hughes (Vancouver), Jesperi Kotkaniemi (Montreal), Lajoie, Zack MacEwen (Vancouver), Trevor Moore (Toronto), Victor Olofsson (Buffalo), Pettersson, Keifer Sherwood (Anaheim), Kristian Vesalainen (Winnipeg), Mikhail Vorobyev (Philadelphia), and Sean Walker (Los Angeles).

Sherwood's assist stands out because it came on a Carter Rowney goal into the empty net with only 24 seconds left in the game, the same game that started with Comtois's quick first goal.

Only two players took shots in the shootout, the aforementioned Poehling, who scored the game winner, and Vancouver's Quinn Hughes, who did not score on his chance.

Of the 134 newcomers, 21 incurred a penalty, but three stand out for having incurred more than just a minor:

Connor Clifton (Boston)	9 PIM (fighting, two minors)
Nathan Bastian (New Jersey)	5 PIM (fighting)
Trent Frederic (Boston)	5 PIM (fighting)

One-Game Wonders

For now, there are 10 players who are on the undesirable one-game wonder list, but many of these are likely to play a second game in 2019–20 or beyond.

Nevertheless, as of the end of the 2018–19 season, these players have but one NHL game to their credit: Vitali Abramov, Brandon Gignac, Dennis Gilbert, Brady Keeper, Rem Pitlick, Poehling, Anthony Greco, Riley Stillman, Anthony Richard, Mark Friedman.

Of the 134 new players to the NHL during the 2018–19 regular season, 55 were Canadian (41.0%) and 38 from the United States (27.8%). Nine other countries were represented:

Canada	55	Latvia	2
United States	38	Denmark	1
Finland	11	France	1
Sweden	11	Slovakia	1
Czech Republic	7	Switzerland	1
Russia	6		

Total 134

Of the 55 from Canada, the breakdown by province is as follows:

Ontario	19	Saskatchewan	2
Alberta	15	Manitoba	1
Quebec	9	New Brunswick	1
British Columbia	4	Newfoundland	1
Prince Edward Island	2	Nova Scotia	1

Total 55

Of the 38 from the United States, the breakdown by state is as follows:

Minnesota	8	Florida	1
Michigan	8	Indiana	1
Massachusetts	4	Iowa	1
New York	3	New Hampshire	1
Ohio	3	New Jersey	1
Texas	2	North Dakota	1
Arizona	1	Oregon	1
California	1	Wisconsin	1

Total 38

Overall by Position:

Defence	49
Forward	75
Goalie	10

Total 134

Making History

Drafted 25th overall by Montreal in 2017, Poehling returned to St. Cloud State that fall for his junior season of NCAA hockey. It wasn't until after his third college season was over that he decided to turn pro, signing with the Habs on March 31, 2019.

The team was in a last-ditch, desperate attempt to make the playoffs, so Poehling was a healthy scratch for two games. But on April 6, the final day of the season and the Canadiens out of post-season contention, coach Michel Therrien dressed the youngster for a game against arch-rivals the Maple Leafs.

Poehling scored three goals on his only three shots, including one late in the third to send the game to overtime. He then scored the game winner in the subsequent shootout.

"It's a surreal moment for myself, and I feel like I'm in a dream," he said in the dressing room after his heroics. "I'm just in shock."

In the shootout, Auston Matthews (Toronto) and Jonathan Drouin (Montreal) scored, making it 1–1 after three shots, but Poehling scored with Montreal's fourth attempt. He twisted and twirled in on goal before ripping a shot over Fredrik Andersen's glove.

The goal was called by Bob Cole across *Hockey Night in Canada*, the last game of his extraordinary broadcasting career. "Yes, sir! What an unbelievable start of a career!" Cole roared as Poehling made history.

Poehling was just the sixth player to score at least three goals in his NHL debut (excluding players from the league's first season), and he was only the fourth to score a shootout winner in his debut after Evgeni Svechnikov, Linus Omark, and Tim Stapleton.

Of course, this being the last game of the season for Montreal, Habs fans had to wait all summer to see what Poehling would do for an encore.

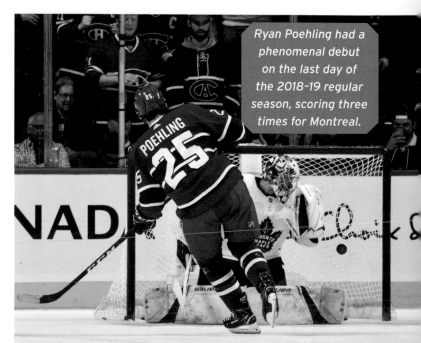

Ryan Poehling had a phenomenal debut on the last day of the 2018-19 regular season, scoring three times for Montreal.

Dude, Where's Makar?

Cale Makar

COLORADO AVALANCHE // APRIL 15, 2019

The first defenceman to score in his playoff debut, Makar capped off a busy week with a goal and victory in Denver.

On Friday, April 12, Makar was named winner of the Hobey Baker Award. The next night, he and his University of Massachusetts-Amherst Minutemen lost the NCAA Frozen Four finals to the University of Minnesota-Duluth, 3–0.

On Sunday, the 20-year-old signed with the Avs, and on Monday he flew to Denver and was in the lineup at the Pepsi Center. It was Game 3 of the Conference quarter-finals, and it came against Calgary, his place of birth, and, of course, the team of his boyhood dreams.

Nathan MacKinnon got the Avs going with two goals, but then Makar made his mark, scoring on his first career shot, at 16:02, off an odd-man rush. Makar took a pass from MacKinnon and barged up the middle, snapping a quick shot between the pads of Mike Smith to make it a 3–0 game.

"I don't think it will be too big of a transition . . . NCAA hockey is pretty fast-paced itself. I don't think the speed or anything will be too much of a challenge for me," he said on game day. "I like the way they [Avs] play. They're fast, and I think I can fit in."

He was right. After the game, he was on cloud nine. "It was a total surreal, pinch-me moment all wrapped into one. It's insane," he enthused. "I couldn't be more excited."

Cale Makar (No. 8) scored in his first game, which came in the 2019 playoffs.

Appendix

Debut Game Records, Skaters

Most Points, Game

5 Al Hill, Philadelphia Flyers, February 14, 1977

Most Goals, Game

5 Harry Hyland, Montreal Wanderers,
December 19, 1917

Joe Malone, Montreal Canadiens,
December 19, 1917

4 Auston Matthews, Toronto Maple Leafs,
October 12, 2016

Reg Noble, Toronto Arenas,
December 19, 1917

Most Assists, Game

4 Dutch Reibel, Detroit Red Wings,
October 8, 1953

Roland Eriksson, Minnesota North Stars,
October 6, 1976

Most PIM, Game

42 David Koci, Chicago Blackhawks,
March 10, 2007

37 Tie Domi, Toronto Maple Leafs,
March 2, 1990

Most Points/Goals/Assists, Period

3 Harry Hyland, Montreal Wanderers,
December 19, 1917 (3 goals, 1st period)

Real Cloutier, Quebec Nordiques,
October 10, 1979 (3 goals, 3rd period)

Al Hill, Philadelphia Flyers,
February 14, 1977 (2 goals, 1 assist, 1st period)

Len Fontaine, Detroit Red Wings,
October 7, 1972 (1 goal, 2 assists, 1st period)

Kent Nilsson, Atlanta Flames,
October 10, 1979 (1 goal, 2 assists, 2nd period)

Roland Eriksson, Minnesota North Stars,
October 6, 1976 (3 assists, 1st period)

Vaclav Nedomansky, Detroit Red Wings,
November 18, 1977 (3 assists, 2nd period)

Winning Shootout Goal in Debut

Tim Stapleton, Toronto Maple Leafs, February 26, 2009

Linus Omark, Edmonton Oilers, December 10, 2010

Evgeni Svechnikov, Detroit Red Wings, April 3, 2017

Ryan Poehling, Montreal Canadiens, April 6, 2019

Shortest Debut

2 seconds Kellan Lain, Vancouver Canucks,
January 18, 2014

Brian White, Colorado Avalanche,
November 21, 1998

Fastest Goal from Start of Career

15 seconds   Gus Bodnar, Toronto Maple Leafs,
October 30, 1943

18 seconds   Danny Gare, Buffalo Sabres,
October 10, 1974

Youngest Debut

16 years, 338 days Bep Guidolin, Boston Bruins,
November 12, 1942

Oldest Debut

43 years, 80 days   Lester Patrick, New York Rangers,
March 20, 1927

38 years, 120 days Connie Madigan, St. Louis Blues,
February 1, 1973

Earliest Calendar Debut

September 29 Bobby Ryan, Anaheim Ducks (2007)
Brady Murray, Anaheim Ducks (2007)
Jonathan Bernier, Los Angeles Kings (2007)

Latest Calendar Debut

May 23   Esa Tikkanen, Edmonton Oilers (1985)

Most Player Debuts, One Day

45   October 10, 1979
October 5, 2005

Most Debuts, One Team, One Game

11   Winnipeg Jets, October 10, 1979

Debut Game Records, Goalies

Longest Shutout in Debut

70 minutes   Tiny Thompson, Boston Bruins,
November 15, 1928

Shortest Debut

7.6 seconds   Jorge Alves, Carolina Hurricanes,
December 31, 2016

2:59   Robbie Irons, St. Louis Blues,
November 13, 1968

Most Goals Allowed

12   Frank Brophy, Quebec Bulldogs, December 25, 1919

10   Ron Loustel, Winnipeg Jets, March 27, 1981

Most Saves

49   Manny Legace, Los Angeles Kings,
October 21, 1998
Laurent Brossoit, Edmonton Oilers,
April 9, 2015

Most Shots

51   Laurent Brossoit, Edmonton Oilers, April 9, 2015

Most PIM

12   Marc D'Amour, Calgary Flames, October 11, 1985

Acknowledgements

The author would like to thank several people who have been integral to getting this book published, notably Jack David and Michael Holmes at ECW for their enthusiastic support of the project from the get go. As well, to designers Kathryn Zante (interior) and Michel Vrana (cover), and the team at ECW for support in one form or another—Jessica Albert, Jennifer Smith, Jennifer Gallinger, Jen Albert, Laura Pastore. To Julie Young and Stuart McComish at the NHL for their help in finding some of the stats, and to Kimmo Leinonen for expert help with some of the Finnish players. As well, to Craig Campbell and Phil Pritchard at the Hockey Hall of Fame for the usual photos and research assistance. To Gord Miller and Damien Cox for providing kind words about the book (and, by extension, moi). And lastly to my wife, LMW TT, who surely knows a good debut when she sees one.

Photo Credits

Getty Images—front cover, 7, 15, 21, 23, 24, 25, 26 (both), 27, 29, 30, 35, 46, 47, 50, 51, 52, 55, 56, 57, 58, 59, 61, 62 (both), 63, 64, 65, 67, 68, 69, 74, 77, 83 (both), 84, 87, 88, 90, 91, 92, 94, 96 (both), 97, 98, 99, 101, 103, 104, 105, 106, 113, 114 (both), 115 (both), 116, 119, 121, 122, 123, 124, 125, 126, 128, 130, 131, 132, 134, 137, 138, 145, 147, 149, 150, 152, 154, 155, 156, 157, 158, 160, 161, 163, 165, 166, 168, 169, 170, 171, 172, 173, 174, 175, 176, 177, 178, 179, 180, 181, 182, 183, 185, 186, 187, 188, 189, 190, 191, 192, 193 (both), 194, 196, 197, back cover

HHOF/Le Studio du Hockey—28, 49, 120, 142
HHOF/O-Pee-Chee—66, 70, 82
HHOF/Turofsky Collection—38, 40, 72
HHOF/Paul Berewsill—111
HHOF/Howie Borrow—80

Temple University Archives—79 (both)

Ilves Hockey Club—109

Author's collection—10, 12 (both), 13, 16, 18, 20, 31, 33, 34, 36, 39, 41, 42, 43, 53, 71, 76, 108, 118, 140, 141, 143, 153